STUDY GUIDE

Paul Heyne
University of Washington

John P. Palmer
The University of Western Ontario

THE ECONOMIC WAY OF THINKING

First Canadian Edition

Prentice Hall Canada Inc.
Scarborough, Ontario

handwritten notes:

$M = 20\%$
$V = 1$
$P = 3\%$
$Q = 3\%$

$MV = PQ$

$\frac{P \cdot Q}{V} \leftarrow$ relate to strong

$MV = PQ$

money supply — ogg price level

real GDP per yr.

ISBN 0-13-681537-5

Acquisitions Editor: Dave Ward
Developmental Editor: Maurice Esses
Production Editor: Mary Ann McCutcheon
Production Coordinator: Janette Lush

Original edition published by Prentice-Hall, Inc., Upper Saddle River, New Jersey
Copyright © 1997.

All photographs © John P. Palmer.

1 2 3 4 5   03 02 01 00 99

Printed and bound in Canada.

Visit the Prentice Hall Canada Web site! Send us your comments, browse our catalogues, and more. **www.phcanada.com** Or reach us through e-mail at **phcinfo_pubcanada@prenhall.com**

Table of Contents

Preface

How to Use this Study Guide

Economics is a fascinating subject, with considerable relevance for everyday, real-world problems. Much of the time economic analysis is straight-forward common sense. Other times, though, understanding the economic way of thinking requires considerable effort, thought, and reflection. After too much painful experience, I have become convinced that the only way to learn almost any subject is to *do* it. You can read and memorize all you want, but you will not be able to use what you have read or memorized until you get considerable practice applying it to new and different situations. That's one reason so many textbooks have study guides to accompany them.

By working through the questions in each chapter of this study guide, you will receive a review of the topics and concepts we think are important. You will also, and perhaps more importantly, be asked to apply these concepts to new situations. Although some of the questions may seem unrelated to the material, be assured that we have considered these questions carefully to make sure they push you to apply the economic way of thinking to a wide variety of situations.

All too often students think that if they read the textbook, underline or highlight the main points, and memorize a bunch of it, they have learned the material. That is only half the job, though. To be sure they have learned the material, students must then be able to *use* what they have underlined, highlighted, and memorized. The questions and problems throughout this study guide help you do this, especially toward the end of each chapter.

This study guide is not a quiz; it is a learning tool. One recommended way to study economics is this: after you have read a chapter *once*, do the questions for that chapter in the study guide, with your textbook open, referring to it whenever necessary. Also, doing the study guide is not a speed contest. Take your time, and study the material. For each multiple-choice question, make sure you understand why the correct answer is correct and why the incorrect answers are incorrect. If there is any part of the material that you do not understand, then work on it – reread the relevant material, study that section in the textbook, discuss it with your classmates, and ask your instructor for help.

If you find any mistakes in the study guide, please let me know. My e-mail address is **jpalmer@julian.uwo.ca**   Also, there is a website available with my (very brief) lecture notes and a separate section devoted to *The Economic Way of Thinking*. The internet address for the website is:

http://www.sscl.uwo.ca/economics/faculty/jpalmer/

While putting together the Canadian edition of this study guide, I had excellent research and editorial assistance from Rachael Connors, Jacob Palmer, Zillah Moss, Matthew Palmer, and Sammy Chen. The photographs that appear at the end of some of the chapters were taken in various parts of Canada during the past year while I was working on the study guide.

Finally, once again I wish to thank Paul Heyne for having written such a superb textbook and such a challenging study guide, on which we could base the Canadian edition, and I wish to thank my wife, Carolle Trembley, for her support throughout this project.

John P. Palmer
Clinton, Ontario

Chapter 1

The Economic Way of Thinking

A. Multiple-Choice Questions on the Principal Ideas of Chapter 1

1. Economic theory originated largely in efforts to understand why it was that many diverse individuals, pursuing their own interests on the basis of extremely limited information,
   A. cooperated more effectively when they were selfish than when they tried to behave generously.
   B. could not coexist peacefully in the absence of a sovereign government to arbitrate their disputes.
   C. managed to cooperate extensively in mutually advantageous ways.
   D. preferred continued social chaos to an ordered, planned society.

2. The system of social coordination described by economic theory is one in which
   A. consumers are sovereign.
   B. producers control both output and prices.
   C. producers decide what kinds of goods will be available, and consumers decide how much ought to be produced.
   D. people adjust to one another's actions by responding to the changing relative advantages that they perceive in the various opportunities open to them.

3. Which one of the statements below best summarizes the point of view from which economic theory views social behaviour? Social behaviour
   A. can be predicted from a knowledge of the biological, cultural, and psychological factors that determine it.
   B. is determined by the interactions of the three major groups in society: consumers, business, and government.
   C. is the outcome of processes created by the reasoned choices of individuals.
   D. is determined by a continuous struggle for supremacy between the wage-earning class and the class made up of the owners of property, especially capital.

4. The use of theory to explain or predict the working of an economic system
   A. enables students of economics to avoid the biases that might otherwise distort their thinking.
   B. will lead to erroneous results unless the theory is based entirely upon close observation.
   C. leads to many conclusions that are correct in theory but false in the real world.
   D. is inevitable because all efforts at understanding are rooted in some theoretical framework.

B. Answers to, and Explanations of, Multiple-Choice Questions on the Principal Ideas of Chapter 1

1. **C.** Economic theory, in assuming that people pursue their own interests, doesn't assume that those interests are selfish. Nor do people as a rule cooperate more effectively when they're selfish than when they're generous. But economic theory does show how a great deal of effective cooperation can occur in the presence of very little generosity and also without a great deal of government

guidance and control. It explains the surprising fact that order and not social chaos is found in the absence of an authoritative central plan.

2. **D**. The three other options are much too simplistic. Some people certainly have more power and control than others do. But the process in which consumers and producers participate is essentially a mutual adjustment process. Money prices are the key signals. Participants in the economic process alter their behaviour largely in response to the changed pattern of relative prices created by the continually changing behaviour of others.

3. **C**. Economic theory assumes that events are the result of people' s choices, that only individuals make choices, that their choices are reasoned — in the sense that people compare expected benefits and costs – and that these choices are largely coordinated through markets of many sorts. "Market" in this context is simply a name for the interactive adjustment process through which people's various interests are made mutually compatible.

4. **D**. Some theory is unavoidable, because in the absence of a theory we don't know what we're observing or what to look for. Good theories are intimately connected with observations of the phenomena they try to explain but can never be based exclusively on observation because observation itself is always guided by theory. Every theory is a partial perspective, which means that it emphasizes some factors while slighting others. This means that every theory contains some biases. Students beginning the study of economics are invited to view the world from a perspective developed over many years by economists; they receive no guarantee that this is the only valid or even the best perspective. But since the test of any theory is its ability to make sense of the real world, no theory can be called correct if it proves false or misleading when applied to actual events.

C. Step-By-Step Review of Chapter 1

1. The text maintains that people find the workings of economic systems bewildering, largely because
    A. they notice the economy only when it's malfunctioning, but the principles by which a system works are best discerned when the system is functioning properly.
    B. they don't like to be reminded of economic problems and so lose many opportunities to learn from looking closely at the causes and consequences of economic failures.
    C. an economic system is such a complex mechanism of social coordination that it can be understood only with the aid of mathematical theories that are beyond most people's comprehension.
    D. everything depends on everything else, so that nothing can be understood until the system is grasped in its entirety.

2. The movement of rush-hour traffic demonstrates that
    A. detailed regulations directing each person's behaviour are necessary to secure cooperation when large numbers of people are involved.
    B. people's pursuits of their own interests while paying little or no attention to the interests of others don't necessarily produce conflict.
    C. general rules or laws are not necessary for a society to function effectively.
    D. people place a very low value on safety.

3. If traffic is to flow smoothly, which pieces of knowledge are important for each motorist to have?
    A. The position, direction of movement, and velocity of a few cars in the immediate environment.
    B. The principal rules of the road (stop at red lights, drive to the right, etc.)
    C. Both of the above.
    D. The destination of other drivers in the immediate environment and the urgency of their trip.
    E. The number of drivers expected to be on the road at the same time and their preferred routes.

4. If we are to achieve the benefits of civilized life, people must be induced to cooperate with one another by engaging in certain very specific acts at exactly the right time and place
   A. because people tend to think only of themselves.
   B. regardless of how selfish or selfless people are.
   C. unless they love one another.
   D. unless they want to rely on government.

5. In *The Wealth of Nations*, published in 1776, Adam Smith tried to show that
   A. the constant attention of government was an essential precondition for effective cooperation among the members of a society.
   B. social cooperation became impossible among the members of a society if government tried to regulate it in any detailed way.
   C. people often are capable of cooperating effectively even when government policies tried to prevent them from doing so.
   D. wealth is produced more by selfish behaviour than by altruistic behaviour.

6. What did Adam Smith mean by the phrase "a commercial society"?
   A. A society in which business people, or what Smith called "merchants and manufacturers," dominate the culture.
   B. A society in which making money is the most important concern in almost everyone's life.
   C. A society in which religious and national holidays are just opportunities to make money.
   D. A society in which specialization has been carried so far that everyone lives by exchanging.

7. What the text calls "the economic way of thinking" is primarily a
   A. body of statistical data.
   B. set of historical generalizations.
   C. series of conclusions directly applicable to economic policy.
   D. method rather than a doctrine.

8. Economic theory assumes that
   A. individuals choose those actions from among the options available that they think will yield them the largest net advantage.
   B. people are selfish in the last analysis.
   C. everyone is more interested in money than in other goods.
   D. there's no difference between rational and irrational behaviour.

9. Economic theory would be much less successful than it is in predicting the consequences of particular actions if it were not the case that
   A. almost everyone in the society prefers more money to less, other things being equal.
   B. economists hold powerful positions in government.
   C. people's basic values and tastes are ultimately the same.
   D. people's incomes are very different.

10. The process of social coordination that economic theory describes is called a mutual adjustment process because
    A. no one has any more power than anyone else.
    B. the actions that people take create the alternatives that others consider before acting.
    C. everyone derives as much benefit from it as everyone else.
    D. it leads to the greatest good for the greatest number.

11. Economic theory explains, to some degree,
    A. the workings of the business sector of society.
    B. the workings of the government sector of society.
    C. the behaviour of consumers.
    D. all of the above.

12. Economic theory assumes
    A. that social groups are less influential than individuals.
    B. that people never behave spontaneously or without careful calculation of the probable consequences.
    C. that everything that happens to a person is a result of someone's conscious choice.
    D. all of the above.
    E. none of the above.

13. The term *market processes* refers to
    A. the interactions or exchanges in which people engage in the course of pursuing their goals.
    B. the buying and selling of commodities.
    C. anything that takes place between people through the use of money.
    D. social interaction not controlled by government.

14. Automobile drivers using the streets of a large city usually manage to reach their destinations without any collisions because almost all motorists
    A. pay strict attention to the rules of the game of traffic.
    B. share the same goals.
    C. value safety more than speed.
    D. want to avoid collisions.

15. Property rights can usefully be thought of as
    A. characteristics exclusively of the private sector in capitalist economies.
    B. obstacles to government coordination of the economy.
    C. rules of the game that facilitate social cooperation.
    D. social institutions that create additional uncertainty.

16. What happens when "the rules of the game" in a society are in dispute or inconsistent or highly unclear for other reasons?
    A. Social cooperation breaks down.
    B. Less voluntary exchange occurs.
    C. Conflict increases.
    D. A, B, and C.
    E. None of the above occurs, but rather people become more considerate of others because they want others to be considerate of them.

17. In order to move from a centrally planned economy to an effective market-coordinated economy, the countries of the former Soviet bloc will have to
    A. abolish the welfare state that had grown up under socialism.
    B. develop a new system of satisfactorily clear and widely accepted property rights.
    C. eliminate almost all government controls and regulations.
    D. lower taxes to provide their people with adequate monetary incentives.

18. The argument that we ought to approach every question with a completely open mind is
    A. excellent advice even if we often have difficulty following it.
    B. absurd advice because a completely open mind is completely empty.
    C. accepted by almost all economists.
    D. only accepted by true liberals.

D. Answers to the Review Questions in Chapter 1

1. A	5. C	9. A	13. A	17. B
2. B	6. D	10. B	14. D	18. B
3. C	7. D	11. D	15. C	
4. B	8. A	12. E	16. D	

E. Mutual Adjustment and Centralized Coordination

Is it really wise to permit all the drivers who use an expressway to choose for themselves the lane in which they will drive? What if 80 or 90 percent of them just happen to decide one morning that they all want to drive in lane four? Wouldn't it be better to assign numbers to motorists as they enter the freeway and thereby guarantee that they'll distribute themselves evenly across the lanes? Better safe than sorry — right?

1. Even without CB radios or cellular phones, drivers are in communication with each other. How would their communication system handle the potential problem if 90 percent of the drivers entering the expressway on a given morning were thinking, "Today I'm going to drive in lane four"?

2. How could a lane-assignment system be enforced?

3. How does the present system handle the problems created by very slow drivers or stalled vehicles in a particular lane? How might the assigned-lane system handle it?

4. A related question: What's going to happen to Thunder Bay and Yellowknife, respectively, when everybody finally realizes how much more pleasant the weather is in southern Ontario or Victoria than in the frigid north?

F. Answers to Questions in Section E

1. Entering drivers would find themselves making such excellent progress in the other three lanes that they would quickly abandon their resolve. And drivers who were already in the fourth lane would leave it in response to the perceived advantages of the other lanes.

2. There would be no enforcement problems if all the drivers were perfectly satisfied with their assignments. But that would hardly ever be the case, given the different distances the drivers plan to travel, their varying skills and temperaments, and the inevitable advantages that some lanes would turn out to have at a given time and place. Allowing drivers to change lanes when they are not satisfied would, in practice, restore the present system. But not allowing them to do so is futile in the absence of an enforcement system. A lane-control system increasingly being used on some U.S. urban expressways prohibits all but car-poolers from using a reserved lane. Enforcement problems have arisen even in this case, in which it is relatively easy for traffic officers to see whether a vehicle contains two or more passengers. Moreover, car-pool lanes are notoriously underutilized.

3. Under the present system, drivers behind the slow or stalled vehicle try to move into another lane. A slow vehicle in lane four will produce a diversion of traffic into lane three; the resulting slowdown in lane three will cause some movement into lane two. Drivers pursue their own narrow interests, using whatever skills they possess, plus available information on the position and velocity of nearby cars. It is hard to conceive of any better way in which the assigned-lane system could handle such problems. Contrary to what many suppose, centrally directed systems for securing social coordination are often not superior in "emergencies." Mutual adjustment processes may demonstrate their superiority most decisively in situations characterized by unexpected problems.

4. A substantial exodus of people from Thunder Bay to Victoria would change the relative advantages of living in each city. Think of the effects that such a migration would have (and has had) on job opportunities, real estate prices, and congestion. The question is designed to make you see that Canadians decide where to live and work by participating in a vast mutual adjustment process. Quite a few questions that begin "What if everyone decided to…" dissolve once we note that people actually decide on the basis of the changing net advantages created by the decisions of everyone else. "Everyone would not make such a decision because the first such decisions would change the relative advantages perceived by later decision makers."

G. Questions to Think about

1. Who are some of the people whose cooperation helps you make it to and through your first class in the morning? Do you make predictions about their behaviour? On what basis, or with what combination of empirical observation and theory?

2. What would be implied in a rejection of what the text refers to as the major biases of economic theory? For example, how would you proceed if you decided to predict or explain events in society on the assumption that people do not really make choices but rather respond to stimuli in a strictly determined way? What are the consequences of dropping the assumption that other people's behaviour is reasoned behaviour, taking account of expected benefits and costs?

H. Answers to Questions in Section G

1. If you had breakfast or even a cup of coffee, you were the beneficiary of extensive cooperative activities. Did you predict that someone would get up early in order to prepare the coffee? You did if you predicted that freshly brewed coffee would be waiting when you arrived in the cafeteria. If you took the bus to school, you probably predicted that the driver would adhere closely to the printed route and schedule. Your confidence in this prediction was surely not a result of simple observation. You worked with a theory. That theory assumes that bus drivers, like almost everyone else, find it in their interest to obey company rules when they have little or nothing to gain from disobeying them. You concluded that whoever happened to be driving your bus this morning would decide to stop at your corner fairly close to the usual time.

2. You probably couldn't survive very long without the knowledge that you possess as a result of assuming that people choose their actions and that improving the benefits or increasing the costs of a particular action affects people's behaviour. When we find someone who does not seem to be responding to the costs and benefits that influence almost everyone else we call that person "disturbed." We might more accurately call such people disturb*ing*: they disturb *us* because we cannot understand, explain, or predict their behaviour.

Chapter 2

Scarcity and Choices

A. Multiple-Choice Questions on the Principal Ideas of Chapter 2

1. The people in every economy must make choices because
   A. people who own businesses have everything and force the rest of us to choose from what is left.
   B. people have unlimited wants.
   C. society has limited productive resources.
   D. both B and C.
   E. none of the above — there would be no scarcity if only people would control their wants and desires.

2. Scarce goods are rationed in every economy. We know this because
   A. we observe that people seek to increase their net advantages by obtaining more of whatever is used to determine who gets what in the economy.
   B. we are issued ration coupons on a monthly basis for those things that are rationed.
   C. people are willing to stand in line only for those things that are rationed.
   D. it says so in the text.

3. When we choose to produce more of one product, typically we must give up the opportunity to produce more of some other product at the same time
   A. in any economy because when we produce more of anything, the costs of doing so will fall.
   B. in market economies, but not in centrally planned economies.
   C. in centrally planned economies, but not in market economies.
   D. in all types of economies because all economies must deal with the problem of scarcity.

4. The choices and trade-offs that people in any economy must make are called "opportunity costs" because
   A. opportunity only knocks once.
   B. people generally take anything they get the opportunity to take, regardless of the costs.
   C. choosing one option means that one must forego other options or opportunities.
   D. the opportunity to trade things with other people involves costs.

B. Answers to, and Explanations of, the Multiple-Choice Questions on the Principle Ideas of Chapter 2.

1. **D.** If we didn't have limited productive resources in the economy, there would no scarcity; and if we didn't have unlimited wants, there would be no scarcity. But we seem to have both limited resources and unlimited wants, and so we are simply unable to produce everything that everyone would like to have. Certainly, if we could control our wants and desires there would be no scarcity, but even various experimental Utopian societies found that people's desires outstripped the societies' ability to produce things, and so even those societies faced the problem of shortages and having to make choices.

2. **A**. Any mechanism that distinguishes between all the people who want something must do so according to some criterion. Once people figure out what the criterion is, they try to satisfy that criterion. For example, getting in line early for tickets to "Star Wars" is one way to make sure one would be able to obtain the tickets. But queuing is not the only way goods are rationed. Other mechanisms that determine who gets what might include "might makes right" or "willingness and ability to pay". Whatever the mechanism, we find that people do indeed try to obtain more of whatever characteristics are required to help them satisfy the rationing criteria.

3. **D**. In a world of scarcity, there are more demands than there are resources, and so people must choose what to produce with their scarce resources. In your own case, you must choose whether to produce, for example, fast food services or an investment in your own "human capital" by increasing your education. Often, an extra hour spent working detracts from your studying and lowers your investment in your education, and you must make a trade-off.

4. **C**. Opportunity costs are a reflection of foregone opportunities. Later, in Chapters 5 and 7, we will see that *all* costs are "opportunity costs". One of the best illustrations of the concept is that for most Canadian students, the biggest cost of attending post secondary school is the foregone income they could have earned working full time instead of attending school.

C. Step-By-Step Review of Chapter 2

1. The combination of unlimited human wants and limited productive inputs leads to the problem of
    A. who gets the output.
    B. what goods should be produced in the economy.
    C. opportunity cost.
    D. scarcity.
    E. trade-offs.

2. When does the problem of scarcity arise?
    A. in the past and in the present, but economic growth means it will go away in the future.
    B. only when people do not maximize their net advantages when they consume.
    C. only when people behave irrationally.
    D. only when people are selfish.
    E. in all types of economies.

3. How does the problem of scarcity affect altruists?
    A. Altruists must decide which starving children to feed.
    B. Altruists must decide which charities to support.
    C. People must decide how much they want to give to various charitable organizations.
    D. All of the above.
    E. None of the above.

4. Of the people listed below, the best example of someone for whom physical attributes help determine the allocation of Canada's output to various people would most likely be
    A. Wayne Gretsky.
    B. Prince Harry.
    C. Bill Gates.
    D. the 7th caller on a radio contest.
    E. your professor.

5. Queuing (first-come, first-served) often fails as a criterion for determining who gets society's output because
    A. people who have low opportunity costs of time stand in line and then, after buying something at a low price, sell it to someone else for a high price.
    B. people who would value the product very highly if they could buy it but who also value their time very highly hire others at a low wage to stand in line for them.
    C. the people selling the tickets or products often keep a quantity aside for political bigwigs, friends, and influential people.
    D. market forces (buying the item from someone who stood in line) tend to overcome the sense of fairness (everyone has an equal chance to get in line early).
    E. all of the above.

∂ can Test it

⚹ 6. Which of the following is a *positive* statement?
    A. "Good work! Keep up the strong effort!"
    B. "The world would be a better place if we all said nice things to each other."
    C. "Negative political messages are really bad."
    D. "We should always try to treat others the same way we would like to be treated."
    E. "The sky is red."   *A Testable Statement of fact, not necessarily correct !*

∂ ought or should

⚹ 7. Which of the following is a *normative* statement?
    A. "Everyone should share their wealth with those less fortunate than they are."
    B. "The distribution of wealth in Canada has become increasingly less nearly equal."
    C. "The social norms of Canadian society are determined exclusively by sociologists."
    D. "Normal body temperature is 37° C."
    E. All of the above.

8. When economists say "There's no such thing as a free lunch," they are saying
    A. nothing in this life is free — you'll pay for it eventually.
    B. to produce more lunches, resources must be diverted from producing something else that people value too.
    C. even if someone buys you a lunch, they're going to expect you to return the favour somehow.
    D. if people are giving away food, there is probably something wrong with it.
    E. if we want more "free lunches", taxes will have to go up.

9. The traditional guns and butter trade-off is based on the idea that
    A. the scarce resources used to produce guns cannot be diverted to produce butter.
    B. the scarce resources used to produce butter cannot be diverted to produce guns.
    C. using scarce resources to produce military materials means that these resources cannot be used to produce food, and vice versa.
    D. scarce resources should not be used to produce guns when there are some many starving children in the world.
    E. we need to produce more guns to make sure the world is a safe place to raise food.

For questions 10 and 11, consider the following possible combinations that can be produced in a fictitious economy. It might be helpful to plot these combinations to show the opportunity cost curve.

Can use these #'s to produce a production possibilities curve!

	Food	Clothing
A	200	0
B	190	60
C	160	100
D	100	160
E	80	200
F	40	270
G	0	300

10. If the economy is presently producing combination **C** (160 units of food and 100 units of clothing), what will it cost to produce 30 more units of food?

    A. $30
    B. 40 units of clothing
    C. 60 units of clothing
    D. 190 units of food
    E. not enough information is provided

    Go from 160 to 190... an ↑ of 30 units of food
    Go from 100 to 60... a ↓ of 40 units of clothing!

11. Why does it cost so much to produce ten more units of food when the economy is producing 190 units of food (at combination **B**), compared with when the economy is producing, say, 40 units of food (at combination **F**)?

    A. producing that last 10 units of food requires using scarce resources that are most likely better suited to producing clothing rather than food.
    B. food producers will have a monopoly and raise the cost of food.
    C. it takes more resources to produce food than to produce clothing.
    D. people need food but they don't really need clothing.
    E. all of the above.

12. How might a country get to some combination of goods that is outside its production possibilities curve (also called an opportunity cost curve)?

    A. if it saves this year (i.e. produces capital goods instead of consumer goods), it will be able to produce more in the future.
    B. if it discovers more resources, it will be able to produce more in the future.
    C. if it implements technological change, it will be able to produce more in the future.
    D. if it trades with other countries, it will be able to have more goods than if it didn't trade.
    E. all of the above.

13. What does an economist mean when she says, "The optimal amount of pollution is certainly greater than zero; some pollution is better than none."?

    A. sometimes pollutants can be good for you.
    B. this economist is most likely being paid by big polluting firms to say things like this.
    C. the cost of getting rid of the last few bits of pollution, in terms of foregone production of other goods and services, is probably extremely high.
    D. some people don't mind the pollution we have.
    E. all of the above.

14. What does an economist mean when she says, "The optimal amount of crime is certainly greater than zero; some crime is better than none."?

   A. some crime can be good for you.

   B. this economist is most likely paid by large criminal organizations to say things like this.

   C. the cost of getting rid of the last few remnants of criminal activity, in terms of foregone production of other goods and services, is probably extremely high.

   D. some people don't mind the excitement of having a little crime in the neighbourhood.

   E. some of her best friends are criminals.

D. Answers to the Review Questions in Chapter 2

1. D	4. A	7. A	10. B	13. C
2. E	5. E	8. B	11. A	14. C
3. D	6. E	9. C	12. E	

E. Who Gets the Goodies?

Recent stories in various media tell us that tickets to major sporting events are sold out even though the price in some cases is over $100. As a result, sports fans offer scalpers prices rumoured to be over a thousand dollars for tickets to such events as Stanley Cup playoff games or the Superbowl. What determines who gets these tickets at various prices?

1. Do people who pay the "face value" of $100 for one of these tickets really pay only $100? What else might they have to "pay" for their tickets?

2. When scalpers charge $1000 for a ticket that has a face value of only $100, who are they hurting?

3. Which is fairer: some people get tickets for only $100 because of who they know, while others must either wait in line for 3 days to get tickets or pay $1000 to a scalper?

queue → 1st come, first served.

F. Answers To Questions In Section E

There are many different possible determinants of who gets tickets at low prices instead of having to pay scalpers' prices. Typically, though not always, the people who queue up early for tickets have a low opportunity cost of time — they don't have jobs that pay them high wages, are homemakers or students, or are unemployed. Others who receive tickets at the lower prices are season ticket holders, some of whom buy season tickets in part because doing so entitles them to playoff tickets at face value. Still others are local politicians and other influential people. Do you think that if the Prime Minister wanted to attend the seventh game of the Stanley Cup finals, there would be some way to find a ticket for him or her? *Yes, of course!*

What about the people who pay over $1000 for a ticket? Some of them are just fanatics. Others are wealthy fans who are happy to pay the money to have someone else get them tickets. Still others are corporations who consider the high price of the ticket just another entertainment expense.

1. There are many different possible costs involved with getting a ticket for only $100. Season ticket holders must buy tickets to games in which they might not otherwise have much interest; people must forego many other options to wait in line for tickets; some people try to "suck up" to those who control the rationing mechanism; others ingratiate themselves with team members or officials to try to get tickets; and still others try to use political pull. Doing these things is costly — time and scarce resources must be used to further any of these attempts to obtain the cheaper tickets.

2. It is difficult to determine who, if anyone, they are hurting. The people who pay $1000 for a ticket signify by doing so that they would rather have the ticket than anything else they could buy for $1000; of course, they would rather pay less, but they are still better off getting a high-priced ticket than not getting a ticket at all. Most often, those who complain about scalpers are those who fantasize that somehow if scalpers hadn't sold a ticket to A for $1000, then that ticket would be available to them for only $100. In their dreams....

3. This is one of those normative issues that we probably shouldn't touch in economics, narrowly defined. In one case the rationing mechanism benefits those who have low-valued alternative uses for their time; in the other case the rationing mechanism benefits those who have cultivated valuable personal contacts; and in the case of scalping the rationing mechanism benefits those who are willing and able to pay the most. In every instance *some* form of rationing must take place to discriminate between all the potential ticket buyers.

G. Changing the Economy's Production Possibilities

Every economy, no matter what its political structure, faces the problem of scarcity. One result of this scarcity is that somehow, people must choose how many of their scarce resources should be used to produce consumer goods and services for consumption this year, versus how many should be used to produce capital goods — things which will enable them to produce even more in future years. These capital goods might be such things as buildings and machinery; they might also include stocks of inventories; and they could include investments in human capital (otherwise known as education). By educating the work force, the people in an economy are deciding *not* to have the students produce consumer goods and services now with the expectation that those who become better educated will produce even more in the future.

Most developed economies devote roughly between ten and twenty percent of their scarce resources to the production of capital goods. Less-developed countries have difficulty emerging from poverty because they find it difficult to bear the *opportunity costs* of foregoing current consumption, when they are so poor, in order to build up their capital stocks.

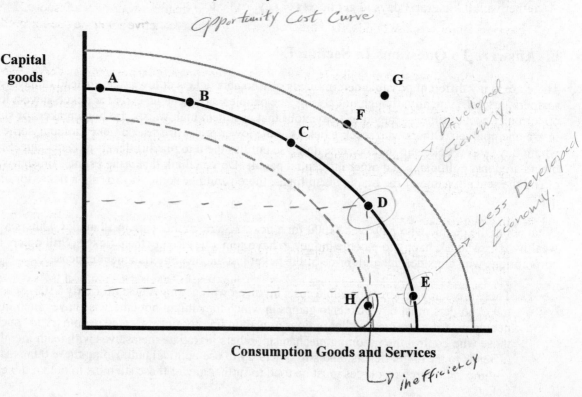

1. In the opportunity cost curves shown on the previous page, which point along the solid black curve represents the combination of capital goods and consumption goods and services chosen by a developed economy? Which point shows the combination chosen by a less developed economy?

2. If the economy were at point **D**, how could it get to point **F**?

3. What might happen to cause an economy to move to point **H**?

4. In a market economy, who makes the decision about which point to choose on the production possibilities curve? How do they make that decision?

H. Answers to Questions in Section G

1. Developed economies most likely choose a combination like that represented by point **D**. They choose to consume most of their output, but they still use many of their scarce resources to produce capital goods so that they can consume even more in the future. Less developed economies end up at points more like point **E**. They produce some capital goods, but nearly all of their scarce resources are devoted to the production of consumer goods; and many of the capital goods that they *do* produce are used to replace old capital goods that have depreciated. An extreme existentialist might choose to produce at the bottom end of the opportunity cost curve — consume all today and not worry about the future. No economies, not even the most austere of the Puritan societies of the 16th and 17th centuries, choose points like **A**, with so little current consumption and so much capital accumulation.

2. It might be able to get to point **F** simply by staying at point **D** this year. The capital goods it produces this year would give it more resources next year, and so it might be able to produce even more of both capital and consumption goods then. If the people in the economy want to get to **F** even quicker or with greater certainty, then this year they might consider choosing to produce at point **C** instead of point **D**. By choosing to forego some current consumption to produce more capital goods, they then would have more productive inputs to use for production next year.

3. Economies move to points like **H**, inside their current production possibilities curves, when they either (a) have fewer productive inputs in the future than they do now or (b) implement policies that encourage less efficient use of their current resources. They might have fewer productive inputs if they choose to produce very little capital — not even enough to replace their current capital stock — or if they have a serious drought or natural catastrophe. They might also get to point **H** if they implement policies that encourage inefficiency, much as what happened in agriculture and other industries in the Soviet Union during its last decade or so of communism and its early years of transition to a market economy.

4. In a market economy, people choose individually how much to consume and how much to save. Their savings are then generally channeled through the financial system for others to borrow for use on capital projects such as clearing land, building factories and homes, or financing inventory expansions. Individuals choose how much to save based on their own expectations, prices, and interest rates, and these economic signals affect their decisions. At the same time individuals choose how much to borrow, also on the basis of their expectations, prices, and interest rates.

Chapter 3

Substitutes Everywhere: The Concept of Demand

A. Multiple-Choice Questions on the Principal Ideas of Chapter 3

1. The word demand is used in economic theory to refer to
   A. the amounts people are willing to purchase at various prices.
   B. those wants or needs that are urgent or pressing.
   C. needs of both households and business firms.
   D. wants that are economic in character, rather than social, cultural, or spiritual.

2. The law of demand asserts that
   A. there is someone somewhere who has a use for anything.
   B. people will spend a constant dollar amount for a good that is in demand.
   C. if people want something, they can always get it.
   D. the quantity of a good that people will want to purchase and the price they must pay for it are inversely related.

3. Which of the following will **not** change the "demand" for movie tickets? *has to do with anything other than the Price of the movie Tickets*
   A. A change in the cost of hiring babysitting services.
   B. A change in the price of movie tickets.
   C. A change in the quality of television programs.
   D. A change in the income of moviegoers.

4. Someone is confusing the demand and the quantity demanded by asserting that an increase in the price of gasoline will
   A. have no effect on gasoline purchases.
   B. force people to do without gasoline.
   C. compel people to spend more of their income on gasoline.
   D. reduce the demand for gasoline.

5. If a good is scarce,
   A. it must be rationed.
   B. its price is too high.
   C. its price is too low.
   D. people cannot purchase as much as they want to purchase.

6. The money cost of purchasing a good is
   A. the only part of the cost of which economic theory takes account.
   B. the most important part of the cost to purchasers.
   C. the least important part of the cost to purchasers.
   D. only one part of the cost of acquiring the good that affects purchasers' decisions.

7. Price elasticity of demand is defined as the
   A. quantity demanded divided by the price.
   B. change in the quantity demanded divided by the change in the price.
   C. percentage change in the price divided by the percentage change in the quantity demanded.
   D. percentage change in the quantity demanded divided by the percentage change in the price.

8. Which of the following sets of goods might, under the right circumstances, be substitutes for a bicycle?
   A. Shoes, a motorcycle, roller skates
   B. Carrots, skim milk, sugar-free soft drink
   C. A chess set, a colour television, a book of crossword puzzles
   D. Barbells, a tennis racket, a non-motorized lawnmower
   E. They could all be substitutes for a bicycle under the right circumstances

B. Answers to, and Explanations of, Multiple-Choice Questions on the Principal Ideas of Chapter 3

1. **A.** The concept of demand asserts nothing about the nature of the good or of the purposes for which it is wanted. The demand for a good merely expresses the relationship between its price and the amount or quantity some set of people will be willing to purchase during some time period.

2. **D.** It would be odd behaviour indeed if anyone chose to buy more of a good because the good costs more to get it, or to buy less because it costs less. If we observe that the price and quantity demanded of the good have moved in the same direction rather than in opposite directions, it is reasonable to assume that something has occurred to change the demand itself.

3. **B.** Almost anything is capable of changing the demand for a good except the price of that good itself. That's a matter of definition. A change in the good's price affects the quantity demanded; it does not affect the relationship between its price and the quantity of it that will be demanded, which would be required if the change in price were to affect the demand. But there may be more to the story. See the next question and its answer.

4. **D.** An increase in the price of gasoline reduces the quantity demanded, not the demand. Of course, a higher price for gasoline also encourages automobile manufacturers to develop more fuel-efficient products. When more fuel-efficient automobiles become available at lower prices, then the demand curve for gasoline shifts downward to the left. So a rise in the price of gasoline might well trigger changes that eventually reduce the demand for gasoline. But the immediate, direct effect of a price increase is a reduction in the quantity demanded, not in the demand. For additional practice on this point, see Questions for Discussion 10 through 13 in the textbook.

5. **A.** Scarcity means that everyone cannot have as much as they would like to have without sacrificing something else that they also value. Chapter 6 will explore further the concept of scarcity and contrast it with the quite different concept of shortage.

6. **D.** The money cost is a part of the cost that can be changed relatively quickly and by a small or large amount. Changes in the money cost of a good are therefore an especially effective way of reconciling the incompatible intentions of people, such as a desire to acquire more of the good than is available. But there certainly are other costs than money costs, and economic theorists will sometimes emphasize them.

7. **D.** If they are to be compared in any meaningful way, the relative changes that price elasticity of demand compares must be stated as percentage changes. This also eliminates the arbitrary influence that would otherwise be exerted by the choice of units (grams versus kilograms, cents versus dollars).

8. **E.** Human purposes and the means for achieving them are almost infinitely diverse, which is why we can safely assume that there are substitutes for any good under at least some circumstances. Is that bicycle wanted for transportation, weight reduction, recreation, or exercise? The answer will determine what goods are substitutes for a bicycle.

C. A STEP-BY-STEP REVIEW OF CHAPTER 2

1. A good is free
    A. if government supplies it.
    B. if it is sold at a zero money price.
    C. to someone who can acquire it without sacrificing anything else of value.
    D. when everyone has it.

2. Most goods are not free to most people under most circumstances because
    A. business is run for profit.
    B. just acquiring a good usually requires the expenditure of time, which has other valuable uses.
    C. people must pay taxes.
    D. most property is privately owned.

3. "The people of Canada want energy independence." This statement is
    A. false.
    B. true.
    C. extremely vague.
    D. unscientific.

4. "Most Canadian citizens do not want this country to be dependent on other nations for energy resources." This statement is
    A. probably false.
    B. probably true.
    C. almost certainly true if the cost of energy independence is very low and almost certainly false if the cost of energy independence is very high.
    D. unscientific.

5. Medical care could be offered free to every citizen who wants it if
    A. medical resources were in such abundant supply that one person's use of them did not deprive anyone else.
    B. the government paid all medical bills.
    C. health-care practitioners were willing to serve without pay.
    D. sick people could be counted on to behave responsibly.

6. If there are 1000 cars that their owners want to park and 800 parking spaces, free parking cannot be provided to
    A. all of the 1000 car owners unless the capitalist system is abolished.
    B. all of the 1000 car owners unless they agree to share fairly.
    C. all of the 1000 car owners under any social system.
    D. any of the 1000 car owners.

7. Intelligent choice requires an assessment of
    A. past costs against past benefits.
    B. past costs against future benefits.
    C. future costs against future benefits.
    D. future costs against past benefits.

8. Economic theory assumes that
    A. buyers and sellers have all the information they can use.
    B. information is often a costly good to acquire and there are substitutes for additional information.
    C. decision makers have a complete knowledge of all the relevant alternatives.
    D. economic decisions result from random behaviour.

9. Economists prefer to talk about the quantity demanded rather than the quantity needed or the quantity wanted because
    A. the quantity demanded is more stable.
    B. needs and wants vary from one person to another.
    C. they associate quantity demanded with the idea of a particular price.
    D. they have nothing else to talk about.

10. "Housing prices rose again last month, so I'm going to buy a house." The person who makes such a statement probably
    A. hates living in an apartment.
    B. is contradicting the law of demand.
    C. would rather buy a house at current prices than at the higher prices expected in the future.
    D. is wealthy enough to ignore prices.

11. "If you don't know which brand is best, buy the most expensive one." The person who makes such a statement probably is recommending
    A. you patronize his own store.
    B. a violation of the law of demand.
    C. that price be used as an indication of quality.
    D. cautious consumer behaviour.

12. Inflation means an increase in the
    A. cost of living.
    B. sacrifice required to obtain desired goods.
    C. money price of goods.
    D. number of people in poverty.

13. If the average of all prices as measured by the Consumer Price Index doubled from 1980 to 1999 while the price of an average pair of jeans rose from $20 to $30, then jeans
    A. cost half again as much to buy in 1999 as they did in 1980.
    B. cost in 1999 about three-fourths of what they had cost in 1980.
    C. cost just as much in 1999 as they had in 1980.
    D. must be of lower quality in 1999 compared with 1980.

14. The demand for a good
    A. is a constant amount.
    B. cannot be expressed simply as an amount.
    C. can always be stated simply as an amount.
    D. is a variable amount.

15. The demand for a good
    A. can only be expressed by a schedule of prices and quantities.
    B. can only be expressed by a curve showing the relationship between prices and quantities.
    C. can be expressed either as a schedule or a curve.
    D. is the specific amount that people want to purchase at the prevailing price.

16. "As the price of gasoline rises, the demand for gasoline will fall." That statement is
    - A. always true empirically.
    - B. basic economic theory.
    - C. probably misleading because it mistakenly substitutes the word *demand* for *quantity demanded*.
    - D. much too dogmatic to be helpful.

17. If we observe an increase in both the price and the quantity demanded of a particular good, we should probably conclude that the
    - A. buyers are being irrational.
    - B. demand for the good has increased.
    - C. law of demand does not apply.
    - D. sellers have conspired to fix prices.

18. If people are willing this year to buy more of a particular good at each and every price than they were willing to buy last year, the
    - A. demand for the good has increased.
    - B. law of demand has been refuted.
    - C. law of demand has been demonstrated.
    - D. cost of living must have risen.

19. A law requiring that all soft drinks be sold in returnable containers for which the customer must pay a deposit
    - A. compels people to return empties.
    - B. encourages people to return empties.
    - C. has an effect only on people with no ecological consciousness.
    - D. resolves the litter problem.

20. Rationing scarce goods by using the criterion of willingness to pay the money price
    - A. distributes scarce goods arbitrarily.
    - B. encourages individuals to economize as their specific situation suggests.
    - C. pays little or no attention to the differences between people.
    - D. prevents the poor from obtaining any until the wealthy have satisfied their wants.

21. There are many excellent substitutes for water because
    - A. people use an inexpensive good like water for so many different purposes.
    - B. so many things contain water.
    - C. people won't die just because they're thirsty for a short time.
    - D. water is recycled by nature.

22. A sizable increase in the price of a consumer good that has suddenly become much more scarce
    - A. compels poor people to do without the good.
    - B. forces every household to spend a larger part of its income on the good.
    - C. gives everyone an incentive to look for and use substitutes.
    - D. will have no effect on the quantity demanded.

23. Higher prices tend to reduce the quantity demanded
    - A. immediately if they're going to have any effect at all.
    - B. by a lesser amount as time goes by because people get accustomed to higher prices.
    - C. by a greater amount as time goes by because time enables consumers and producers to devise better substitutes.
    - D. only until people become accustomed to the higher prices.

24. If the quantity demanded of a particular good changes very little when the price of the good changes substantially, the demand for the good is
    A. perfectly elastic.
    B. relatively elastic.
    C. unit elastic.
    D. relatively inelastic.
    E. perfectly inelastic.

25. If a very small change in the price of a good causes a huge change in the quantity demanded, the demand for the good is
    A. perfectly elastic.
    B. relatively elastic.
    C. unit elastic.
    D. relatively inelastic.
    E. perfectly inelastic.

26. If Canadians spend about the same amount of money on beef when its price is relatively high as when it is relatively low, the demand for beef is [make sure you understand *why*!]
    A. perfectly elastic.
    B. relatively elastic.
    C. unit elastic.
    D. relatively inelastic.
    E. perfectly inelastic.

27. If a 20 percent tuition increase leads to a 10 percent decline in enrolment, the price elasticity of demand is
    A. 2
    B. 0.2
    C. 0.5
    D. 0.3
    E. 0.1

28. For which of these goods would you expect the demand to be most elastic?
    A. Food
    B. Pasta
    C. Spaghetti
    D. Old Neapolitan Brand spaghetti

29. An increase from $5 to $6 in the price of movie tickets is a larger percentage increase in the cost of an evening's entertainment for
    A. unmarried students than for a couple who must hire a babysitter in order to go to a movie.
    B. a couple who must hire a babysitter in order to go to a movie than for an unmarried student.
    C. poor people than for rich people.
    D. people who like movies than for those who don't.

30. For the reason suggested in the preceding question, the price elasticity of demand for movie tickets among students is likely to be
    A. greater than among couples with small children.
    B. less than among couples with small children.
    C. less for poor students than for rich ones.
    D. less for people who like movies than for those who don't.

31. A business firm selling in a very competitive market faces a
    - A. highly elastic demand curve
    - B. highly inelastic demand curve
    - C. demand curve of unit elasticity
    - D. small demand curve.

32. Percentage markups tend to be low on food items in grocery stores because
    - A. people can always grow their own food
    - B. food is a necessity of life.
    - C. there are usually many excellent substitutes for the food items handled by any particular grocery store.
    - D. the demand for grocery food is highly inelastic.

33. The vast increases in oil revenues received by OPEC members after 1973 demonstrated that the demand for oil was
    - A. completely inelastic in 1973.
    - B. inelastic at the original 1973 price levels.
    - C. elastic at the original 1973 price levels.
    - D. under the control of the multinational oil companies.

34. Price elasticity of demand determines the relationship between price changes and changes in total sales revenue. When demand is inelastic,
    - A. price and total revenue move in opposite directions
    - B. price and total revenue move in the same direction
    - C. total revenue increases whether price goes up or down
    - D. total revenue decreases whether price goes up or down.

35. We can be confident that the demand for clean air on the part of people who must pay the cost of obtaining cleaner air will be
    - A. perfectly inelastic because there is no substitute for clean air
    - B. highly elastic because air is available in such abundance
    - C. less than completely inelastic.
    - D. larger than the demand for clean water.

36. The law of demand asserts that, over the whole range of possible prices, there is no such thing as
    - A. a completely elastic demand
    - B. an inelastic demand.
    - C. a unit elastic demand.
    - D. a completely inelastic demand.

D. Answers to the Review Questions in Chapter 3

1. C	7. C	13. B	19. B	25. B	31. A
2. B	8. B	14. B	20. B	26. C	32. C
3. C	9. C	15. C	21. A	27. C	33. B
4. C	10. C	16. C	22. C	28. D	34. B
5. A	11. C	17. B	23. C	29. A	35. C
6. C	12. C	18. A	24. D	30. A	36. D

E. Demand: Schedules, Curves, and Elasticity

The schedule on the next page shows the number of cans of tennis balls that would be purchased during each summer month in Footfault, Ontario, at a variety of prices:

Price per Can	Cans Demanded Each Month
$5	100
4	200
3	290
2	350
1	370

[handwritten: P↓] *[handwritten: Qd↑ Qd Demand Increases as Price falls]*

[handwritten: ↱ should say "Quantity Demanded"]

1. "The demand for tennis balls in Footfault increases as the price falls." This statement

    A. is true if the above schedule is reliable.
    B. should cause you to say: "No, only the quantity demanded increases. The demand is the entire schedule." *[circled B]*

2. In order to show a genuine increase in the demand for tennis balls, you would have to cross out the numbers under "Cans Demanded Each Month" and write in

    A. larger numbers, because an increase in demand means a larger quantity is being demanded at each price than was formerly demanded. *[circled A]*
    B. the name of your favourite brand of tennis balls.

3. Which one of the events listed below could reasonably be expected to cause a genuine increase in the demand for tennis balls in Footfault?

    A. A rainy summer.
    B. Reduced prices on tennis rackets and tennis clothes. *[circled B]*
    C. Shutting off of lights on courts to conserve energy .
    D. Lower prices for tennis balls.
    E. Opening of new golf courses and handball courts.

4. Which one of the events listed in the preceding question will have no effect on the demand for tennis balls in Footfault? *[handwritten: Lower Prices on Tennis Balls.]*

5. Between $5 and $4, the relationship between price and total revenue shows that the demand for tennis balls is

    A. elastic. *[circled A]*
    B. inelastic.

    [handwritten: P↓ TE↑   (P↓ Qd↑) = Elastic.]

6. Between $3 and $2, the relationship between price and total revenue shows that the demand for tennis balls is

    A. elastic.
    B. inelastic. *[circled B]*

    [handwritten: Because the Qd did not remain constant.]

7. What is the exact price elasticity of demand between $5 and $4? Calculate the answer so that you obtain the same answer whether you begin with the higher or the lower price. *[handwritten: ? 7 100/1 What?]*

F. Answers to Questions in Section E

1. B. (Sorry to harp on it, but the distinction is important, and many students have trouble grasping it).

2. A.

3. B. (A, C, and E would cause a decrease in the demand for tennis balls.)

4. D. (by definition).
5. A. (Price and total revenue change in opposite directions.)

6. B. (Price and total revenue change in the same direction.)

7. The change in quantity demanded is 100 and the change in price is $1. But what are the percentage changes? They will be affected by our choice of the base from which to calculate each percentage change. In order to obtain the same result whether you calculate from $5 to $4 or from $4 to $5, use as the base the average of the two quantities and prices from between which you are calculating the elasticity. In this case that would be 150 for quantity and $4.50 for price. So the percentage change in quantity is 100 ÷ 150 and the percentage change in price is $1 ÷ $4.50. The coefficient of elasticity is consequently 2/3 ÷ 2/9 = 3.

    This method of calculating elasticity yields what we call *arc elasticity* of demand. If we had used 100 and $5 as the bases for quantity and price, respectively, we would have obtained a considerably different answer: 100% ÷ 20% = 5.

    If the question had asked for the elasticity between $4 and $5 and this had prompted us to use 200 and $4 as the bases for quantity and price respectively, our answer would have been 50% ÷ 25% = 2.

    To avoid misleading or arbitrary answers, especially when the percentage changes are large, always use as the base the *average* of the two quantities and prices (i.e. use *arc elasticity of demand*).

G. Questions to Think about

1. Two firms offer supplemental hospitalization insurance to their employees. Firm I pays the entire premium for an insurance plan that pays 75 percent of hospital costs incurred. Firm II pays only 50 percent of the premium, requiring employees to pay the other half; but the insurance plan pays 100 percent of hospitalization costs. Think through the different implications of each insurance plan by filling in the blanks in the following paragraph:

    The quantity of hospital care demanded per insured employee will tend to be greater in Firm _II_ . The cost of entering the hospital relative to the cost of not entering in any given case will be higher for insured employees in Firm _I_ . Physicians will more readily instruct their patients to enter the hospital for observation if the patients are insured employees of Firm _II_ . A greater eagerness to get out of the hospital quickly will tend to be observed among insured employees of Firm _I_ .

2. Many people who could significantly improve their health and lengthen their life expectancy by eating less, drinking less, exercising more, and not smoking fail to follow these good health practices. What does this imply about the elasticity of their demand for health? *Completely Inelastic.*

3. If the Canadian government suddenly and unexpectedly increased the federal gasoline tax enough to bring the price of gasoline up to European levels, would the quantity of gasoline demanded by Canadians per person decline to the European level? *No*

4. Suppose the total dollar revenue from wheat sales by Canadian farmers rises 20 percent in a year when the total number of bushels sold falls by 20 percent.

    A. What would this tell you about the price elasticity of demand for wheat? *Inelastic*
    B. Does this imply that less wheat is more valuable than more wheat? *See answer guide.*

H. Answers to the Questions in Section G

1. II, I, II, I.

2. The demand is less than completely inelastic; the high cost causes people to "purchase" less "good health."

3. No. There are many reasons why the demand for gasoline is greater in Canada than in Europe, including longer average travel distances, heavier automobiles, and less adequate public transportation systems in Canada than in Europe. With time these differences could be expected to narrow if the Canadian gasoline price remained at the European level.

4. A. The demand is inelastic. If you answered "unit elastic," you were confusing a 20 percent rise in total revenue with a 20 percent rise in price. For total revenue to rise 20 percent when the quantity sold declines by 20 percent, the price will have to rise by considerably more than 20 percent.
    B. To whom? Not to consumers of wheat products. And not to individual wheat farmers, who would always prefer to have a larger crop to sell. But for wheat farmers collectively, a smaller total crop may well be exchangeable for a larger money income.

Chapter 4

Behind the Demand Curve

A. Multiple-Choice Questions on the Principal Ideas of Chapter 4

1. Even though we assume that human wants are unlimited, we also assume that after some point, consuming more of a particular good adds less and less to your overall sense of satisfaction. This assumption is called

    A. the assumption of *diminishing marginal utility*.
    B. the point of *diminishing returns*.
    C. the assumption of *diminishing total utility*.
    D. the point of *diminishing utility*.
    E. the assumption of *diminishing indifference*.

    [handwritten: ↳ utility]

2. If you eat one hamburger, and then eat a second one, usually eating the second one will add less to your overall utility than eating the first one did. Will eating the second one make you worse off?

    A. Not if the marginal utility of eating it is positive and you don't have to buy the hamburger.
    B. Only if eating it reduces your total utility.
    C. Yes, if eating it gives you negative marginal utility.
    D. All of the above.
    E. None of the above.

3. *Consumer surplus* measures

    A. the difference between total utility and marginal utility that a person receives from consuming the last unit of a good.
    B. the extra utility that a consumer receives from consuming an additional unit of a good.
    C. the difference between the most a consumer would be willing to pay for something and the amount s/he actually ends up paying.
    D. the amount of a good that a consumer has left over (as a surplus) after the maximum total utility has been achieved.
    E. the number of surplus, or extra, consumers wanting to purchase a product which is in short supply.

4. A *budget line* is analogous to a production possibilities curve (or opportunity cost curve) because it shows

    A. all the combinations of goods it is possible for consumers to consume, given their limited resources.
    B. absolutely nothing about which combination of goods and services the consumer will actually choose from among the possible ones.
    C. the trade-off a consumer must make if s/he would like to consume more of one particular good.
    D. the opportunity costs of deciding to consume more of one particular good.
    E. All of the above.

5. An *indifference curve* shows
    A. all the combinations of goods that a consumer will want to consume.
    B. all the combinations of goods that a consumer is able to consume, given his income and the prices of the goods.
    C. all the different consumption bundles that yield the same total utility to the consumer.
    D. the point at which each consumer becomes indifferent between consuming more or less of a good.
    E. the attitude of students toward taking economics courses.

6. A map with a consumer's indifference curves and budget line will indicate the combination the consumer should consume in order to maximize her utility as
    A. an endpoint of the budget line
    B. an endpoint of one of the indifference curves
    C. the highest indifference curve
    D. the lowest indifference curve
    E. the highest possible indifference curve the consumer can reach while still on the budget line (usually the point of tangency between the two).

7. When the price rises for the good on the horizontal axis of an indifference-map-budget-line graph,
    A. the consumer will choose to buy more of that good.
    B. the indifference curves will shift toward the origin of the graph.
    C. the budget line rotates clockwise.
    D. the budget line rotates counter-clockwise.
    E. the budget line shifts inward, toward the origin.
    F. the budget line shifts outward, away from the origin.

B. Answers to, and Explanations of, the Multiple-Choice Questions on the Principle Ideas of Chapter 4.

1. **A.** As you consume more of something, the *additional* utility you receive from it begins to decline. Consuming more still adds to your total utility, but doings so adds less and less, the more you consume.

2. **D.** Eating an additional hamburger will increase your total utility if that burger still has a positive marginal utility. If you have to pay for the burger, though, you might be better off spending the money on something else that will add more to your overall, total utility. If the second burger has a negative marginal utility, consuming it will subtract from your total utility and make you worse off (unless someone pays you a lot to eat it and you can use the money to increase your utility some other way).

3. **C.** Most sellers don't know how much we'd be willing to pay for something; in fact in many situations, even if they knew the maximum we'd be willing to pay, say, for a litre of milk, they can't charge that much because there are so many other sellers competing with them. As a result, even if we'd be willing to pay seven dollars for a litre of milk, we don't have to pay that much. The difference between what we'd be willing to pay and the amount we actually pay is called *consumer surplus*. Geometrically, it is the area between the demand curve and the price we pay for a good.

4. **E.** A budget line is just like a production possibilities curve or opportunity cost curve. The difference is that the location of an opportunity cost curve is determined by production technologies and scarce resources [see Chapter 2]. The location of a budget line, however, is determined by a consumer's income and the prices of the goods. Otherwise, they both show what is *possible*, but they give no indication which combination of goods will actually be chosen. Also, they both show trade-offs, or opportunity costs, as you move from one combination to another.

5. **C**. Indifference curves and indifference maps are geometric representations of consumer preferences. An indifference curve is drawn through all the points representing the same total utility. For most goods, points to the left of (or below) the curve represent bundles of goods yielding lower total utility; and points to the right of (or above) the curve represent bundles yielding higher total utility. Indifference curves do *not* say anything about what the consumer would be able to consume — that is shown with the budget line. And one more thing: different consumers have different-shaped indifference curves if they have different tastes and preferences.

6. **E**. We assume that consumer attempt to maximize their utility, that they are rational maximizers. Maximizing their utility is the same thing as get to the highest possible indifference curve. But the key to this equivalence is that the highest possible indifference curve is the highest one they can reach, given the constraint represented by their budget line.

7. **C**. When the price of the good on the horizontal axis increases, the consumer would not be able to buy as much of it if she spent all her income on it. Consequently the endpoint of the budget line along that axis must move closer to the origin. But the consumer could still buy just as much as before of the good measured along the vertical axis, so that endpoint of the budget line doesn't move.

C. Step-by-Step Review Of Chapter 4

1. Why do diamonds have a higher price per ounce than water? We need water to survive, but we don't need diamonds.

    A. Diamond sales are controlled by an international monopoly but water sales are not.
    B. An extra ounce of diamonds adds more to the total utility of most people than an extra ounce of water.
    C. Diamonds are harder than water.
    D. Diamonds are provided by the capitalistic, market economy; water is usually provided by governments or by government-regulated firms.
    E. None of the above.

2. What is the optimal (rational, utility-maximizing) amount to eat at an "all-you-can-eat" buffet?

    A. As much as possible, regardless of whether it makes you sick.
    B. As much as possible, but stop just before you actually get sick.
    C. Equal amounts of everything.
    D. Just enough to make sure that the price per serving for everything you *do* eat is less than it would be if you ordered those same things from the menu.
    E. Up to the point at which the marginal utility from consuming another serving of anything would be less than or equal to zero.

3. Which of the following choices better expresses a consideration of total utility than of marginal utility?

    A. A household moves from a four-room to a five-room apartment.
    B. A family discovers just the right antique picture frame for Uncle Bill's picture.
    C. A shopper decides to purchase the large size of laundry detergent instead of the medium size.
    D. A woman trades in her car for a slightly larger model.
    E. The Smiths decide to install a whirlpool tub instead of a regular bathtub when they are remodeling their bathroom.

4. Suzy has the opportunity to buy coolers and small bags of pretzels. Table 4.1 shows the total utility she receives from consuming various quantities of each. We have also provided a column for you to calculate the marginal utilities.

Number of Coolers	Total Utility	Marginal Utility	Number of Small Bags of Pretzels	Total Utility	Marginal Utility
Table 4.1 Suzy's Total Utility from consuming coolers and pretzels					
1	24		1	10	
2	56		2	18	
3	83		3	24	
4	103		4	29	
5	113		5	33	
6	113		6	36	

How many coolers and how many bags of pretzels should Suzy consume to maximize her utility?

A. 5 coolers and 6 bags of pretzels.
B. 6 coolers and 6 bags of pretzels.
C. 5 coolers and 1 bag of pretzels.
D. 2 coolers and 1 bag of pretzels.
E. There isn't enough information provided to answer this question.

5. Suppose the price of coolers is $2 each and the price of small bags of pretzels is $1 per bag. How many coolers and how many bags of pretzels should Suzy consume to maximize her utility?

A. 5 coolers and 1 bag of pretzels.
B. 4 coolers and 1 bag of pretzels.
C. 3 coolers and 1 bag of pretzels.
D. 5 coolers and 4 bags of pretzels.
E. There isn't enough information provided to answer this question.

6. Suppose that the price of coolers is $2 each, the price of small bags of pretzels is $1 per bag, and Suzy has $9 to spend on coolers and pretzels. How many of each should she consume to maximize her utility?

A. 4 coolers and 1 bag of pretzels.
B. 3 ½ coolers and 2 bags of pretzels.
C. 3 coolers and 3 bags of pretzels.
D. 2 coolers and 5 bags of pretzels.
E. There isn't enough information provided to answer this question.

7. An example of a "marginal" value would be

A. your mark on the 3rd economics quiz.
B. the average temperature in Lennoxville in December.
C. the $255.44 that I paid for beverages to host a party last weekend.
D. your monthly rent when you've signed a 12-month lease.
E. the "save percentage" of an NHL goalie.

8. Suppose that Sammy is consuming both apples and oranges and that he is maximizing his utility. The marginal utility of the last apple he eats is 20, and the marginal utility of the last orange he eats is 10. If the price of an apple is 50¢, then what must be the price of an orange?

    A. 5¢
    B. 10¢
    C. 25¢
    D. 50¢
    E. $1.00

    Use this information to answer questions 9 - 12:
    Phebe is willing to pay $7 for the first litre of milk she purchases each week, $6 for the second one, $5 for the third one, and so on. The current market price of milk is $2 per litre. (Assume for this problem that she buys the larger quantity if she would be indifferent between two different quantities)

9. What is Phebe's total consumer surplus?

    A. $28
    B. $27
    C. $15   ?
    D. $12
    E. $5

10. What is the total dollar value of the milk (that she buys) to Phebe?

    A. $28
    B. $27   ?
    C. $15
    D. $12
    E. $5

11. What is the consumer surplus to Phebe of the *last litre* of milk that she buys

    A. $4
    B. $3
    C. $2   ?
    D. $1
    E. zero

12. How much money will Phebe spend on milk each week?

    A. $28
    B. $23   ?
    C. $15
    D. $12
    E. $5

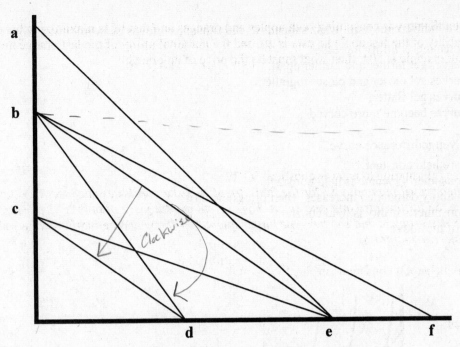

Figure 4.1   Budget Lines for Veronica

13. Suppose that line *be* in Figure 4.1 shows Veronica's budget line for chips and chocolate bars. What should be measured on the vertical and horizontal axes?
    A. the price of chips and the price of chocolate bars.
    B. the price of chips and the quantity of chips.
    C. the price of chocolate bars and the quantity of chips.
    D. the price of chocolate bars and the quantity of chocolate bars.
    E. the quantity of chips and the quantity of chocolate bars.

14. If chocolate bars are measured along the horizontal axis of Figure 4.1, what will happen to Veronica's budget line if the price of chocolate bars doubles? *Rotate Clockwise*
    A. Nothing. She will move from one point on *be* to a different point on *be*.
    B. It will rotate from *be* to *bd*.
    C. It will rotate from *be* to *bf*.
    D. It will rotate from *be* to *ae*.
    E. It will shift inward (toward the origin) from *be* to *cd*.

15. What will happen to Veronica's budget line if her income is cut in half?
    A. Nothing. She will move from one point on *be* to a different point on *be*.
    B. It will rotate from *be* to *bd*.
    C. It will rotate from *be* to *bf*.
    D. It will rotate from *be* to *ae*.
    E. It will shift inward (toward the origin) from *be* to *cd*.

16. If chocolate bars are measured along the horizontal axis in Figure 4.1, and her original budget line is *be*, what would happen to Veronica's budget line if you told her she could have all the chocolate bars she wants and doesn't have to pay for them?
    A. It would become vertical at point *e*.
    B. It would become horizontal at point *b*.
    C. It would rotate from *be* to *bf*.
    D. It would rotate from *be* to *ce*.
    E. It would disappear; you cannot show a budget line for a product for which there is no price.

⌐D deals w̄ utility

17. On a typical indifference map, what happens as the consumer moves outward, away from the origin?
    A. The consumer's utility increases.
    B. The curves get farther and farther apart.
    C. The curves get closer and closer together.
    D. The curves get flatter.
    E. The curves become more curved.

18. Along a given indifference curve,
    A. Price are held constant.
    B. The consumer's income is held constant.
    C. The quantity demanded increases when prices increase.
    D. The consumer's utility is held constant.   *Because indifference curves don't deal*
    E. None of the above.   *with price.*

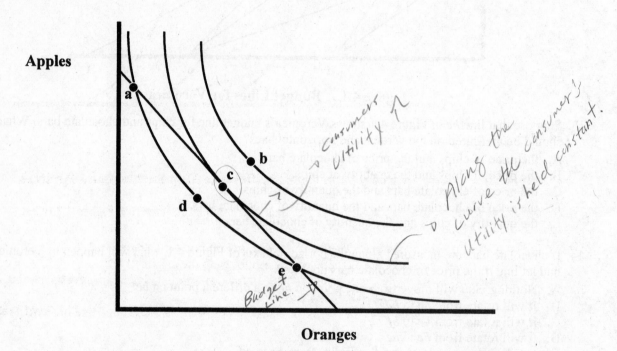

→ consumers utility ↑

Along the curve the consumer's utility is held constant.

Budget Line.

Figure 4.2
Rachael's Indifference Map and Budget Line for Apples and Oranges

19. Given her income and preferences, and given the prices of apples and oranges, all shown by the budget line and indifference map in Figure 4.2 , what combination of apples and oranges should Rachael choose to consume in order to maximize her utility?

    A. *a*, because it is the highest point in the graph.
    B. *b*, because it is on the highest indifference curve.
    C. *c*, because it is on the highest indifference curve she can reach, given her budget constraint.
    D. *d*, because it represents the most utility.
    E. *e*, because it represents the most oranges.

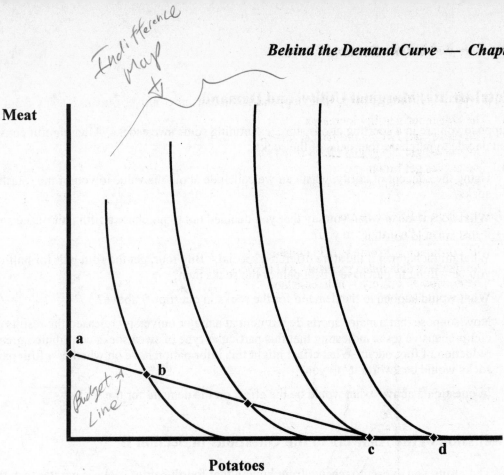

Indifference map

Meat

Budget Line

a

b

c   d

Potatoes

Figure 4.3   Daniel's Budget Line and Indifference Map for Meat and Potatoes

20. Given Daniel's budget line and preferences for meat and potatoes, as shown in Figure 4.3, what combination of meat and potatoes should Daniel buy?

A. *a*, because it represents the best he can do. It is the highest point in the graph.
B. *b*, because it is on the indifference curve which is closest to the origin.
C. *c*, because it is on the highest indifference curve Daniel can reach, given his budget constraint.
D. *d*, because it is on the highest indifference curve.
E. None of the above. Daniel should look for a tangency between his budget line and his indifference map to maximize his utility.

21. Why are demand curves downward-sloping from left to right?

A. When the price of the good goes up, the opportunity cost of purchasing it increases.
B. When the price of the good goes down, your purchasing power increases, and that will usually induce you to purchase more of the good.
C. When the price of the good goes down, the additional utility of purchasing this good, in comparison with what you might have used the money for, makes this good more attractive to you.
D. A, B, and C above.
E. None of the above.

D. Answers to the Review Questions in Chapter 4

1. B	4. E	7. A	10. B	13. E	16. B	19. C
2. E	5. E	8. C	11. E	14. B	17. A	20. C
3. B	6. A	9. C	12. D	15. E	18. D	21. D

E. Total Utility, Marginal Utility, and Demand

Suppose you are in a sporting goods store, examining some sweatsocks. After careful consideration, you decide to purchase four pairs of the socks.

1. Using the concept of utility, what can we conclude about the value to you of the fourth pair of socks?

2. What does it mean when you say that you decided not to purchase a fifth pair of the socks because it just wasn't "worth it" to you?

3. What might happen if the store offered a special: "Buy four, get the fifth pair for half price"? Might you be willing to purchase a fifth pair of the socks then?

4. What would happen to the demand for the socks in question 3 above?

5. Now suppose that a major sports department at a major university released the results of comprehensive tests, indicating that this particular type of sweatsocks contributed greatly to the reduction of foot odour. What effect might this information have on whether a fifth pair of the socks would be "worth it" to you?

6. In question 5 above, what would be the effect on the demand for the socks?

F. Discussion of the Answers to the Questions in Section E

1. The utility you expect to receive from buying that fourth pair of socks is greater than the utility you would expect to receive from any other potential use of the money you would have to give up to buy that pair of socks.

2. But the utility you would expect to receive from the fifth pair of sweat socks is not enough to compensate you for the utility you would expect to lose from having to give up some other use of the money.

3. You might buy a fifth pair in these circumstances. Certainly some people would.

4. Nothing would happen to the demand for sweat socks. The demand curve would not shift. Instead, there would be a movement downward and to the right, along the demand curve. This movement is known as an *increase in the quantity demanded*.

5. The socks themselves haven't changed, but your perception of their quality has changed as a result of this new information. Consequently, the utility you would expect to receive from consuming the fifth pair of socks has increased, perhaps enough to compensate you for the lost utility you would experience from having to forego the consumption of something else in order to buy the fifth pair of socks. So you might be more likely to buy the fifth pair.

6. This new information will change consumers' preferences such that overall they will want to buy more socks, even if the prices don't change. The demand curve will shift to the right. This is known as an *increase in demand*.

G. Using a Budget Line and Indifference Map to Derive a Demand Curve

Mary has a huge flower garden in which she would like to raise silver bells and cockle shells. Her preferences for the flowers involve trade-offs. If one is too expensive, she'll plant less of it and more of the other. Her preferences are shown in Figure 4.4a on the next page. You will use the graph in Figure 4.4b to derive her demand for silver bells.

Figure 4.4a Mary's Preferences for Silver Bells and Cockle Shells

Silver Bells and Cockle Shells

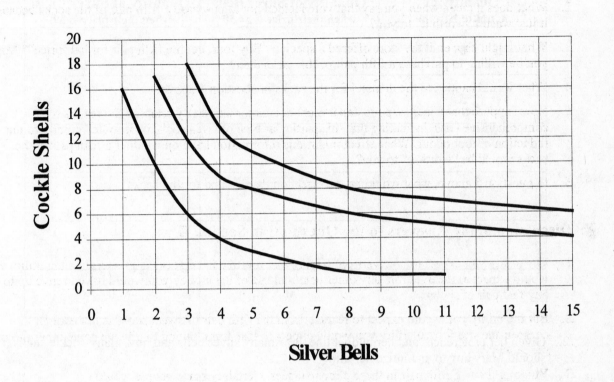

Figure 4.4b Mary's Demand for Silver Bells

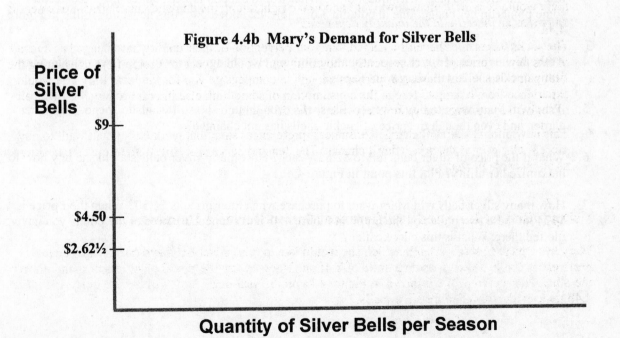

1. Mary has allotted $45 to spend on her garden this season. The price of silver bells is $4.50 each, and the price of cockle shells is $3 each. Complete the first two columns of Table 4.2 below to calculate some of the points on her budget line. Plot these points and connect them to show her budget line in Figure 4.4a.

Table 4.2   Mary's Budget Line for Silver Bells and Cockle Shells

Quantity of Cockle Shells	Quantity of Silver Bells when their price is $4.50	Quantity of Silver Bells when their price is $9
0		
3		
	6	3
9		
12		
	0	0

2. Given her preferences and her budget line, how many silver bells and how many cockle shells should Mary buy to maximize her utility?

3. Suppose the price of silver bells increased from $4.50 apiece to $9 each. What would happen to Mary's indifference map (trick question!)? What would happen to her budget line? Recalculate some points on her budget line in column 3 of Table 4.2 above. Plot this new budget line in Figure 4.4a.

4. At the higher price of silver bells, assuming nothing else changes, how many silver bells and how many cockle shells will Mary want to buy?

5. Why will Mary want to buy fewer cockle shells even though she still wants to spend $45 on her garden and even though the price of cockle shells has not changed?

6. What if the price of silver bells fell to $2.62½ each? How many silver bells should she buy now to maximize her utility? Plot this point in Figure 4.4b.

7. How many silver bells will Mary want to purchase when their price is $4.50? When their price is $9? Plot these two points on the graph in Figure 4.4b and connect all three of the points you have plotted there. What is this curve called?

H. Solutions and Answers to the Questions and Problems in Section G.

1. **Mary's Budget Line for Silver Bells and Cockle Shells**

Quantity of Cockle Shells	Quantity of Silver Bells when their price is $4.50	Quantity of Silver Bells when their price is $9
0	10	5
3	8	4
6	6	3
9	4	2
12	2	1
15	0	0

2. When the price of silver bells is $4.50 each, to maximize her utility Mary should move to the tangency point between the middle budget line and indifference curve shown in Figure 4.5a on the next page. She should buy 4 silver bells and 9 cockle shells.

3. Nothing happens to her indifference map. Her indifference map shows only her preferences and is not affected by changes in prices. However, her budget line rotates clockwise when the price of silver bells increases. Her new budget line is shown as the dotted budget line in Figure 4.5a, connecting the endpoints of 15 cockle shells and 5 silver bells.

4. When the price of silver bells rises to $9 each, Mary will want to buy only 6 cockle shells and 3 silver bells.

5. When the price of silver bells increases, the purchasing power of the money that Mary has set aside for her garden will fall. Because the purchasing power of her $45 declines, she will buy less of everything. Here, the "income effect" is very strong. But it doesn't always work this way. Notice what happens in question 6.

6. When the price of silver bells drops, Mary's budget line rotates out, counter-clockwise, and she will choose to buy 8 silver bells and 8 cockle shells. She chooses to buy fewer cockle shells in this case because the price of silver bells has fallen so much that they are much more attractive to her. Here, the "substitution effect" is very strong.

7. It's a demand curve.

Figures 4.5a and 4.5b   Solutions to Section G.

Silver Bells and Cockle Shells

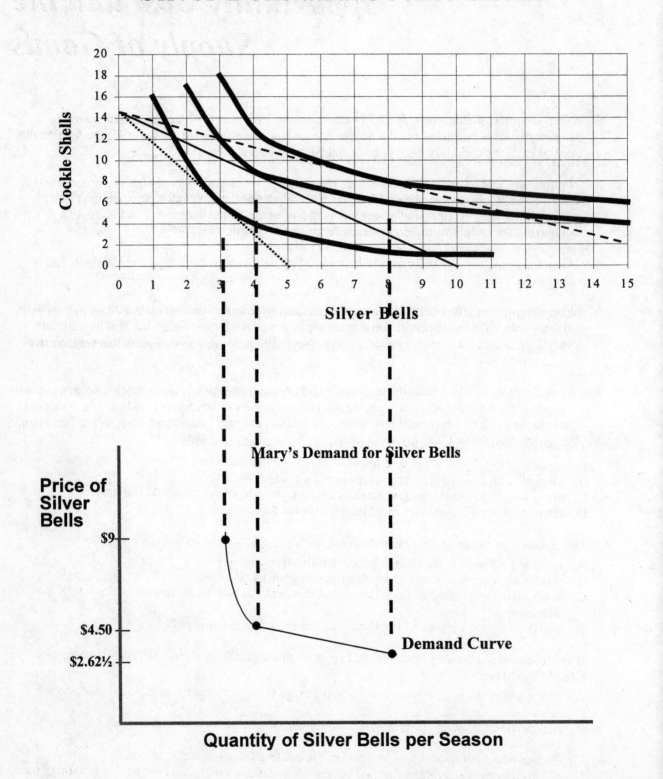

Mary's Demand for Silver Bells

Demand Curve

Quantity of Silver Bells per Season

Chapter 5

Opportunity Cost and the Supply of Goods

A. Multiple-Choice Questions On The Principal Ideas Of Chapter 5

1. All costs that affect people's decisions and consequently all costs capable of affecting demand or supply are
   A. expenditures of human effort, representing someone's "toil and trouble."
   B. embodied in goods through past productive efforts.
   C. costs that involve monetary expenditures.
   D. the value of the opportunities people expect to give up by making those decisions.

2. The opportunity cost of producing a good will depend on the cost of using the inputs required for its production, which in turn will depend on
   A. the value the owners of those inputs expect them to have in their next most valuable alternative use.
   B. the cost of producing those inputs.
   C. everything in the past that has contributed to the creation of those inputs.
   D. the quantity of labour embodied in those inputs.

3. The cost of obtaining a particular kind of resource is likely to rise when
   A. owners of that kind of resource begin receiving smaller incomes.
   B. owners of that kind of resource begin receiving larger incomes.
   C. more valuable alternative opportunities become available for that kind of resource.
   D. alternative opportunities for that kind of resource diminish.

4. The cost of a particular government decision, such as using tax dollars to buy up eggs,
   A. is the net addition to the budget which that decision causes.
   B. is the sum of the value of the opportunities forgone by taxpayers.
   C. is the difference between the dollar cost of that decision and the dollar cost of the least expensive alternative.
   D. will be different for federal legislators, taxpayers, and egg consumers.

5. If the federal government prohibited the export of lumber to Japan, the cost of building houses in Canada would probably
   A. not be affected because other costs would change to compensate for any change in materials costs.
   B. rise because Canadian lumber sellers would have to charge more to make up for the lost export business.
   C. decline because this action would reduce the bidding for construction materials.
   D. not be affected because the demand for lumber in Japan cannot affect the cost of building houses in Canada.

6. Compared with a system in which resource ownership is not clearly established, when resources are clearly and definitely owned by someone,

   A. resources will be withheld from use more frequently and thus wasted.
   B. the price that resource users must pay will tend to be lower.
   C. resources will tend to be used less efficiently.
   D. resource users will more frequently be compelled to pay the value of those resources in their next best use.

B. Answers to, and Explanations of, Multiple-Choice Questions on the Principal Ideas of Chapter 5

1. **D**. Only decisions (actions) have costs. Decision makers recognize that the cost of a contemplated action will be the value of the opportunities that will have to be forgone if the action is taken. They decide by weighing this loss against the expected benefit from the action.

2. **A**. Past events do not determine costs. Expected benefits forgone determine costs. Monetary costs of inputs are established by the competing bids of those who do not want to forgo the opportunities that control of those inputs will provide.

3. **C**. The incomes of resource owners are by and large irrelevant to the prices those resources will command. What you will have to pay for the services of a plumber is not determined by whether the plumber is wealthy or poor but by the demand of other people for plumbers' services in relation to the number of capable plumbers available. Plumbers cannot charge more because business is bad and their incomes are down, contrary to a popular belief.

4. **D**. If costs are valuable opportunities forgone, there can be no costs that are not costs to some particular people.

5. **C**. Anything that eliminates potential bidders for a valuable resource tends to reduce the demand for that resource, thereby lowering its price. And its price is its cost to potential users of the resource.

6. **D**. When resources are clearly and definitely the property of particular people, those people tend to hold out for the best offer. They thereby compel resource users to pay the value of the resources in their next best use, which in turn implies that resources will not be used in one place when they could be producing more someplace else.

C. A Step-By-Step Review Of Chapter 5

1. What the economist calls opportunity costs underlie

   A. demand curves.
   B. supply curves.
   C. both demand and supply curves. — *Both these have opportunity costs.*
   D. people's thinking but not the real economy.

2. The demand for goods reflects people's values

   A. and so does the supply of goods.
   B. but the supply of goods rests on objective realities rather than values
   C. insofar as they are material values.
   D. insofar as they can be satisfied by spending money.

3. The opportunity cost of an action is

   A. everything that produced that action.
   B. the sum of the events that made that action possible.
   C. the value of the opportunities that must be sacrificed in order to take that action
   D. the payments made to those who contributed toward that action.

4. The economic theory of demand assumes that

   A. demanders choose among alternatives by comparing their anticipated net benefits
   B. demanders choose what suppliers offer
   C. no one can demand what is not supplied
   D. no one can supply what is not demanded.

5. The economic theory of supply assumes that

   A. suppliers choose among alternatives by comparing their anticipated net benefits
   B. supply depends entirely upon technical production possibilities.
   C. nothing is supplied unless it is demanded.
   D. nothing is demanded unless it is supplied.

6. The cost of the inputs used to produce any good will depend on

   A. the time required to produce them.
   B. the amount of human effort that went into their creation
   C. their availability in relation to the demand for them
   D. whether they were produced for profit.

7. An increased demand for lawyers' services to prosecute damage suits

   A. has no effect on the cost of hiring a lawyer to draw up a will.
   B. raises the cost of hiring a lawyer to draw up a will.
   C. lowers the cost of hiring a lawyer to draw up a will.
   D. reduces the number of damage suits filed.

8. Opportunity-cost theory implies that if the public lost most of its interest in spectator sports,

   A. the cost of hiring professional athletes would rise
   B. the cost of hiring professional athletes would fall.
   C. this would have no effect on the cost of hiring professional athletes
   D. athletes would have to charge more for their services in order to survive.

9. Someone who wants to rent an urban lot in order to grow vegetables should expect the rental cost to reflect the

   A. property taxes paid on the lot.
   B. expenses incurred in developing that lot.
   C. fact that land is a free gift of nature.
   D. value of that lot to other people who would also like to use it.

10. If all barbers were "born to be barbers" and wouldn't for a moment think of earning their living in any other way, haircut prices would have risen over the last 40 years

    A. more rapidly than they actually did.
    B. less rapidly than they actually did.
    C. at the same rate as they did.
    D. at the same rate as the wages of artists and musicians rose.

11. In a community where poor people do not associate with members of the opposite sex until they are 21 years old, the cost of hiring a babysitter on weekends will be

    A. lower than in other communities
    B. higher than in other communities
    C. prohibitive.
    D. zero.

12. Opportunity-cost theory predicts that rising unemployment among teenagers during a recession will

    A. increase the high-school dropout rate
    B. lower the high-school dropout rate
    C. encourage teenage drinking.
    D. increase the number of teenagers.

13. The phrase "the cost of a university education" has no clear meaning
    - A. because it does not specify whose cost is under consideration.
    - B. because it does not distinguish costs of obtaining from costs of supplying.
    - C. for both of the reasons above.
    - D. because a monetary value cannot be placed on education.

14. If the Ministry of Defense hires only volunteers, the armed forces will be staffed predominantly by people who
    - A. do not have better alternatives available to them than enlistment in the armed forces
    - B. are incompetent.
    - C. care only about money.
    - D. are patriotic.
    - E. are members of minority races.

15. If the Department of Energy hires only volunteers, the nation's energy bureaucracy will be staffed predominantly by people who
    - A. do not have better alternatives available to them than working for the Department of Energy.
    - B. are incompetent.
    - C. care only about money.
    - D. are patriotic.
    - E. are members of minority races.

16. A military draft and the National Hockey League's annual draft of junior hockey players have in common that they both
    - A. preserve competitive balance, whether among branches of the armed forces or hockey teams.
    - B. are essential to the survival of the Canadian way of life.
    - C. leave both types of draftees worse off than they would otherwise be and reduce the cost of employee compensation to those who must pay the bill.
    - D. promote greater fairness.
    - E. None of the above.

17. Resources tend to be utilized in ways that create goods with a higher monetary value when
    - A. the cost of obtaining them is low.
    - B. users must pay the opportunity cost of obtaining them.
    - C. users don't have to worry about their cost.
    - D. there is no competition for them.
    - E. None of the above.

18. Users are more often compelled to pay the opportunity cost of obtaining the resources they use when those resources are
    - A. clearly and definitely owned by someone. *farm land example.*
    - B. not private property but belong to the society at large.
    - C. government property.
    - D. natural resources.
    - E. None of the above.

19. The rental rate that students must pay for privately owned rooms in the vicinity of their college or university will tend to reflect the
    - A. value of those rooms to other students looking for housing.
    - B. greed or generosity of landlords.
    - C. level of tuition charges.
    - D. income of their parents.

20. Rooms in university-owned dormitories are less likely to reflect the value of those rooms to other students who would like to live in them because

    A. corruption is rampant in college administrations.
    B. universities are operated in the public interest.
    C. university dormitories are not the clearly owned property of anyone.
    D. first-year students are given special privileges.
    E. All of the above.

21. Price elasticity of supply is defined as

    A. the change in the quantity supplied divided by the change in the price.
    B. the change in supply divided by the change in demand.
    C. the percentage change in the price divided by the percentage change in the quantity supplied.
    D. the percentage change in the quantity supplied divided by the percentage change in the price.

22. The supply of any good is likely to be highly elastic if

    A. additional resources to produce the good can be readily obtained at no increase in the cost of obtaining them.
    B. the demand for the good is highly elastic.
    C. the demand for the good is highly inelastic.
    D. very little time elapses between the change in price and the measured change in quantity supplied.

23. The usual way in which the opportunity cost of employing resources is determined in Canada is through

    A. an estimate of their cost of production
    B. an estimate of their cost of reproduction.
    C. competing bids for the use of the resources.
    D. government price controls.

24. "Cost of production rather than demand determines prices in the long run." This statement is misleading because

    A. we never reach the long run.
    B. cost of production also determines prices in the short run.
    C. the cost of producing a particular good is not independent of the demand for that good and for other goods that compete for the same resources.
    D. no one knows.

25. The prices that consumers must pay to obtain the goods they want reflect the

    A. greed of sellers.
    B. value of those goods to other people.
    C. total benefit that consumers receive from using the goods.
    D. incomes of the consumers.
    E. None of the above.

26. Larger quantities of any good will usually be supplied at higher prices because

    A. the more that can be earned by using resources in a particular way, the more costly it is to use them in any other way.
    B. people are lazy and usually require financial incentives before they will do anything
    C. people are greedy and respond only to financial incentives.
    D. less is usually demanded at higher prices.

D. Answers to the Review Questions in Chapter 5

1. C	7. B	13. C	19. A	25. B
2. A	8. B	14. A	20. C	26. A
3. C	9. D	15. A	21. D	
4. A	10. B	16. C	22. A	
5. A	11. A	17. B	23. C	
6. C	12. B	18. A	24. C	

E. Costs, Demand, And Prices: Everything Depends On Everything Else

One way to appreciate the interrelatedness of costs, demand, and prices is to trace the sequence of effects that might follow from an event such as a drought in Ukraine. Here's a practice example. In each case, should we expect an increase or a decrease?

A severe drought in Ukraine, the so-called bread basket of the former USSR, will (1) ___↓___ the quantity of wheat available to the people of Ukraine. If the government of Ukraine then buys wheat from Canadian grain dealers, the price of Canadian wheat will (2)___↑___ . This will (3)___↑___ the cost of flour to Canadian millers and (4)___↑___ the cost of bread in Canadian grocery stores. It will also (5)___↑___ the cost to Pakistan of purchasing wheat from Canada, which will (6)___↑___ the demand in Pakistan for domestically produced wheat and (7)___↑___ its price. This will (8)___↑___ the demand for land on the part of Pakistani wheat growers and thus (9)___↑___ the cost of growing cotton on land that is also suitable for wheat production. This will (10)___↓___ the quantity of cotton produced, (11)___↑___ the price of cotton, and (12)___↑___ the cost of purchasing cotton clothing. This will (13)___↑___ the demand for wool.

Meanwhile, back in Canada, the demand for land suitable for wheat production will (14)___↑___, which will (15)___↑___ the cost of growing feed grain for cattle. This will (16)___↓___ the quantity of cattle grown and cause beef prices to (17)___↑___ . This will (18)___↑___ the demand for chickens.

F. Answers to Questions in Section E

1. decrease	2. increase	3. increase	4. increase	5. increase	6. increase
7. increase	8. increase	9. increase	10. decrease	11. increase	12. increase
13. increase	14. increase	15. increase	16. decrease	17. increase	18. increase

G. Questions to Think about

1. Suppose you're the driver of a city bus. The official fare is one dollar. Someone gets on the bus and asks to be transported without charge because he says he has to get downtown for a job interview but has no money. If you let him ride without paying, what will be the cost to the bus company, to you, and to other passengers on the bus?

If you refuse to let him ride, what will be the cost to him, to you, and to other passengers on the bus?

2.   What does it cost you to get your automobile tuned up? What would it cost you to do it yourself? Which is cheaper?

H. Answers to Questions in Section G

1.   If he really does have one dollar and will pay the fare if you insist, your action will cost the bus company one dollar. But it won't cost the company anything if he really doesn't have any money. Of course, if this encourages other passengers to try to avoid the fare in the future, it could be quite costly to the bus company.

The cost to you will depend in part on the probability that you will be disciplined for letting him ride without paying.

As for the other passengers, do they want to avoid delay and an embarrassing scene at the front of the bus? You might be benefiting them by letting him ride free. On the other hand, some may deeply resent his obtaining a free ride when they had to pay. Hassle and resentment are both costs. It also makes a difference whether the bus is crowded or empty. Suppose he takes a seat and a subsequent boarder has to stand…

The cost of not letting him ride might be a lost job for him, an unpleasant encounter for you, and embarrassment for all the other passengers. At the same time, your decision might entail good exercise for him.

2.   It isn't always a simple matter to compare the cost of having it done at a garage with the cost of doing it yourself. Do you already have access to the required tools or must you purchase some? What is the cost of having the car not available for the longer time it takes you to do the job in your spare time? What is the value of your time? To what extent is the job recreation to you? And if you must pay taxes on the money income you earn in order to pay the garage to do the job, that lowers the relative cost of doing it yourself. Also, you must also decide whether you and the garage are likely to produce tune-ups of equal quality.

Chapter 6 _____

Supply and Demand: A Process of Coordination

A. Multiple-Choice Questions on the Principal Ideas of Chapter 6

1. Supply and demand
   A. is the basic law of economics.
   B. cannot function where the government controls prices.
   C. controls only money prices in a commercial society.
   D. is a process of cooperation and mutual accommodation.

2. Which of the following could reasonably be expected to increase the transaction costs that often interfere with productive cooperation among members of a society?
   A. A breakdown of law and order
   B. A lower level of trust among the members of society
   C. Growing diversity of languages, customs, and fundamental beliefs within a society
   D. Rapid inflation
   E. All of the above

3. A market-clearing price (sometimes referred to as an equilibrium price) is a price that
   A. causes everyone to be better off than any other price.
   B. causes the demand to equal the supply.
   C. causes the quantity sold to equal the quantity purchased.
   D. causes the quantity people want to sell to equal the quantity people want to purchase.
   E. is fair to both consumers and sellers.

4. If a good is scarce,
   A. someone must be withholding it from the market.
   B. everyone cannot have all that they want without being required to sacrifice something else that is also wanted.
   C. it must be privately owned.
   D. it must be rare.

5. If a good is scarce,
   A. that scarcity can be reduced by lowering the good's price.
   B. it must be impossible to expand the quantity available.
   C. the good must be rationed according to some discriminatory criteria that people will then compete to satisfy.
   D. there is no reason why people should compete to obtain it.

6. Which of the following does *not* help to explain why most exchanges in contemporary commercial societies occur through the medium of money prices?

    A. A barter system would enormously increase the amount of time and energy people would have to spend searching for others with whom they could exchange.
    B. It is usually easy for people who want to exchange to agree on the value of a unit of money.
    C. The use of money makes it easier to avoid income taxes.
    D. Unlike many of the other costs of acquiring a good, the money cost can be easily adjusted up or down by small amounts.

7. A shortage of a good means that

    A. there is not enough of it to satisfy everyone, regardless of its price.
    B. at the prevailing price the quantity demanded is greater than the quantity supplied.
    C. the price of the good is higher than people are willing to pay.
    D. the good is scarce only because someone is withholding it from the market.

8. If by law we suppress the rationing device of monetary prices,

    A. there will be no alternative way to make the quantity demanded conform to the quantity supplied.
    B. scarcity will be reduced or eliminated.
    C. shortages will be reduced or eliminated.
    D. other criteria will come into play to ration scarce goods.

9. Deadweight costs in an exchange are costs *eg. Standing in Line @ a checkout.*

    A. charged for goods that are not actually scarce.
    B. that have nothing to do with the sacrifice of valuable opportunities.
    C. that have no effect on either the quantity demanded or the quantity supplied.
    D. to one party in the transaction that are not simultaneously benefits to the other party.

10. If a surplus of a good exists,

    A. the prevailing money price is too high for the quantity demanded to be as large as the quantity supplied.
    B. the good is not scarce.
    C. more of the good must have been produced than people have any use for.
    D. the good must not be privately owned.

11. We more frequently observe persistent, continuing shortages of goods produced by government agencies than of goods produced by privately owned firms because

    A. higher prices for goods generally don't benefit the government officials who are in charge of supplying the goods.
    B. people who work for government are less competent.
    C. those who control privately owned firms are more greedy.
    D. those who work for government usually don't pursue their own interests.

12. Money prices are an extremely effective device for promoting social cooperation because

    A. they help to clarify the options available to people.
    B. they provide people with incentives to use sparingly resources that other people value highly.
    C. they provide useful information about the relative scarcity of different resources.
    D. they serve all the functions above.

B. Answers to, and Explanations of, Multiple-Choice Questions on the Principal Ideas of Chapter 6

1. **D**. If supply and demand is a law, it's an odd law because it doesn't prohibit any particular actions. Even if the government rigidly legislates prices, supply and demand will still operate to determine who will obtain the price-controlled goods and on what nonmonetary terms they will be supplied.

Supply and demand is the economist's name for a process of continuing negotiation and accommodation among those who desire goods and those with the means to provide them.

2. **E**. Transaction costs are the costs of arranging contracts or agreements to exchange, including the costs of acquiring adequate assurance that the other party will actually do what has been agreed to. A breakdown of law and order in a society will obviously increase these costs, as will anything that reduces people's willingness to trust one another or their ability to understand one another. Rapid inflation increases transaction costs by creating uncertainty about the future value of the medium of exchange that enters into the terms of most agreements to exchange.

3. **D**. A market-clearing price is neither the "best" price from everyone's standpoint nor the price that everyone is likely to consider fair. Since demand and supply, as we have agreed to use the terms, are schedules or curves, they will never be equal. The quantity sold is always equal to the quantity purchased. How could they possibly differ? Nothing can be sold unless it is also purchased. A market-clearing price equates the quantity people want to purchase with the quantity people want to offer for purchase. It balances desires or intentions.

4. **B**. A good can be abundant but still scarce, or rare but not scarce at all. Scarcity is a relationship between desirability and availability.

5. **C**. There are many ways to ration scarce goods but no way of avoiding the necessity to do so. There are also many ways in which people can attempt to satisfy the criteria being used to ration scarce goods. To assume that they will not compete, however, is to assume that they don't actually want the goods, which implies that the goods are not scarce.

6. **C**. The other options recapitulate points made in the chapter. But because the income tax is basically a tax on money income, barter might be used to reduce taxes. The surgeon could take out the plumber's appendix and the plumber could install a new set of water pipes in the surgeon's basement. If they each purchased these services with money, they would first be liable for taxes on the money income earned to pay for the services. (This is *not* tax advice. Revenue Canada is quite hostile to barter arrangements that are undertaken for the purpose of evading taxes.)

7. **B**. The quantity actually purchased cannot be greater than the quantity supplied. But people can and will want to purchase more than is being supplied if the price being charged is low enough. A sufficiently higher price can eliminate any shortage.

8. **D**. Scarce goods must be rationed. If the quantity demanded is not adequately restrained by the money price, other costs of acquisition will begin to appear and will increase until the quantity demanded no longer exceeds the quantity supplied.

9. **D**. Deadweight costs, such as the cost of waiting in line, represent a using-up of resources. A seller who notices that people are lining up to buy his product for $1.50 plus a 20-minute wait will be tempted to wonder how many of those in line would be willing to pay another 50 ¢ to avoid the 20-minute delay. Those who would rather pay $2.00 and avoid the queue are by definition better off when allowed to do so, and they obviously make the seller better off.

10. **A**. A sufficiently high price will eliminate any shortage, and a sufficiently low price will eliminate any surplus of a *good*. But even a zero price will not be low enough to eliminate the surplus supply of a "bad," such as crude oil gushing into the ocean from a blown-out underwater well.

11. **A**. No good evidence exists that people employed by government are less competent, less greedy, or less intent on pursuing their own interests than are people who own private businesses. We don't require any of these assumptions to predict that prices will be raised less often in response to a shortage when those with the power to raise them have nothing to gain from doing so. The difference in behaviour emerges from the difference in the rules of the game.

12. **D.** Consider the following example. If there aren't enough pizza parlours in the area to satisfy all the pizza lovers, it is not necessary to form committees to assess the relative merits of pizza parlours and other establishments, the nutritional value of thick and thin crusts, the costs and benefits of various hours of operation, and so forth. Relatively small adjustments in expected relative prices induce people to change their behaviour in ways that promote "solutions." The other dimensions of goods can more easily be simplified and standardized when the money-price dimension is free to move.

C. A Step-by-Step Review of Chapter 6

1. The textbook attributes the spectacular failures of cooperation that occurred as the USSR disintegrated in the late 1980s and early 1990s to

   A. growing hostility among different regions and ethnic groups.
   B. inability to recognize that a problem existed.
   C. the absence of clearly defined and generally accepted property rights.
   D. the collapse of the central planning system.

2. Supply and demand is a process of coordination that generates more benefits for participants when

   A. demand is greater than supply.
   B. equality of power exists between demanders and suppliers.
   C. supply is greater than demand.
   D. transaction costs are low.

3. Which of the following statements about transaction costs is true?

   A. Transaction costs are paid by sellers, not by consumers.
   B. Transaction costs are the costs of arranging agreements between demanders and suppliers.
   C. Transaction costs are wasted in the sense that they do not have to be covered in order for exchange to occur.
   D. Transaction costs benefit only sellers, not consumers.
   E. Transaction costs do not affect prices.

4. Which of the following statements best explains the relationship between clearly defined property rights and transaction costs?

   A. Clearly defined property rights increase transaction costs by necessitating more negotiation among people who want to exchange.
   B. Clearly defined property rights tend to lower transaction costs.
   C. Social revolutions tend to reduce transaction costs by creating new and therefore more clearly defined systems of property rights.
   D. Transaction costs would be lower in a society where all property was clearly owned by a single central authority.

5. In commercial societies, allocation of tasks and benefits is negotiated by the affected parties primarily

   A. by majority vote.
   B. in a highly haphazard and unsystematic way.
   C. in regular committee meetings.
   D. through money bids and offers.

6. Why do most exchanges in Canada occur through the medium of money?

   A. Barter is prohibited by law because it encourages tax evasion.
   B. People have grown so accustomed to money that they can no longer recognize its inefficiency.
   C. The government supplies money in response to the demand for it.
   D. The use of money lowers transaction costs.
   E. Those who buy and sell often confuse money with wealth.

7. If a large increase in the demand for wheat produces no significant increase in the price of wheat, we may reasonably conclude that
   A. the demand for wheat is elastic.
   B. the demand for wheat is inelastic.
   C. the supply of wheat is elastic.
   D. the supply of wheat is inelastic.

8. If a small reduction in the supply of wheat produces a huge increase in the price of wheat, we may reasonably conclude that
   A. the demand for wheat is elastic.
   B. the demand for wheat is inelastic.
   C. the supply of wheat is elastic.
   D. the supply of wheat is inelastic.

9. The price of buying land in and around cities that are growing rapidly will tend to increase
   A. faster than the inflation rate because the demand for land is highly elastic.
   B. faster than the inflation rate because the supply of land is highly elastic.
   C. faster than the inflation rate because the supply of land is highly inelastic.
   D. slower than the inflation rate because land is a natural resource in abundant supply.

10. Legislated price controls
   A. allocate resources equally to all who need them.
   B. assure that low-income people will be able to purchase the goods they need.
   C. make sure that the quantity demanded matches the quantity supplied, especially in emergencies.
   D. suspend the working procedure for securing social cooperation in a commercial society.

11. The market-clearing price of a good (also sometimes called the equilibrium price) is the price that
   A. equates the quantity purchased and the quantity sold.
   B. equates the quantity people want to purchase and the quantity people want to sell.
   C. assigns the gain from voluntary exchange equally between demanders and suppliers.
   D. satisfies both demanders and suppliers.

12. What the text calls "the Popular Perspective" assumes that
   A. the demand and the supply of most goods are both completely elastic.
   B. the demand and the supply of most goods are both completely inelastic.
   C. the demand for most goods is completely elastic while the supply is completely inelastic.
   D. the demand for most goods is completely inelastic while the supply is completely elastic.

13. If the Popular Perspective were correct, then changing prices would *not*
   A. persuade users of goods to economize.
   B. persuade producers of goods to adjust their activities to consumer preferences.
   C. adjust the quantity of goods demanded to the quantity supplied.
   D. affect the allocation of resources.
   E. do any of the above.

14. The ready availability in retail stores of most items that we want when we want them
   A. indicates that most goods are not scarce.
   B. would not be possible if there were no one to supervise the overall coordination of production and distribution.
   C. depends on the continuing achievement of a long series of balances between willingness to sell and desire to buy.
   D. proves that surpluses are widespread.

15. Social coordination on the scale regularly displayed by the Canadian economy depends on
    A. extensive data collection by government.
    B. an extensive and continuous exchange of information.
    C. detailed agreement among people on what should be produced and who should get it.
    D. intimate knowledge of one another's needs and capabilities.

16. Relative money prices
    A. are not used to ration goods produced by government.
    B. are information on the relative scarcity of goods.
    C. rarely have any systematic relationship to the relative scarcities of goods.
    D. correspond directly to the costs of production.

17. Scarcity of a good can be reduced only by
    A. increasing the availability of the good.
    B. reducing the desirability of the good.
    C. either increasing its availability or reducing its desirability.
    D. lowering its price.
    E. raising its price.

18. If there are two plumbers *(Supply)* and four electricians in Cambridge Bay, we know
    A. that plumbers are scarcer than electricians in Cambridge Bay.
    B. nothing about their relative scarcity until we find out about the demand for plumbers and for electricians in Cambridge Bay.
    C. that there is more electricity than water in Cambridge Bay.
    D. that electricians earn more than plumbers in Cambridge Bay.

19. To a thirsty hiker by the side of a pure mountain stream, drinking water is, not counting his time,
    A. a scarce good because it is in demand.
    B. a scarce good because there is not as much pure water in the world as everyone wants.
    C. not a scarce good because he can drink all he wants without giving up any other good in order to do so.
    D. not a scarce good because its cost of production is zero.

20. If a good is scarce, it
    A. will be rationed in some way.
    B. ought to be rationed in some way but may not be.
    C. cannot be rationed so that everyone gets at least a little.
    D. must be rationed by money price.

21. The rationing of scarce goods requires that
    A. someone decide how much each person ought to have.
    B. goods be allocated exclusively to those who are willing to pay.
    C. goods be allocated in accordance with some criteria that discriminate between those who will and those who will not be able to obtain the good.
    D. goods be assigned to people in a fair manner.

22. The criteria according to which rationing of scarce goods occurs
    A. must be legal.
    B. must be set down clearly in advance.
    C. do not have to be consistent, fair, or even well understood.
    D. must be moral.

23. The criteria used to ration scarce goods

    A. must be divisible, portable, and tangible.
    B. make no difference because any criteria can be used to ration.
    C. make a difference because people will tend to behave in ways that they think will enable them to satisfy the criteria
    D. must be the same for everyone.

24. High prices for scarce goods are

    A. a cause of their scarcity.
    B. an effect of their scarcity.
    C. both cause and effect of their scarcity.
    D. neither cause nor effect of their scarcity.

25. Any shortage can eventually be eliminated by allowing the price of the scarce good to rise

    A. unless there is a finite amount of the scarce good.
    B. because higher prices usually lead to larger quantities being supplied and eventually must result in smaller quantities being demanded. ↑P Qd↓
    C. unless the good is a basic necessity.
    D. unless either the demand or the supply is completely inelastic.

26. A shortage means that people

    A. are getting poorer.
    B. are buying more than is being sold.
    C. want to buy more than is available, given the price they are being asked to pay.
    D. are getting wealthier.

27. A larger increase in price is required to eliminate a shortage of a good

    A. the greater the demand for the good.
    B. the more inelastic the demand and the supply.
    C. the more elastic the demand and the supply.
    D. the less the supply of the good.

28. If a maximum or ceiling price is imposed on a good by law and the quantity demanded at that price is greater than the quantity supplied,

    A. the good will not be sold.
    B. competition among demanders will tend to raise the nonmonetary cost of obtaining the good.
    C. competition among suppliers and among demanders is prevented.
    D. potential buyers are made better off.

29. An increase in the nonmonetary cost of purchasing a good

    A. raises the monetary cost also.
    B. reduces the monetary cost.
    C. has no effect on the quantity people will want to purchase.
    D. reduces the quantity of the good that people will want to purchase at any price.

30. The money someone pays to buy a movie ticket is not a deadweight cost because

    A. the movie is a tangible good.
    B. the movie can be shown over and over.
    C. giving up mere money is not a genuine sacrifice of valuable opportunities.
    D. the buyer's loss is the seller's gain.

31. Sellers usually have an incentive to
    A. eliminate deadweight costs by raising the monetary price.
    B. increase deadweight costs in order to stimulate demand for their products.
    C. turn money costs into deadweight costs.
    D. increase deadweight costs for buyers.

32. Sellers who are prevented by law from raising their prices when deadweight costs exist will
    A. have no way of turning the situation to their own advantage.
    B. search for procedures that reduce their selling costs even though these procedures increase the cost to purchasers.
    C. go out of business.
    D. sell their deadweight costs to the highest bidder.

33. Changing money prices in a changing world are
    A. the only way in which suppliers and demanders can be induced to cooperate.
    B. one way by which suppliers and demanders can be induced to search for ways to accommodate one another.
    C. the best way in all cases to secure cooperation among suppliers and demanders
    D. equally advantageous to everyone.

34. When a scarce good is rationed by means of money price,
    A. each rich person will obtain more of it than any poor person will.
    B. a poor person who wants that good intensely will obtain more of it than will some rich people.
    C. poor people will get none until rich people have obtained all they want.
    D. sellers gain at the expense of buyers.

35. If all people had the same amount of money income to spend,
    A. it would make no sense to ration scarce goods by means of money prices because everyone would simply want the same amount of everything.
    B. people would still be willing to pay very different prices to obtain particular scarce goods.
    C. everyone would obtain the same satisfaction.
    D. all incentives would be destroyed.

36. At the beginning of a period of rapid inflation, residential rents tend to rise
    A. because housing becomes more scarce.
    B. more rapidly than the average of all prices.
    C. less rapidly than the average of all prices.
    D. when everyone realizes that the inflation is occurring.

37. In a period of unanticipated, rapid inflation, residential rental space tends to become
    A. available to almost anyone because the real price falls.
    B. underpriced, which produces low vacancy rates.
    C. overpriced, which produces low vacancy rates.
    D. unavailable at any price.

38. A system of rent controls legislated during a time of low vacancy rates and designed to last only until the problem of low vacancy rates disappears will tend to
    A. perpetuate the problem and therefore the system of rent control.
    B. eliminate the problem and thereby the need for rent controls.
    C. make the vacancy rate rise.
    D. increase the supply of rental units by reducing landlords' incomes.

$Q^S > Q^D$

39. If a surplus of a good exists and persists for a long time, we can most reasonably assume that
    A. the quantity supplied is not responsive to price.
    B. the good is not scarce.
    C. there is no demand for the good.
    D. something is preventing the price of the good from declining.

40. Persistent surpluses of many farm commodities in Canada during most of the years following 1930 were the consequence of
    A. migration from cities to farms.
    B. government programs to support the price of farm commodities.
    C. advances in agricultural productivity that temporarily ended the scarcity of farm commodities in Canada.
    D. low farm prices that compelled farmers to produce more in order to survive.

41. When the Canadian Medical Association predicts an imminent surplus of physicians by comparing the quantity of physicians' services that they expect to be supplied with the quantity they expect to be demanded, the CMA is
    A. performing a public service.
    B. assuming a continuing high price for physicians' services.
    C. predicting that physicians' services will no longer be scarce goods.
    D. predicting that physicians' incomes will rise.

42. Suppliers are unlikely to take steps to raise the money prices of the good they are supplying despite a continuing shortage of the good when
    A. a shortage is in the public interest.
    B. the suppliers work for nonprofit institutions.
    C. the demand is highly elastic.
    D. the demand is highly inelastic.

43. Cooperation among numerous people in using what's available to obtain what they want
    A. cannot occur under a competitive system.
    B. requires that the people cooperating be well acquainted with one another's wants and abilities.
    C. depends primarily on numerous acts of exchange between people who are almost wholly unacquainted with one another.
    D. requires suspension of the pricing system.

44. Extensive and productive exchanges among people who barely know one another
    A. are impossible.
    B. require coordination through committees of some sort.
    C. require that the terms of exchange be relatively clear, simple, and standardized.
    D. depend for their success upon a dictator of some kind.

45. A system of money prices promotes mutually advantageous exchanges
    A. because more money or less money can usually compensate for an enormous range of other advantages and disadvantages perceived by potential parties to a transaction.
    B. because most people prefer money to almost anything else.
    C. because people will do anything for a price.
    D. because money is the ultimate good.

D. Answers to the Review Questions in Chapter 6

1. C	2. D	3. B	4. B	5. D	6. D	7. C	8. B	9. C	10. D	11. B	12. D
13. E	14. C	15. B	16. B	17. C	18. B	19. C	20. A	21. C	22. C	23. C	
24. B	25. B	26. C	27. B	28. B	29. D	30. D	31. A	32. B	33. B	34. B	
35. B	36. C	37. B	38. A	39. D	40. B	41. B	42. B	43. C	44. C	45. A	

E. Changing Supply Curves and Demand Curves

The concepts of supply and demand enable us to think more clearly and consistently about causes and consequences. Learning to use these concepts, however, requires much more than the ability to see where supply curves and demand curves intersect. Their effective use requires us to recognize what factors are likely to influence supply and demand respectively and in what direction this influence is likely to be exerted. The exercises of this section were designed to give you practice in doing this.

The good in question is soybeans, with the quantity measured in bushels per year and the price in dollars per bushel. You will probably find this exercise most helpful if you use pencil and paper to sketch the original curves and then shift them in the predicted direction. Assume for the sake of simplicity that the supply curve and demand curve for soybeans in Canada form a standard supply and demand "cross," as in the figure below.

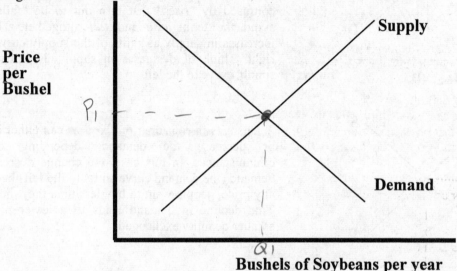

Bushels of Soybeans per year

Your task is to decide what effect each of the changes described below will have on "the price of soybeans paid by buyers to Canadian growers and the quantity exchanged."

a. Will the event described affect the supply of soybeans or the demand for soybeans?
b. Will it cause the supply or the demand curve to increase (shift to the right) or decrease (shift to the left)?
c. What effect will this shift have on the price and the quantity exchanged?

Remember that the idea behind the exercise is not to spark arguments on facts about soybeans but to help you begin seeing what kinds of events have what kinds of effects on supply and demand.

1. Wages of farm workers increase substantially. *Supply*
2. Consumers suddenly become very concerned about potential pesticides sprayed on soybeans. *Demand.*
3. The supply of corn declines dramatically because of warnings about the effects of hybrids. *Demand.*
4. Improvements in soybean harvesting technology making production of soybeans less costly. *Supply*
5. Scientists develop new soybean hybrids permitting farmers to raise two crops per year in Canada. *Supply*
6. An association of soybean farmers conducts a successful advertising campaign to persuade people that soybeans are a tasty snack. *Demand*
7. A new chemical is discovered that can be added to soybean oil at an insignificant cost to make promote weight loss. *Demand.*
8. Foreign countries begin exporting soybeans to Canada. (Remember that the exercise deals with Canadian-grown soybeans.) *Demand.*
9. The federal government pays Canadian growers 50¢ for each bushel of soybeans marketed. *Supply*
10. The government agrees to purchase, at a price 50 percent above the current price, all of the soybeans that Canadian growers cannot sell at that higher price.

F. Answers to Questions in Section E

(The original supply and demand curves are shown as solid lines. The new ones are dotted)

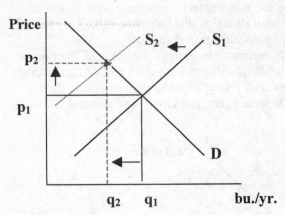

1. An increase in the cost of producing soybeans will decrease the supply, leading to a higher price and smaller quantity exchanged. Note that a decrease in supply looks like an upward movement of the supply curve. Look carefully and notice that when the supply curve "rises" in this way, a smaller quantity is supplied at each price. That constitutes an actual decline, or "fall," in supply. The simplest way to avoid being confused by "rises" that turn out to be "falls" is to avoid the terms *rise* and *fall* altogether. Think of increases in supply as shifts of the supply curve to the right. Think of decreases in supply as shifts of the supply curve to the left

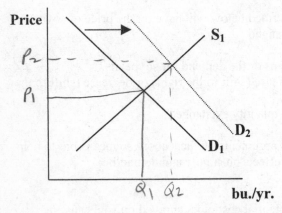

2. Changes in consumer preferences can either increase or decrease the demand, depending on the circumstances. In this case, the change decreases the demand (the demand curve shifts to the left) because at any price, people want to buy less than they did before. This decline in demand leads to a lower price and smaller quantity exchanged.

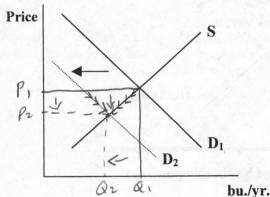

3. Corn is a substitute for soybeans in many uses. A decline in the supply of corn will raise the price of corn, and that, in turn, will cause an increase in the demand for soybeans.

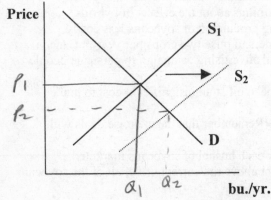

4. The improvement in harvesting technology means that more farmers will be willing to sell more beans at each possible price. In general, anything that lowers the cost of production will lead to an increase in supply. The supply curve shifts to the right, prices fall and output increases.

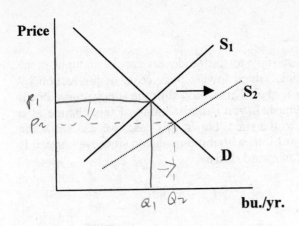

5. The tremendous increase in productivity would lead to an increase in supply. The supply curve shifts to the right.

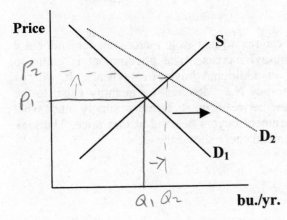

6. To the extent that the advertising campaign is successful, it would change consumers' tastes and preferences, this time causing an increase in demand. The equilibrium price and quantity would increase.

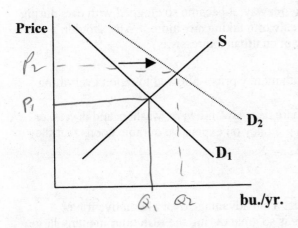

7. This change would lead to an increased demand for soybean oil, which in turn would lead to an increased demand for soybeans. The demand curve shifts rightward. The equilibrium price and quantity increase.

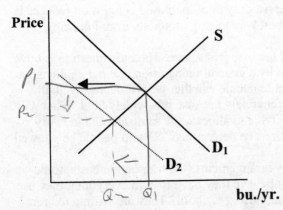

8. The demand for Canadian-grown soybeans will decline because foreign soybeans are an excellent substitute. This is *not* an increase in the supply of Canadian-grown soybeans.

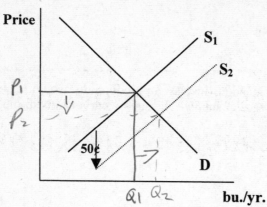

9. The subsidy to the producers can be thought of as something, which lowers their costs of production by 50¢ per bushel. This would shift the supply curve down by 50¢/bushel (you can also think of this change as a shift it to the right, but in this case, we can show the downward shift with more precision since we know it is a 50¢ downward shift).

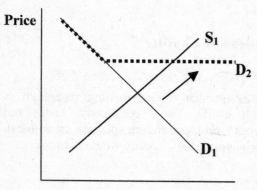

10. You can regard this as an increase in demand, but it is an unusual increase. The government is going to become an additional buyer of soybeans. It will be willing to buy (i.e. "demand") a quantity equal to the difference between what farmers supply and what nongovernment buyers demand at that price. The kink in the demand curve shows the effect.

G. Questions to Think about

1. "Within one week after they turned the tollway into a freeway, it became so clogged with cars during the morning and evening rush hours that it wasn't even worth taking any more." Why shouldn't you be surprised to hear that this had occurred in the case of an urban expressway?

2. Should gasoline be rationed during an emergency?

3. Should basic goods be rationed according to need, with money prices allowed to ration everything else?

4. Why do so few neighbours devise arrangements to share their lawnmowers, washers and dryers, or automobiles? Do Canadian households enjoy spending money on expensive durable goods that they use only a few hours each week?

H. Answers to Questions in Section G

1. People shift toward any mode of travel that offers them a net advantage over alternative travel arrangements. The demand for transportation services is so great during the rush hour in many large cities that the net advantage of a freeway is liable to persist only until increased congestion reduces it to zero. The imposition of a rush-hour toll may be the best way to stop motorists from imposing wasteful congestion costs on one another.

2. It will in fact be rationed and has always been rationed because it is scarce. The only question is how. Public discussion of the issue could be vastly improved by a general recognition that our challenge is to compare alternative rationing systems carefully—not to decide whether we will have any at all.

3. This proposal is worth thinking through carefully and concretely because it is widely held. What will be counted as "basic goods"? Will it be possible or desirable to allocate the same amount to every person? If not, how should individuals' varying allocations be determined? Should people be allowed to sell their allocations of basic goods to others?

4. They apparently expect the costs of making satisfactory arrangements (the transaction costs) to be greater than the benefits. It's not simply that Canadians believe they have to own everything they use. How many Canadian households own their own hospital, farm, or school? They are willing to "rent" or share in other suways if the cost of making satisfactory corrangements is low enough.

Chapter 7

Marginal Values and Economic Decisions

A. Multiple-Choice Questions on the Principal Ideas of Chapter 7

1. When economists say that only "marginal costs and benefits" affect decisions, they mean that
   - A. effective decision makers take into account only those factors that their decisions change.
   - B. it is always possible to begin again from the beginning.
   - C. seemingly unimportant factors will in total be more significant than factors normally taken into account.
   - D. the past does not influence the present.

2. Water is more important and valuable than diamonds
   - A. as shown by the fact that most people will be willing to pay more for a litre of water than for a litre of diamonds.
   - B. at some margins where very few people happen to be at any time.
   - C. in use but not in exchange.
   - D. to anyone with a normal sense of values.

3. Which of the maxims below does **not** express a characteristic of all costs capable of affecting decisions to supply goods?
   - A. Costs always lie in the future.
   - B. There are no impersonal costs because all costs are costs to particular persons.
   - C. Costs belong to actions, not to things.
   - D. Costs are previous efforts embodied in goods.

4. Sunk costs are irrelevant to the decisions of suppliers because
   - A. sunk costs reflect demand and demand has no relationship to supply.
   - B. valuable opportunities forgone in the past are not available to present decision makers.
   - C. the past has no effect on the present.
   - D. the past has no effect on the future.

5. The proper stance for making cost calculations is not looking back to the past but forward to the future. This implies that, considering only the short-run, a newspaper carrier with three papers left over at the end of the route should be willing to sell them at any price above
   - A. their value as waste paper.
   - B. the amount the carrier will have to pay for them at the end of the week.
   - C. the cost to the publisher of printing them.
   - D. the regular newsstand price.

6. A business firm should refuse to sell any item for which it cannot obtain a price at least as large as

   A. the firm's cost to produce that particular item.
   B. the item's worth to the firm if not sold.
   C. the firm's cost to produce another item of that precise kind.
   D. the firm's cost on average to produce items of that sort.

7. The "cost per kilometre of owning a car" is a misleading notion because

   A. this cost will vary between city and country.
   B. automobile owners drive in very different ways.
   C. no two cars are exactly the same.
   D. owning is not a decision that produces kilometres.

8. If a business firm operates indefinitely without covering any of its sunk costs, what happens to those costs?

   A. Nothing happens to them; they have ceased to exist.
   B. They are distributed across the whole economy.
   C. They continue unpaid for as long as the firm fails to make a profit large enough to cover them.
   D. They reduce the wealth of the investors who risked their wealth to make mistaken decisions possible.

9. Which of the statements below best expresses the relationship between the cost of a legal education and the fees charged by lawyers?

   A. The greater the expected cost of a legal education, the fewer lawyers there will be and the higher their fees.
   B. The greater the cost of a lawyer's education in both money and effort, the higher the fees they can legitimately set for their services.
   C. The greater the cost to lawyers of obtaining a legal education, the higher the fees they will charge in order to recover those costs.
   D. The greater the average cost of a legal education, the higher the fees that lawyers will be able to set.

10. The cost to a physician of tending a patient is

    A. the value of the time so spent in its next-best use.
    B. dependent on the number of years over which the physician practices.
    C. higher for a recent medical-school graduate than for a physician with a well-established practice.
    D. zero under a system of complete and comprehensive medical insurance.

11. The "marginal dollar cost" to a patient of a visit to the doctor when that patient's bill will be paid entirely by insurance is

    A. zero if the patient does not pay the insurance premiums.
    B. the same as if the patient had no insurance.
    C. the value of the care not received by some other patient who couldn't get an appointment.
    D. zero.

12. Your landlord's cost of continuing to rent to you is

    A. the sum of his operating costs.
    B. the amount he could get by renting to the highest bidder.
    C. the sum of his operating costs plus depreciation and interest on the rental property.
    D. zero, once the apartment has been constructed and all costs are sunk.

Could Be A,B&C they say.

✗ 13. An <u>increase</u> in the "demand for a good" will tend to bid up the cost of acquiring the good more

   Ⓐ. if suppliers respond by quickly making larger quantities available.
   B. if the cost of transferring resources out of other uses into production of this good is low.
   C. if the supply curve is highly elastic.
   D. in the short run than in the long run.

14. Goods will be supplied only when the expected benefit from supplying is greater than the expected marginal cost. This principle

   A. applies only to capitalist societies.
   Ⓑ. states the general rule for efficient resource use by anyone in any society.
   C. Both of the above are correct.
   D. None of the above is correct.

B. Answers to, and Explanations of, Multiple-Choice Questions on the Principal Ideas of Chapter 7

1. **A.** Because marginal costs and benefits are the additional, or incremental, costs and benefits that a decision creates, they are the only costs and benefits that should be taken into account by someone contemplating a decision. Outside of economics, the word marginal commonly means unimportant, implying that marginal costs and benefits would be costs and benefits too trivial for the decision maker to be concerned about. This is decidedly different from how the word is used in economics. A synonym for marginal in economic thinking is additional. But additional fails to capture the full meaning of the word marginal, which also means "on the edge" or "on the frontier." The economic way of thinking calls attention to the many margins on which decisions can be made, the many edges, frontiers, or directions in which decision makers can move, the many trade-offs that are available.

2. **B.** Only someone close to dying of thirst would be likely to offer more money in exchange for water than for an equal volume of diamonds. That's true, not because value in use has no essential relationship to value in exchange, but because most people are "on a margin" where they have all the water they want readily available to them. Goods don't have any value, in use or exchange, that is independent of the circumstances.

3. **D.** Because nothing can be done now about efforts already exerted, those efforts are not costs capable of affecting decisions. They are the spilt milk over which the proverb says you shouldn't cry.

4. **B.** This restates the same idea as the previous question. Should you sit and watch the final quarter of a boring football game because you've already sat through three boring quarters? You ought to watch that boring last quarter only if you expect all the options available to you in the next 45 minutes to be less valuable than suffering through until the end of the game.

5. **A.** If all undelivered newspapers end up in the wastepaper stack, the carrier's cost of selling them is the opportunity forgone to add three newspapers to the pile. However, selling them at a discount might cause some problems. The carrier might have a contract with the publisher forbidding sales at low prices; or the carrier might soon find that regular buyers stop paying the full price if they learn that they can purchase "leftovers" at a discount.

6. **B.** This option includes many different possibilities. The cost of selling an item today will be very high if someone is coming in tomorrow to pay a fancy price for it, close to zero if the item will spoil before tomorrow, and negative if the item, in spoiling, will contaminate the entire store.

7. **D.** All the other statements are correct, of course. But the notion is misleading, at best, because "owning" a car costs exactly as much whether you drive it 100 kilometres or 100,000 kilometres. The cost per kilometre of driving it, once you have already made the decision to own it, is unaffected by the cost of owning it.

8. **D.** The party who pays sunk costs is the party who already paid and now fails to be repaid.

9. **A.** Supply and demand determine prices. To understand the economic way of thinking, try to see what actually affects supply and demand. It's the expected cost (compared with the expected benefits) of obtaining a law-school education that influences the supply of lawyers and thereby the price of

their services. This takes time, of course—a lowering of the expected cost won't produce more lawyers very quickly. Note, however, that if Canadians experienced a sudden and dramatic conversion to using do-it-yourself legal guides, lawyers could not continue to charge high prices merely because they had spent a lot of time and money on their education.

10. **A.** The cost to the physician thus depends on what the physician would otherwise do with the time. See another patient? Play golf ?

11. **D.** Ignore the premiums because they will be the same to this patient whether or not the patient visits the doctor. The marginal cost of any action is the additional cost that the action generates. Notice carefully that the question asks about the cost *to the patient*. Notice, too, that the question refers to the marginal *dollar* cost — the patient will still face extra costs in the form of traveling and waiting each time s/he visits the doctor.

12. **B.** You get the answer by asking what benefit the landlord does not receive because of the decision to rent to you. The demand on the part of potential tenants thus determines the cost to landlords of allocating the space to any particular use.

13. Options **A**, **B**, and **C** all describe a highly elastic supply curve, in which case an increased demand will produce a substantially larger quantity in response to a slightly higher price. But supply curves tend to be more elastic in the long run and relatively inelastic in the short run.

14. **B.** Application of the rule will produce different results in capitalist and socialist economies because the systems of resource ownership and control will differ. But the general rule for efficiency requires resource controllers to compare the expected marginal cost with the expected marginal benefit of contemplated actions.

C. A Step-by-Step Review of Chapter 7

1. Larger quantities of <u>any good</u> will be supplied at higher than at lower prices because
    A. higher prices include more sunk costs.
    B. higher prices attract resources from other uses.
    C. people are naturally lazy and have to be bribed to give up their leisure.
    D. price and quantity supplied are inversely related.

2. Marginal costs are
    A. costs that are too insignificant to enter into a decision maker's calculations.
    B. the addition to costs that a particular action or decision entails.
    C. costs of obtaining goods now by promising to pay later.
    D. costs that cannot be affected by anyone's decision.

3. Someone who says he loves his mother far more than he loves football but who nevertheless attends a football game when he could be visiting his mother
    A. displays weakness of will.
    B. is a hypocrite.
    C. is behaving inconsistently with his own stated values.
    D. places a lower marginal value on visiting his mother than on attending a football game.

4. Many people who think having clean air to breathe is important still drive their cars quite a bit. These people most likely
    A. drive only non-polluting cars.
    B. are hypocrites and should give up their cars in favour of public transportation.
    C. value their own contribution toward are pollution as minor, at the margin, compared with the personal benefits they receive from driving a bit more.
    D. try to obtain legislation banning cars from cities.

✗ 5. Marginal analysis tends to "reject"
   A. all-or-nothing approaches to choice situations.
   B. compromises.
   C. government intervention.
   D. trade-offs.

   But Accepts these!

6. Past expenses are irrelevant to supply decisions because
   A. no one remembers the past.
   B. supply decisions depend on opportunities that will have to be forgone, not opportunities already forgone.
   C. expenses incurred in the past never affect opportunities available in the present.
   D. it is essential to avoid bankruptcy.

✗ 7. An expense is not a "genuine cost," in the economist's way of thinking, if it
   A. has not yet been incurred.
   B. does not use up either human time and effort or non-renewable natural resources
   C. represents no opportunity for choice.
   D. is merely expected in the future.

✗ 8. An increase in a retailer's "overhead" expenses, such as utilities and rent,
   A. amounts to an increase in marginal costs.
   B. enables the retailer to raise the prices on all items sold.
   C. compels the retailer to raise the prices on all items sold.
   D. does not by itself make an increase in prices desirable, possible, or necessary.

✗ 9. The schedule of tolls that will "maximize" the net revenue received by the owner of a bridge
   A. varies directly with the cost of constructing the bridge.
   B. varies inversely to the cost of constructing the bridge.
   C. does not depend on the cost of constructing the bridge.
   D. is the highest toll anyone is willing to pay rather than forgo the opportunity to cross the bridge.

10. Marginal cost means
   A. cost that can be ignored.
   B. average cost.
   C. additional cost.
   D. sunk cost.

11. Opportunity costs are
   A. always incremental, or marginal, costs.
   B. sometimes marginal costs.
   C. never marginal costs.
   D. unrelated to marginal costs.

12. Marginal—rather than average or per-unit—costs should guide decisions because marginal costs
   A. are the consequences of decisions.
   B. have to be paid regardless of what is decided.
   C. are deductible for tax purposes.
   D. are contractual obligations.

13. The marginal costs relevant to any decision will always be the costs
    - A. that the decision cannot affect.
    - B. anticipated from making that decision.
    - C. already incurred as a result of that decision.
    - D. that are trivial.

14. Business firms whose total revenue in a given year falls short of total expenses in that year
    - A. must file for bankruptcy.
    - B. must raise their prices.
    - C. must stop operating.
    - D. may find that their most profitable course is to continue in the same way.

15. Homeowners who make monthly mortgage payments are paying
    - A. sunk costs.
    - B. the cost of constructing the house.
    - C. the cost of constructing a new house.
    - D. the cost of retaining ownership of the house.

16. If a Canadian constructs a hot dog stand in Moscow on Red Square but fails to sell any hot dogs, who will pay the cost of constructing the hot dog stand?
    - A. No one, because it is a sunk cost.
    - B. The Russian economy if the Russians supplied the resources.
    - C. The Canadian economy if a Canadian citizen owned the stand.
    - D. Whoever put up the money, expecting to get it back

17. The argument that psychiatrists charge high fees because they must go to school for so many years to qualify as psychiatrists is confirmed by
    - A. evidence that psychiatrists whose brilliance enables them to graduate early set lower fees.
    - B. evidence that clients are willing to pay more for any psychiatrist's services if they discover that the psychiatrist spent five years as an undergraduate rather than four.
    - C. evidence that psychiatrists don't raise their fees merely because they have many clients requesting their services.
    - D. none of the above.

18. If the cost of becoming a psychiatrist were lowered,
    - A. psychiatrists' fees would not be affected in the long run because education is a sunk cost.
    - B. new psychiatrists would charge less than old psychiatrists.
    - C. the increased supply of new psychiatrists over time would tend to reduce the price that old psychiatrists could charge.
    - D. psychiatrists' fees would immediately decline.

19. The most important determinant of the cost to you of having your car repaired by an auto mechanic is the
    - A. income you have to spend.
    - B. demand for the services of auto mechanics in relation to the number of auto mechanics available.
    - C. value of the time spent by the auto mechanic in acquiring the necessary training.
    - D. value you place on having an auto mechanic fix your car.

20. An increased demand for the services of psychiatrists
    - A. may cause their fees to rise but cannot affect their costs.
    - B. may cause their fees to rise by raising the cost to a psychiatrist of providing service to a particular client.
    - C. will lower the cost of psychiatrists' services by causing more psychiatrists to be trained.
    - D. will not affect the fees they charge because demand doesn't affect costs.

21. Your employer announces the following change in your medical insurance plan: You will pay $2 more each month in premiums and the insurance company will begin paying for up to 12 visits annually to a psychiatrist. Under this new system, the dollar cost to you of making the first visit to the psychiatrist in a year will be

    A. $0.
    B. $2.
    C. $24.
    D. $24 plus the employer's contribution to the premiums.

22. Higher-quality service is most likely to be demanded by those who

    A. have the highest incomes.
    B. must pay the marginal cost of improved-quality service.
    C. do not have to pay any additional cost for improved-quality service.
    D. are willing to pay only for what they receive.

23. The owner of a laundromat posts the following announcement: "We regret that rising costs compel us to raise our prices." You may most safely assume that the owner

    A. does not want to raise prices but has no choice.
    B. wants customers to believe that the price increases are fair.
    C. doesn't know the difference between sunk costs and marginal costs.
    D. hasn't really raised prices.

24. In a city that is rapidly losing population, the cost of renting apartments will tend to

    A. decline only from the landlord's point of view.
    B. decline only from the tenant's point of view.
    C. decline for landlords and for tenants.
    D. be unchanged so long as the existing housing stock remains unchanged.

25. The relative cost to a shopper of buying rib-eye or flank steaks is determined largely by the relative

    A. nutritional value of rib-eye steaks and flank steaks.
    B. cost of producing rib-eye steaks and flank steaks.
    C. demand by other consumers for rib-eye steaks and flank steaks.
    D. size of rib-eye steaks and flank steaks.

26. An increased demand for a good is more likely to raise its price in the

    A. short run if the supply is highly elastic.
    B. short run than in the long run.
    C. long run than in the short run.
    D. long run if the supply is highly elastic.

27. If the quantity of a good that is supplied can be increased at a cost per unit about equal to the current cost per unit, an increase in the demand for that good will tend to

    A. reduce its price substantially.
    B. reduce its price only a little
    C. raise its price very little.
    D. raise its price substantially.

28. An increase in the demand for pork will

    A. raise the cost of growing beef.
    B. have no effect on the cost of growing beef.
    C. lower the cost of growing beef.
    D. have a completely unpredictable effect on the cost of growing beef.

29. Supply curves tend to be *less* elastic

  A. in the short run than in the long run.
  B. in the long run than in the short run.
  C. if demand curves are inelastic.
  D. if demand curves are elastic.

30. Marginal costs are the costs relevant to the guidance of production

  A. in any economic system where resources are scarce.
  B. only in economic systems characterized by private ownership of resources.
  C. only in economic systems where private profit is more important than the welfare of people.
  D. only when resources are used for the welfare of all.

31. Competitive offers to buy and sell resources establish money prices that reflect relative scarcities in

  A. economic systems characterized by clear and private ownership of resources.
  B. any economic system.
  C. any economic system in which efficient use of scarce resources is important
  D. economic systems that are regulated by government.

32. In a centrally planned economy that does not use markets, there is no

  A. effective way to find out what prices supply and demand would set if they were allowed to do so.
  B. reason why the central planners would want to find out what prices supply and demand would set if they were allowed to do so.
  C. pursuit of private interest.
  D. difference between individual interest and public interest.

D. Answers to the Review Questions in Chapter 7

1. B	2. B	3. D	4. C	5. A	6. B	7. C	8. D
9. C	10. C	11. A	12. A	13. B	14. D	15. D	16. D
17. D	18. C	19. B	20. B	21. A	22. C	23. B	24. C
25. C	26. B	27. C	28. A	29. A	30. A	31. A	32. A

E. Marginal Cost, Supply, Demand, and Prices: a Review

1. What effects would you expect a sudden large increase in the public's desire to play golf to have on the cost of playing golf?

  A. If more people suddenly crowd onto available courses, what will happen to the cost of playing a round?

  B. Would privately owned or publicly owned courses be more likely to raise their fees quickly in response to this new situation

  C. Will new golf courses be constructed in response to the increased demand? Under what circumstances?

  D. What determines the price that will have to be paid for land on which to build new golf courses?

  E. Would you expect the cost of playing a round to come down again after a long-enough time had passed?

  F. Why would you or would you not expect a similar sequence of events to occur affecting the cost of obtaining golf balls and golf clubs?

2. Three supply curves are shown on the next page. You may also think of them as marginal cost curves, or curves showing the cost at which additional quantities can be supplied.

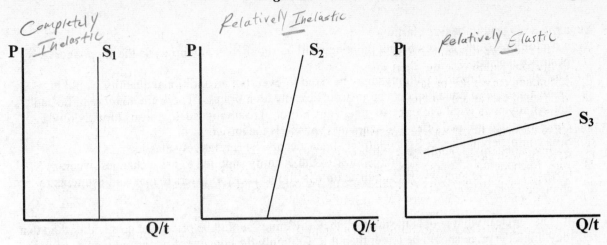

Completely Inelastic S_1 *Relatively Inelastic* S_2 *Relatively Elastic* S_3

A. Which one might best represent the supply of Rembrandt paintings? *S_1*

B. Would your answer be the same if the words "to Canadian art museums and other Canadian collectors" were added to the preceding question? *S_2*

C. What can you say about the price elasticities of supply in each case? *Completely inelastic, relatively inelastic, relatively elastic*

D. Someone tells you that S_2 and S_3 both show the supply curve of rental housing in some area. How could those two curves both be supply curves for a single good? *See answer — D*

3. A letter to the campus newspaper complains because the authorities raised the fees for parking near the chemistry building on campus. The writer asserts, "The price for parking should be set 'at cost'".

A. What does the letter writer mean by "at cost"?

B. What costs do you think the letter writer is omitting in the calculation?

C. How might the letter writer want the spaces to be rationed if the quantity demanded exceeds the quantity supplied?

F. Answers to Questions in Section E

1. A. Even if the fees aren't raised, players will experience additional delays and other unpleasant consequences of congestion. They may be compelled to play at very inconvenient times if they want to play at all.

B. The managers of a publicly owned course do not profit in any direct way from higher fees. The owners of a private course would find an advantage to themselves in reducing congestion costs by raising the monetary cost to players.

C. Increased demand doesn't build anything new. The expectation of higher returns is what induces people to supply additional quantities of goods. In the case of golf courses, which take a long time to build and where returns are obtained only over a lengthy period of time, more are not likely to be created unless the larger demand is expected to persist. Even then, an increased quantity will be supplied only after a considerable interval.

D. Prospective builders of golf courses must bid the land away from such uses as housing, crop production, and pasture. Land far from cities will tend to be available at lower cost, but courses close to cities will be more attractive to more golfers.

E. It probably would come back down again after a while except for the fact that the demand for suitable land for other uses may be rising even faster than the demand for the land as a golf course.

F. The quantity of golf balls and clubs can be increased much more quickly. The additional resources required to produce additional clubs and balls also would not make much of a dent in the overall stock, so that we wouldn't expect a doubled demand for "woods" to have any noticeable effect on the price of lumber. Finally, there is little reason to expect a relatively increased demand for any of the goods that are major users of the inputs that go into clubs and balls. So you probably should predict a larger quantity to be supplied at little or no increase in price in response to the enlarged demand.

2. A. No additional genuine Rembrandt paintings will be supplied at any price, so the supply curve is perfectly inelastic — S_1.
    B. The stock of Rembrandt paintings may be fixed forever, but an additional quantity would be made available to Canadian collectors at sufficiently high prices. "There are no more to be had" is not synonymous with "No one can obtain any more." To supply usually means to withdraw a good from one use and offer it for another. Thus S_2 is the answer.
    C. S_1 is completely inelastic, S_2 is relatively inelastic, and S_3 is relatively elastic.
    D. S_2 could well show the short-run response of the quantity supplied to price changes, whereas S_3 might show the response when adequate time is allowed for producers to make adjustments to changed relative prices.

3. A. It is never clear what people mean when they say things should be priced "at cost" other than that they think the price should be lower than it is. Certainly the concept of opportunity costs was the farthest thing from the mind of this writer.
    B. Most obviously, the writer is omitting the opportunity costs of using the land. If the most valuable use of the land is as a parking lot, the authorities might find out about opportunity costs by renting the lot to the highest bidder, letting a management company operate the parking lot. Aside from this approach to opportunity costs, the writer is omitting the costs imposed on others when he takes a parking place in a full lot. These costs are often substantial.
    C. The writer does not like using price to ration scarce resources because the increased demand for these limited parking places means he will have to pay a higher price. He might prefer a scheme that gives priority to graduate students or laboratory assistants or professors, depending on his own status. Or he might prefer first-come, first-served.

G. Questions to Think about

1. If malpractice insurance premiums increase, do lawyers increase their fees to cover them?
2. Is the probability of being robbed part of the cost of owning and operating a bank? Will banks that have frequently been robbed be able to charge higher service fees and interest rates on loans than banks that have never been robbed?

H. Answers to Questions in Section G

1. Almost everyone assumes they do. But if (that's an important "if") lawyers were previously charging "what the market will bear," the increase in insurance costs won't enable them to raise their prices. Could any particular plumber start charging more because the insurance company had raised the liability premiums on her truck in response to a negligent driving record?

2. It's certainly a cost. But will anyone be willing to pay more to patronize a bank preferred by bank robbers? It is more likely that frequently robbed branches will be closed, or that some banks will incur additional security costs. Higher costs exert their effect on prices through effects on supply. In some areas, higher crime rates and higher costs might still not drive a branch out of business if the local customers would rather pay higher prices for banking services than travel farther to do their banking. But with national banks in Canada and with the growth of "bank-by-phone" and internet banking, it is unlikely that any one of the branches could charge more for its services than any other branch.

Chapter 8

Price Setting and the Question of Monopoly

A. Multiple-Choice Questions on the Principal Ideas of Chapter 8

1. The concept of monopoly is fundamentally ambiguous because
   A. sellers never admit that they are monopolists, but buyers think every seller is a monopolist.
   B. every seller is a monopolist if we define the product narrowly enough, and no seller is a monopolist if we define the product broadly enough.
   C. every seller is a monopolist if we define the product broadly enough, and no seller is a monopolist if we define the product narrowly enough.
   D. it is basically a legal concept, and all legal concepts are fundamentally ambiguous.

2. Sellers have less power to raise their prices above their costs
   A. the poorer the substitutes and the more elastic the demand for their product.
   B. the better the substitutes and the more elastic the demand for their product.
   C. the poorer the substitutes and the less elastic the demand for their product.
   D. the better the substitutes and the less elastic the demand for their product.

3. In the early years of Canada and England, the term monopoly usually referred to an organization to which the government had given an exclusive right to engage in a particular commercial activity. In Canada today,
   A. national, provincial, and municipal governments grant exclusive privileges that prevent some who would otherwise do so from competing with established firms.
   B. such grants of exclusive privilege are extended only to confer benefits upon the wider public.
   C. it is unconstitutional for government to extend exclusive privileges to private citizens.
   D. business firms no longer receive grants of exclusive privilege from government.

4. The distinction between price takers and price searchers is that price takers
   A. are always small firms, and price searchers are always large firms.
   B. never enjoy grants of exclusive legal privileges, whereas price searchers always do.
   C. are buyers, whereas price searchers are sellers.
   D. cannot raise their prices without losing all their sales, whereas price searchers can.

5. Competition tends to produce, in price-takers' markets,
   A. quantities of output at which the marginal dollar cost equals the dollar price.
   B. a situation in which buyers are able to obtain every unit of output for which they are willing to pay the sellers' marginal opportunity cost.
   C. a situation in which sellers have no incentive to withhold from the market any output whose marginal cost of production is less than the prevailing price.
   D. a situation described by all of the above.

6. Firms that are price searchers tend to set prices that

    A. are not limited by the demand.

    B. are unrelated to marginal cost.

    C. have nothing to do with supply or demand.

    D. they think will provide them with a net revenue that is as large as possible.

7. Firms that are price takers sell at prices that

    A. are not limited by the demand.

    B. are unrelated to marginal cost.

    C. have nothing to do with supply or demand.

    D. they think will provide them with a net revenue that is as large as possible.

B. Answers to, and Explanations of, Multiple-Choice Questions on the Principal Ideas of Chapter 8

1. **B**. Here's an interesting implication: You can force yourself as a consumer to purchase entirely from monopolists by being sufficiently difficult to please.

2. **B**. Good substitutes mean good options for buyers, so that they can at low cost reduce their purchases of any item whose price has increased. That's the definition of an elastic demand.

3. **A**. There are many ways for governments to do this, many fine-sounding reasons for doing it, and much lobbying on the part of established sellers who do not appreciate increased competition.

4. **D**. Some price takers are large firms, and many price searchers are very small firms. Some price takers enjoy grants of exclusive legal privilege, and many price searchers do not. Both price takers and price searchers can exist on either side of the market, as buyers as well as sellers. The distinction between them is the ability to raise their prices without losing all their sales (if they are sellers) and to lower their prices (if they are buyers) without thereby becoming unable to purchase any at all.

5. **D**. Each of the first three options describes the same situation from a different perspective.

6. **D**. In searching for the price that will maximize their net revenue, price searchers must pay close attention to buyer demand, the supply curves of competitors, and their own marginal costs. Not all firms attempt to maximize net revenues all the time, however. Most firms tend to try, though.

7. **D**. The difference is that price takers don't have to search for the price at which to sell. Market demand and market supply tell them exactly what they can charge. Price takers will not want to supply any output whose marginal cost is expected to exceed the price.

C. A Step-by-Step Review of Chapter 8

1. The literal meaning of the word monopolist is

    A. huge organization.

    B. price gouger.

    C. mortgage holder.

    D. one seller.

2. A tiny dry-cleaning establishment comes close to being a monopolist from the standpoint of a customer who

    A. wears clothes that have to be dry-cleaned.

    B. lives next door and has no low-cost way to get back and forth from more distant dry-cleaning establishments.

    C. is unwilling to bargain with the dry cleaner about prices.

    D. can't afford to pay for any dry cleaning.

3. Which of the following would make that dry-cleaning establishment look less like a monopolist to the customer?
   A. Customer buys a car.
   B. Customer buys all wash-and-wear clothing.
   C. Customer marries someone who likes to take long walks in the city.
   D. All of the above.

4. Every economics teacher is a monopolist
   A. if the product is defined as instruction of the precise type and style the teacher offers.
   B. because students are incapable of evaluating the product.
   C. because they have captive audiences.
   D. if economics is a required course.

5. Even though it is virtually impossible for anyone to compete with the Canada Post in offering certain services, Canada Post is not necessarily a monopolist, because
   A. it is inefficient.
   B. it hires people of every race, creed, and sex.
   C. there are substitutes for every product sold by Canada Post.
   D. it operates at a loss.

6. When there is only one seller of a product for which no close substitutes are available,
   A. quality is usually guaranteed.
   B. buyers receive the close and undivided attention of the seller.
   C. users of that product have difficulty inducing the seller to give them good quality at low prices.
   D. there are no restrictions on what price the seller can charge.

7. A true and pure monopolist would be a seller facing a
   A. perfectly inelastic demand curve.
   B. perfectly elastic demand curve.
   C. demand curve of unit elasticity throughout its length.
   D. demand curve under the seller's control.

8. The market power of sellers, defined as the percentage by which they can maintain their selling price above marginal cost, decreases as the demand curve facing the sellers becomes more
   A. elastic.
   B. inelastic.
   C. definitely known.
   D. uncertain.

9. Legal grants of exclusive privilege to favoured sellers
   A. assure buyers of higher quality.
   B. restrict competition.
   C. do not really benefit anyone.
   D. are unconstitutional in Canada.

10. If a large Saskatchewan wheat farmer withholds his entire crop from the market to wait for a higher price, his action will
    A. raise the price only in the short run.
    B. raise the price of wheat significantly but only for other farmers.
    C. have no discernible effect on the price of wheat.
    D. raise the price only in the long run.

11. If the nation of Saudi Arabia withholds its entire output of oil from the market to wait for a higher price, its action will
    A. force other sellers to reduce their prices.
    B. raise the price of oil significantly for producers who continue to sell.
    C. have no discernible effect on the price of oil.
    D. increase the demand for oil.

12. If the owner of a single producing oil well in Alberta withholds the well's entire output from the market, that action (in the absence of any legislated price controls) will
    A. raise the price only in the short run.
    B. raise the price of oil only for other sellers.
    C. have no discernible effect on the price of oil.
    D. raise the price only in the long run.

13. Sellers who are price takers
    A. face perfectly elastic demand curves.
    B. cannot affect the price at which they sell.
    C. lose all their sales if they raise their price above the price prevailing in the market.
    D. can sell as much as they want to at the price prevailing in the market.
    E. are in all of the situations described above.

14. Sellers who are price searchers lose
    A. all of their sales if they raise their prices.
    B. none of their sales if they raise their prices.
    C. some of their sales if they raise their prices.
    D. their licenses if they raise their prices.

15. Sellers who are price searchers
    A. face no competition.
    B. can ignore the demand for their product in setting their prices.
    C. Both of the above are true.
    D. None of the above is true.

16. (Questions 16 to 18 refer to Figure 8.1 in the text.) If the minimum price for house painters is set by law at $20 per hour, the quantity of hours that painters will want to supply will be
    A. over twice the quantity buyers are willing to purchase.
    B. equal to the quantity demanded.
    C. less than the quantity demanded.
    D. determined by the quantity demanded.

17. The hours suppliers will be able to sell under a legislated price of $20 per hour will be
    A. over twice the quantity buyers are willing to purchase.
    B. equal to the quantity demanded.
    C. less than the quantity demanded.
    D. equal to the quantity they want to supply.

18. The legislated price of $20 per hour prevents suppliers from selling
    A. any house painting services at all.
    B. 2000 additional hours of house painting for which customers would be willing to pay more than the suppliers' opportunity cost.
    C. inferior services to customers who have been duped into supposing that they benefit from low prices.
    D. in competition with other housepainters.

19. Price-takers' markets are more likely than price-searchers' markets to result in situations

   A. in which all goods are being produced for which buyers are willing to pay the marginal cost of their supply.
   B. in which marginal cost is less than price.
   C. in which sellers advertise extensively.
   D. in which marginal cost is more than price.

20. Price-takers' markets differ from price-searchers' markets in that price takers

   A. earn less than price searchers.
   B. have no incentive to reduce production in order to secure a higher price.
   C. have no desire to secure exclusive legal privileges from government.
   D. face all of the conditions above.

D. Answers to the Review Questions in Chapter 8

1. D	2. B	3. D	4. A	5. C
6. C	7. A	8. A	9. B	10. C
11. B	12. C	13. E	14. C	15. D
16. A	17. B	18. B	19. A	20. B

E. Prices and Resource Allocation: Review and Prelude

Tom Sawyer has plans for this Saturday. He wants to sleep late, go swimming, see a movie, and goof off. He would also like to earn some money, which he can do by raking leaves.

Tom knows seven neighbours who want their yards raked. He doesn't know how much each is willing to pay him to do the job, but we do.

	Maximum Each Neighbour Is Willing to Pay Tom to Rake Leaves this Saturday
Mrs. Hannibal	$7
Mr. Carthage	6
Ms. Punic	5
Mr. Fabian	4
Ms. Cunctator	3
Mr. Cato	2
Mrs. Sippi	1

Tom can rake two yards by giving up his plan to goof off this Saturday, which he would be willing to do for $2 per yard. He can rake two more by not sleeping late, which he would be willing to do for $3 per yard. He would give up the movie matinee, which would enable him to rake another two yards, for $4 per yard. For $5 a yard, he would give up swimming and be able to rake an additional two yards.

1. On the graph on the following page, graph both the demand for Tom's services and the marginal opportunity cost to Tom of mowing lawns.
2. If Tom decides to set his price at $3.50, how many yards will he be asked to rake? How many will he be willing to rake?
3. What would have happened had Tom set his price at $2.50? Would he have come to regret setting this price?
4. Suppose Tom had set his price at $4.50. How many yards would he have been asked to rake? How many would he have wanted to rake?
5. If Tom had known as much as we know about the demand for his services, what pricing policy would he have decided on?

Figure 8.1

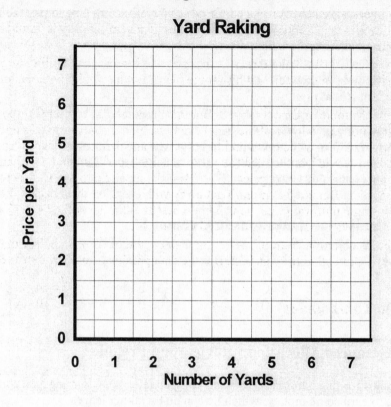

Yard Raking

6. From the point of view of everyone--Tom and his neighbours--what is the best pricing policy for Tom to follow?

F. Answers to the Questions in Section E

1.   **Figure 8.2**

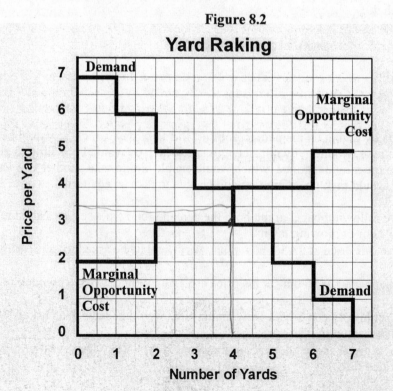

Yard Raking

2. The quantity demanded and the quantity supplied will both be four yards.

3. He would have been asked to rake five yards, which he would not have been willing to do, because $2.50 is only enough to persuade him to sacrifice goofing off. He would have raked only two yards while wondering if he couldn't have charged a higher price from some of his neighbours.

4. He would have been asked to rake three. At that price he is more than willing to give up goofing off plus all of his late time in the sack and his movie plans. But he would not have found six neighbours willing to hire him at that price.

5. Pricing policy is the topic of Chapters 9-12. But the marginal cost of studying the demand and cost curves for a moment is low and the benefit may be high. If the marginal opportunity cost curve represents the cost to Tom as he rakes additional yards, and the demand curve represents the benefits as he does so, Tom would want to rake the yards of neighbours Hannibal, Carthage, Punic, and Fabian and charge each a different price: $7 to Mrs. Hannibal, $6 to Mr. Carthage, $5 to Ms. Punic, and $4 to Mr. Fabian. But maybe he can't get away with charging them each a different price. If he has to charge a single uniform price, he would do best at either $6 or $5. Do you see why? If not, come back to this question after you have read Chapter 11.

6. Do they all share a common point of view? There may be some pricing policy that, after long discussion, they would all agree was best. But the data provided certainly don't tell us what it would be.

G. Questions to Think about

1. Would you expect to be able to persuade the owners or managers of some business firm that it was a monopoly?

2. Think of some sellers who come close to being (or are) the only seller of the product they offer. Then ask yourself what options would be available to customers if that seller doubled the price of the good.

H. Answers to Questions in Section G

1. You're an optimistic sort if you think you could succeed at such a task. So far as sellers are concerned, a monopoly is a firm that faces no competition, and there aren't any sellers for whom competition poses no threat at all. When buyers say "monopoly," they often mean anyone able to charge them a price higher than they think it ought to be. Widely divergent and even unrelated definitions, plus the emotional connotations that surround it, are good reasons for avoiding the word monopoly in favour of more precise substitutes.

2. There are products for which the substitutes are so poor that a doubled price would have little effect on the quantity purchased. But how often is there only one seller of such a product? Even in cases in which the law supports the exclusive privilege of some seller additional options are likely to appear when the seller begins to take full advantage of this favoured position. Some new options may be illegal. But does everyone obey the law regardless of the cost of doing so, especially if the law is widely perceived as an unfair law granting unwarranted privileges to special interests?

Chapter 9

Costs Again:
Behind the Supply Curve

A. Multiple-Choice Questions on the Principal Ideas of Chapter 9

1. When firms are deliberating about how much to produce, they don't always make the correct decisions because
   A. the future is uncertain, and sometimes expectations are not born out.
   B. the decision makers do not always understand marginalist principles.
   C. it is sometimes too costly to acquire all the information that would be needed to make the correct decision.
   D. all of the above.

2. The total output of a firm increases from 700 units per day to 800 units per day when the firm increases the number of workers hired from 7 to 8. The marginal physical product of the eighth worker is
   A. increasing.
   B. decreasing.
   C. constant.
   D. 100.

3. When average physical product is at a maximum,
   A. marginal physical product is decreasing as the rate of output increases.
   B. net revenues are being maximized.
   C. the total output of the firm is also at a maximum.
   D. marginal physical product is at a maximum.

4. Eventually, as more of a variable input is used, the law of diminishing marginal returns sets in because
   A. the total output of the firm will eventually decline.
   B. the additional output resulting from using more of the variable input declines.
   C. marginal physical product eventually becomes negative.
   D. marginal physical product eventually falls below average physical product.

5. When marginal costs are less than average total costs,
   A. marginal costs are less than average variable costs as well.
   B. average variable costs are declining as output increases.
   C. average total costs are declining as output increases.
   D. marginal costs are declining as output increases.

6. A necessary condition for a firm to maximize its net revenues is that it must produce that rate of output for which
   A. marginal revenue is increasing.
   B. marginal cost is at a minimum.
   C. marginal revenue equals marginal cost.
   D. average total cost is minimized.
   E. Total revenue is maximized.

7. What is the short run?
   A. a period of between three and four months.
   B. a period during which the quantities of all the inputs into the production process can be changed.
   C. a period during which the quantities of only some of the inputs can be changed.
   D. a period during which the technology of the firm remains unchanged.

8. What is the shape of the graph of the demand curve faced by a firm that is a price taker?
   A. It is downward-sloping due to consumer choice.
   B. It is horizontal at the market price.
   C. It is horizontal at the minimum point on the firm's average total cost curve.
   D. It is downward-sloping due to the law of diminishing marginal productivity.

9. What is the nature of the marginal revenue curve for a price taker?
   A. It is horizontal and congruent with the demand curve.
   B. It is horizontal, but below the demand curve.
   C. It is downward-sloping and congruent with the demand curve facing the firm.
   D. It is downward-sloping, but lies below the firm's demand curve.

10. In which of the following circumstances will a price-taking firm earn positive net revenues?
    A. P > AVC
    B. MR > ATC
    C. ATC > MC
    D. ATC > MPP
    E. MR > MC

11. When net revenues are zero,
    A. no one will want to produce the product, even in the short run.
    B. no one will want to produce the product, even in the long run.
    C. no one will have an incentive to enter this industry.
    D. revenues are not covering the firm's opportunity costs.
    E. firms will exit from this industry.

12. When the price increases in an industry made up of price-takers,
    A. firms have an incentive to expand their production to a point where ATC is no longer minimized.
    B. some firms may decide *not* to go along with the price increase in order to capture a larger market share.
    C. firms have an incentive to exit from the industry.
    D. firms will continue producing the same rate of output, even in the short run.

B. Answers to, and Explanations of, the Multiple-Choice Questions on the Principal Ideas of Chapter 9.

1. **D**. The graphs and the tables used in economic examples make everything look like a precise science. If economics were that precise, bankruptcy rates would be much lower. The major difficulty is that decisions must be made now on the basis of our *expectations* about what the net benefits will be of those decisions. Since we cannot possibly know everything about the future, and because it is costly to refine our expectations, we are sure to make some mistakes.

2. **D**. When marginal physical product equals average physical product, it is unlikely that *MPP* is increasing. It might be constant, or it might be decreasing, but there is no way to tell which, using the information provided. However it is easy to see that the 8th worker added 100 units to the total output of the firm.

3. **A**. When the margin is above the average, it pulls the average up. When the margin is below the average, it pulls the average down. *MPP* just equals *APP* at the maximum of *APP*, and for typical production relationships, *MPP* is declining at that rate of output.

4. **B**. The concept that is important is diminishing *marginal* returns. As you put more and more of a variable input into the production process, eventually the extra output you get begins to decline. At that point, extra units of the input still add to the total output — they just add less than the earlier units did. The point of diminishing marginal returns sets in long before total output falls.

5. **C**. It is easiest to answer this question by sketching a graph of a firm's "u-shaped" cost curves. Make sure you draw the *ATC* above the *AVC*, but with the two curves getting closer and closer as output expands. Also, make sure you draw the *MC* curve so it goes through the minimum points of both the *ATC* and the *AVC* curves. Now, if you've sketched the curves correctly, you can see that along the *MC* curve between the *ATC* and *AVC* curves, *MC* is rising, *ATC* is falling, and *AVC* is *rising*.

6. **C**. This rule applies for all firms, whether they are price takers or price searchers. It is, for firms, just a restatement of the idea that anything we do should be done only so long as doing it adds more to our benefits than to our costs. Notice that $MR = MC$ is only a necessary condition; it is not a sufficient condition. If, at the rate of output for which $MR = MC$, total revenue is less than variable costs, the firm should ordinarily shut down in the short run.

7. **C**. Although we don't ordinarily think of technology changing during the short run, that is not the criterion we use in the definition. The types of things that might be held constant in the short run could include: long-term labour contracts with substantial severance pay commitments, a lease, some insurance premia, or some tax obligations.

8. **B**. If a price taker tried to raise its price, it wouldn't be able to sell any of its output. And it has no reason to lower its price since it believes it can sell all it wants at the market price.

9. **A**. If a price taker sells one more unit at the going price, it adds an amount equal to the price to its total revenue, and it was able to do so without having to lower the price for other units sold. So for a price taker, $P = MR$.

10. **B**. Because price always equals marginal revenue for a price taker, if the $MR > ATC$, then it must also be the case that $P > ATC$, which is just another way of saying that total revenue exceeds total cost, or that net revenues are positive. In choices A, C, and E, the firm *might* be earning positive net revenues, but it might not, too.

11. **C**. When net revenues are zero, the firm is covering *all* of its opportunity costs, including the opportunity costs of using its owners' financial investment. Consequently the owners have no incentive to leave the industry. But because there are no returns greater than normal to be earned in this industry, there is no incentive for others to enter it, either.

12. **A**. When the price rises for a price taker, so does the marginal revenue. If the firm has the typically positively-sloped marginal cost curve, the firm will then have an incentive to increase its output. But at this higher rate of output, even though net revenues will be maximized, average total costs will be a bit greater than the minimum.

C. A Step-by-Step Review of Chapter 9

1. In calculating the marginal physical product of any one particular input,
    A. the quantities of the other inputs used in the production process must be held constant.
    B. the quantity of that input must be held constant and the quantities of the other factors varied.
    C. the quantities of that factor and all other factors must be held constant.
    D. the quantities of the other factors may, but need not be, varied over time.
    E. the quantity of that input is held constant in the short run but not in the long run.

2. The point of diminishing marginal productivity is reached at the same point as the point at which
    A. total output begins to decline as more of the variable input is used.
    B. average product reaches a maximum.
    C. marginal physical product reaches a maximum.
    D. total output reaches a maximum.
    E. marginal revenue reaches a maximum.

3. A field of soybeans is ready for harvest, and labour is the only variable input. The total possible output from hiring different numbers of workers is

Number of Workers	Bushels Harvested
0	0
1	6
2	14
3	20
4	24

With which worker is the point of diminishing marginal returns reached?

A. the first
B. the second
C. the third
D. the fourth
E. The point of diminishing marginal returns has not yet been reached. Total output is still increasing as the number of workers increases.

4. Which of the graphs in Figure 9.1 represents diminishing marginal physical product for the entire range of its output? Output is measured on vertical axes, and the quantity of a variable input is measured on the horizontal axes.

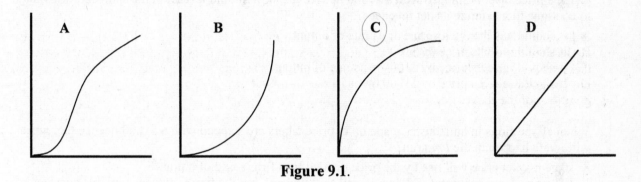

Figure 9.1.

5. Which of the graphs in Figure 9.1 represents constant marginal physical product throughout?

A.   B.   C.   D.   E. None of them does.

6. Consider a firm with just one variable input, *i*, and several fixed inputs. With *MC* = the marginal costs of producing an additional unit of the output, *w* = the rental price or wage of input *i*, *TC* = total costs, *VC* = variable costs, and *Q* = the total rate of output for the firm. Using this notation, marginal cost is equal to

A. *w•MP*
B. *(TC + MC)/w*
C. *MP/w*
D. *w/MP*
E. *TP•w*

7. Which of the following relationships between production and costs is true?

A. When *MPP* is increasing, *MC* is also increasing.
B. When *MPP* is constant, *MC* is increasing.
C. When *MPP* is decreasing, *MC* is increasing.
D. There is no relationship between *MPP* and *MC*.

8. Which of the following is *not* true of a firm's short-run cost curves, as conventionally drawn?
    A. *AFC* declines continuously as the rate of output increases.
    B. *AFC* + *AVC* = *ATC*.
    C. *ATC* decreases so long as *MC* < *ATC*.
    D. *AVC* increases and then decreases as the rate of output increases.
    E. *AVC* and *ATC* get closer and closer together as the rate of output increases.

9. When the market price of a price taker's output increases, the firm should
    A. raise its price even further to take advantage of the increase in demand.
    B. raise its price, but by less than the market increase, to increase its market share.
    C. keep its price where it was originally so as not to appear to be price gouging its customers.
    D. increase its output.
    E. none of the above.

10. If the market price of a price taker's output is less than the firm's average total costs, the firm should
    A. declare bankruptcy.
    B. shut down its operations.
    C. raise its price until the price at least covers its average total costs.
    D. shut down only if the price is less than its average variable costs.
    E. all of the above.

11. When a price taker is slapped with a $1000 licence fee, how should it react in the short run if it wants to continue to maximize its net revenues?
    A. It should not change its price or its rate of output. *Deals with A FC!*
    B. It should raise its price by $1000.
    C. It should raise its price by $1000 ÷ its rate of output.
    D. It should raise its price by $1000 times its rate of output.
    E. None of the above.

    — Lo only ATC shifts

12. When all the firms in an industry made up of price takers are slapped with a $1000 licence fee, what will likely happen in the *long* run?
    A. The market price will rise by the price divided by a firm's rate of output.
    B. The firms' average total cost curves will shift upward, but the firms' average variable costs and marginal costs will remain unchanged.
    C. There will be fewer firms in the industry.
    D. The firms left in the industry will each be producing at a larger rate of output.
    E. All of the above.

13. When a price taker is unexpectedly charged a $10 per unit tax on its output, what will likely happen in the *short* run?
    A. It will increase its rate of output.
    B. Its *ATC, AVC,* and *MC* will all shift upward by $10.
    C. It should raise the price of its output by $10.
    D. Other firms will enter the industry to capitalize on the situation.
    E. All of the above.

14. When all the firms in an industry made up of price takers are charged a $10 per unit tax on their output, what will likely happen in the *long* run?
    A. Output in the industry will decline, but the firms in the industry will be producing the same amounts as were being produced by firms before the tax.
    B. There will be fewer firms left in the industry.
    C. The market price will rise by about $10 per unit.
    D. The marginal revenue curves facing the firms will now be higher by $10 per unit.
    E. All of the above.

D. Answers to the Review Questions in Chapter 9

1. A	2. C	3. B	4. C	5. D	6. D	7. C
8. D	9. D	10. D	11. A	12. E	13. B	14. E

E. Production and Costs: an Example   *They have to give us VC!*

The first two columns of Table 9.1, below, shows the number of wooden planters that Brian's firm can produce each week (*Q/t*) with various numbers of employees per week (*L/t*). Complete the columns for Marginal Physical Product (column 3) and Average Physical Product (column 4).

L/t (1)	Q/t (2)	MPP (3)	APP (4)	FC (5)	VC (6)	TC (7)	MC (8)	AFC (9)	AVC (10)	ATC (11)
0	0	Δ Q/t	Q/t ÷ L/t	100	0	100	ΔTC/ΔQ/t FC÷Q/t	VC÷Q/t	FC+VC	
1	10	10	10	100	400	500	40	10	40	50
2	40	30	20	100	800	900	13.33	2.5	20	22.5
3	65	25	21.67	100	1200	1300	16	1.538	18.46	20
4	85	20	21.25	100	1600	1700	20	1.176	18.82	20
5	100	15	20	100	2000	2100	26.67	1	20	21
6	110	10	18.33	100	2400	2500	40	0.909	21.82	22.73
7	119	9	16.57	100	2800	2900	66.67	0.862	24.14	25
8	125	6	14.88	100	3200	3300	133.33	0.840	26.89	27.73
9	126	1	13.33	100	3600	3700	400	0.833	30	30.53

Some ↑ by 400

In Figure 9.2 on the next page, plot a graph of the relationship between total number of planters produced each week (on the vertical axis) and the number of employees (on the horizontal axis). *Pg. 82*

In Figure 9.3 on the next page, plot a graph of the marginal physical product and the average physical product of labour. *Pg. 82*

Draw a straight line up from the maximum point on the ***MPP*** curve from Figure 9.3 to the curve in Figure 9.2. Notice that this line hits the inflexion point of the curve in Figure 9.2.

Production of Planters

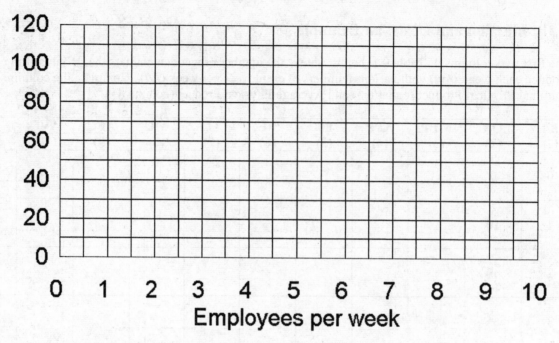

Figure 9.2 A Production Function with One Variable Input

Marginal and Average Physical Products

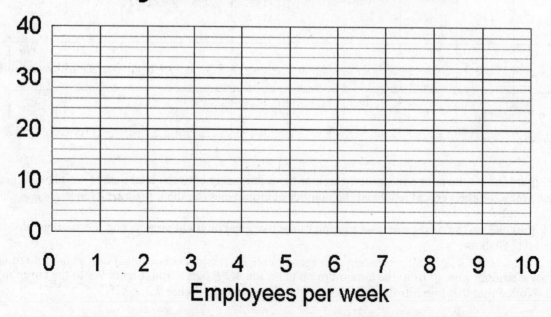

Figure 9.3 Marginal and Average Products of Labour

Brian's fixed costs are $100 per week. In Figure 9.4, below, plot Brian's *AFC, AVC, ATC,* and *MC*.

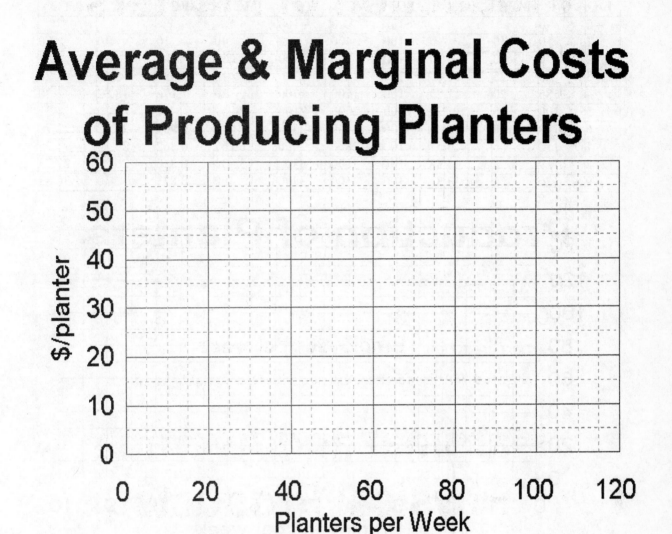

Average & Marginal Costs of Producing Planters

Use the data from Table 9.1 and the graphs in Figures 9.2, 9.3, and 9.4 to answer the following questions:

1. When marginal physical product is increasing, marginal cost is _Decreasing._

2. When marginal physical product is above average physical product, average physical product is _Increasing_

3. As the rate of output increases, average fixed costs _Decline, Decreases._

4. Marginal costs equal average variable costs when average variable costs are _@ a minimum_

5. Marginal costs equal average total costs when average total costs are _@ a minimum_

6. What is the relationship between average variable costs and average total costs as the rate of output increases?   _AVC & ATC get closer together (approach each other) as the rate of output increases._

F. Answers to the Questions in Section E

L/t	Q/t	MPP	APP	FC	VC	TC	MC	AFC	AVC	ATC
0	0			100	0	100				
1	10	10	10	100	400	500	40	10	40	50
2	40	30	20	100	800	900	13.33	2.5	20	22.5
3	65	25	21.67	100	1200	1300	16	1.538	18.46	20
4	85	20	21.25	100	1600	1700	20	1.176	18.82	20
5	100	15	20	100	2000	2100	26.67	1	20	21
6	110	10	18.33	100	2400	2500	40	0.909	21.82	22.73
7	116	6	16.57	100	2800	2900	66.67	0.862	24.14	25
8	119	3	14.88	100	3200	3300	133.33	0.840	26.89	27.73
9	120	1	13.33	100	3600	3700	400	0.833	30	30.83

Production of Planters

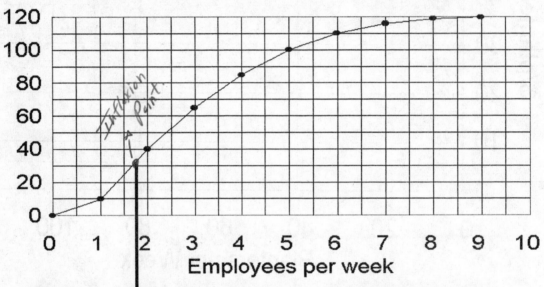

Employees per week

Marginal and Average Physical Products

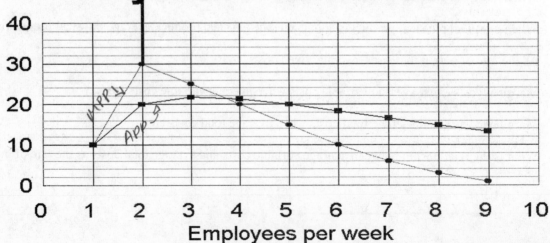

Employees per week

Average & Marginal Costs
of Producing Planters

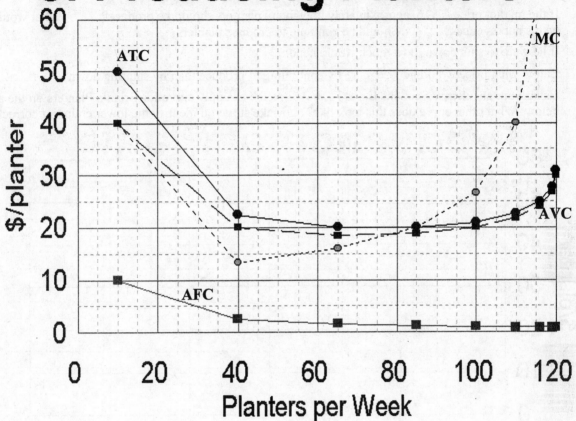

1. Decreasing.
2. Increasing.
3. Decline.
4. At a minimum.
5. At a minimum.
6. *AVC* and *ATC* get closer and closer together (asymptotically approach each other) as the rate of output increases.

G. Net Revenue Maximization and Supply by a Price Taker

1. What are the *two* conditions that a price taker must satisfy if it wishes to maximize its net revenues?

   A. $MR = MC$

   B.

2.   Continuing from sections E and F, suppose the market price of planters is $40 apiece. How many should Brian produce each week in order to maximize his net revenues?

3.   If the market price is $27, approximately how many planters should he produce each week?

4.   If the market price is $20, how many should he produce?   What would be his net revenues? Should he keep producing planters?

5.   If the market price of planters is $19, approximately how many planters should he produce? What would be his net revenues?   Should he keep producing planters?

6.   If the market price is $16, approximately how many planters should he produce?   What would be his net revenues?   Should he continue to produce planters?

7.   If he were to shut down, how much would he lose?

8.   Below what price would he lose more by continuing to produce than by shutting down?

9.   Using your answers to Sections E and F, above, sketch a supply curve for Brian's Planters on the axes below. What other curve does this look like?   Make sure you identify the lower endpoint correctly.

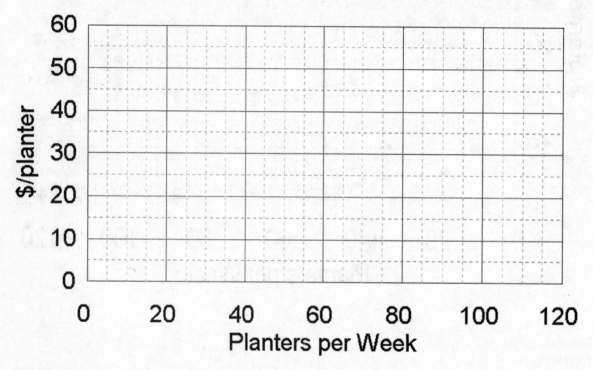

H. Answers to the Questions in Section G

1.   A. Produce that rate of output for which marginal revenue equals marginal costs.
     B. Produce the rate of output identified in part A only if total revenue ≥ variable costs, or equivalently if price is greater than or equal to average variable costs.

2.   When the market price is $40, Brian should produce 110 planters each week.

3.   When the price is $27, he should produce 100 planters per week.

4.   When the price is $20, he should produce 85 planters. His net revenues would be zero, but since he is covering all his opportunity costs (including what he could earn with his labour and his invested capital in some other industry), he has no reason to stop producing the planters. He is earning a normal rate of return.

5.   When the market price is $19, he should produce approximately 83 planters, assuming he can hire some employees part-time. Judging from the graph, at a price of $19 and a rate of output of 83, the price would be slightly below Brian's average total costs, and so his net revenues would be slightly negative. He should continue to produce in the short-run: the price still exceeds his average variable costs. He is more-than-covering variable costs and is making some contribution toward fixed costs.

6. At a price of $16, *MR = MC* at a rate of output equal to 65 planters per week. But at this price-output combination, the firm's revenue is only $1040, while its costs are $1300.

7. If it continued to produce, its net revenues would be -$260, whereas if it shut down, the firm would lose only its fixed costs — $100.

8. It should continue to produce in the short run so long as the market price is greater than about $18.46.

9. The points trace out the short-run supply curve for the firm. This curve is just the firm's marginal cost curve above $18.46. But be careful. A firm's *MC* curve is its supply curve only if the firm is a price taker.

I. Long-Run Adjustments

Continuing the example from sections E - H, above, what would happen in this industry if the price started at $40 per planter:

1. What would be the firm's net revenues?
2. Would firms have an incentive to enter or exit this industry?
3. As a result of #2 above, what would happen to the *industry* supply curve?
4. After the supply curve shifts, what would happen to the market price for planters?
5. How long would this process continue?
6. What would happen in this industry if the market price dropped below $20/planter?

J. Answers to the Questions in Section I

1. The firm would choose to produce 110 planters/week, and would earn net revenues of $1900.
2. Because the net revenues are positive, other firms would have an incentive to enter this industry.
3. Entry causes the industry supply curve to shift to the right (an increase in supply).
4. As supply increases, the market price is driven downward.
5. Entry will continue, supply will increase, and the price will be driven downward so long as firms believe they can earn positive net revenues. This will happen until the price is driven down to $20 per planter and net revenues are equal to zero.
6. If the price dropped below $20, firms would be earning negative net revenues and would have an incentive to exit. As they exit, the industry supply curve shifts leftward (supply decreases), and the price rises until the price reaches $20/planter, and net revenues are once again zero.

Chapter 10

Information,
Intermediaries,
and Speculators

A. Multiple-Choice Questions on the Principal Ideas of Chapter 10

1. The costs and benefits that affect decisions to supply or demand
    A. can be known with certainty only in the case of old, established products.
    B. can be known with certainty only in the case of old, established firms.
    C. can be known with certainty only in the case of old, established products turned out by old, established firms.
    D. are never known with certainty because they are always expected costs and benefits.

2. People make economic decisions that turn out to be mistaken
    A. only when they themselves don't have to pay the cost of their mistakes.
    B. only when they are guided by considerations of private, rather than social, profitability.
    C. because avoiding mistakes sometimes is more costly than making mistakes.
    D. because mistakes are sunk costs, and sunk costs are irrelevant.

3. Retailers and other intermediaries provide benefits to those who patronize them
    A. only because their customers are irrational.
    B. because people don't realize how much they could save by cutting out intermediaries.
    C. but the intermediaries benefit far more.
    D. by lowering the cost to their customers of acquiring valuable information.

4. Information is a scarce good in exchange transactions
    A. because the interests of buyers and sellers are opposed.
    B. because its possession is valuable but acquiring it is costly.
    C. unless sellers are required to disclose all relevant facts about their products.
    D. unless all parties to the transaction are completely honest.

5. When a customer says, "I have enough information to make a decision; I'm not going to shop any more," she is asserting that
    A. she has all the information available about the product she is buying.
    B. she believes that the last merchant she visited was being completely honest with her.
    C. she expects the extra benefits she might get from continuing to shop will be outweighed by the extra costs.
    D. she will wait until tomorrow before she resumes her shopping.

6. Markets provide people with valuable information
    A. in the private sector of the economy but not in the government sector.
    B. in capitalist but not in socialist societies.
    C. by summarizing the terms on which many people are willing to buy or to sell.
    D. but most people look only at prices and ignore the information markets provide.

7. We all behave as speculators in our economic transactions

    A. unless we use the services of intermediaries.
    B. unless we never buy on credit.
    C. because we all act in the hope of benefits from a correct anticipation of future events.
    D. because everyone likes to gamble.

8. We all use the services of speculators as information in reaching our own economic decisions

    A. if we buy or sell commodities through an organized exchange.
    B. because we all use prices that were set by bids and offers based on predictions of the future.
    C. if we play the stock market.
    D. because speculators are aggressive about marketing the information they produce.

9. If illegal insider trading is defined as trading on the basis of information not available to everyone else in the market,

    A. all parties to a trade will have better information.
    B. less information of value to the society will be assembled by traders.
    C. market trades will be fair except in rare circumstances.
    D. the advantages of large traders will be reduced and small traders will benefit.

10. Legislation and court rulings that put all responsibility for product inadequacy on the seller

    A. induce buyers to take advantage of low-cost opportunities to acquire valuable information.
    B. benefit buyers.
    C. induce sellers to provide more quality than most buyers want to pay for.
    D. reduce the net cost of acquiring information.

B. Answers to, and Explanations of, Multiple-Choice Questions on the Principal Ideas of Chapter 10

1. **D**. Many old, established firms supplying old, established products have found that actual costs and benefits were very different from what they had expected when they took particular actions. The Great Atlantic and Pacific Tea Company (A&P) is a prime example. So is the Manville Corporation, which suffered enormous losses when the dangers of asbestos became well established. And what about energy exploration companies in the 1980s? Or IBM in the 1990s?

2. **C.** People will tend to make more mistakes when they don't have to pay the costs of those mistakes. But they will tend to make "too few" mistakes when they don't have to pay the cost of acquiring additional information, which is to say that costs of acquiring some information will be greater than the costs of the mistakes thereby avoided.

3. **D**. There is, of course, no guarantee that anyone will receive a net benefit from patronizing a particular intermediary. The benefits and costs that induce people to use the services of intermediaries are *expected* benefits and costs.

4. **B.** Laws may help to make information less scarce and high ethical standards will surely help. But information would be a scarce good in a society of saints because the best of intentions cannot fully overcome the results of limited knowledge.

5. **C**. So long as the expected marginal benefits of search exceed the expected marginal costs of search, people will continue to search, whether it be for information, a marriage partner, or a job. They stop searching when the expected marginal costs exceed the expected marginal benefits of additional search.

6. **C**. Markets tend to work more satisfactorily where information about people's desire to supply or demand can be distilled into money prices.

7. **C**. Some people are more interested than others in reducing risk, as evidenced by the fact that some insure against more events than do others. But no one can entirely avoid acting in the face of uncertainty about the consequences.

8. **B**. It's important to note both that current relative prices reflect speculation about future events and that we use these price data in formulating our own plans. For example, the current price of housing clearly reflects expectations about future events, and these prices are information people use in deciding how they want to be housed.

9. **B**. Who will go to the trouble and expense of acquiring valuable information if they are prohibited from taking advantage of that information? Society usually benefits from the acquisition of information as does the individual who first dug up and then used the information. There is little reason to suppose that such legislation (How would it be enforced?) would reduce fraudulent trading or enable small traders to transact more successfully with larger traders.

10. **C**. People have differing abilities and advantages in the production of valuable information, and it will not benefit buyers if sellers are compelled to produce, at buyers' expense, information that buyers could have obtained at lower cost.

C. A Step-by-Step Review of Chapter 10

1. The costs and benefits that affect decisions to demand or supply are always
    A. expected and therefore uncertain.
    B. past costs and benefits that can be known with precision.
    C. monetary costs and benefits.
    D. real costs and benefits rather than speculative costs and benefits.

2. If mistakes can be reduced through the acquisition of more information,
    A. it always pays to acquire more information before acting.
    B. it will not pay to acquire information indefinitely because information is costly to acquire.
    C. it will never pay to make a mistake.
    D. those who make mistakes will eventually go out of business.

3. The primary benefit for which real estate brokers are able to charge their commissions is
    A. legal advice.
    B. professional appraisal of property value that helps both buyers and sellers.
    C. improved information about available opportunities.
    D. assistance in arranging financing.

4. It usually pays a family selling its house to
    A. find that one buyer who would submit the very highest bid in a competitive auction in which all potential homebuyers participate.
    B. sell to someone other than that particular buyer who would be willing to pay the highest price anyone would offer.
    C. sell at a price midway between what the seller asks and what the buyer offers.
    D. sell as quickly as possible after the house has been put on the market.

5. Intermediaries promote efficiency and thereby increase people's wealth
    A. by providing additional jobs.
    B. by acting as low-cost producers of valuable information.
    C. only because people are too lazy and ignorant to decide what they really want and then find it.
    D. to the extent that they are regulated by law.

6. Employment agencies benefit

    A. only employees.
    B. only employers.
    C. employees and employers.
    D. only the owners of employment agencies.

7. A man who goes to the mall to buy some new clothes

    A. is avoiding the use of intermediaries.
    B. often finds out what he wants by studying what the clothing stores have to offer on their counters and racks.
    C. must know in advance exactly what he wants to avoid being taken advantage of by sellers.
    D. would do better if he patronized a wholesaler rather than a retailer.

8. University bookstores can often buy used textbooks from students and then sell them at a higher price to other students on the same campus

    A. only because students are willing to be exploited.
    B. and thereby earn a profit at the expense of students.
    C. because it would often cost more than the bookstore's margin for sellers and buyers to find and deal with each other directly.
    D. because used textbooks are just as valuable as new textbooks.

9. The term "markets" as used in economic theory refers to

    A. all social transactions except those involving government.
    B. places where goods of a particular kind are regularly bought and sold.
    C. a process of bids and offers between buyers and sellers.
    D. fraudulent selling.

10. The difference between a well-organized and a less well-organized market is that in well-organized markets we are more likely to see

    A. a single price for goods of fairly uniform type and quality.
    B. sellers taking advantage of buyers.
    C. fees charged for admission to the market.
    D. fraudulent selling.

11. In a mostly *un*organized market, transactions usually cannot be completed

    A. without extensive fraud.
    B. to the advantage of both parties in an exchange.
    C. without negotiations between buyers and sellers.
    D. without government intervention.

12. When the terms at which people can trade are widely and precisely known,

    A. all sales occur at identical money prices.
    B. people have more opportunities and therefore greater wealth.
    C. the cost of making exchanges will be higher because competition will be greater.
    D. no one can gain from exchange.

13. Someone who sells short

    A. is selling goods for future delivery without currently possessing them.
    B. expects the price of the good being sold short to rise before delivery has to be made.
    C. sits down rather than standing up while making a sale.
    D. doesn't have enough cash to carry inventory.
    E. "shorts" the customer by not providing everything the customer paid for.

14. Which of these sellers is selling short?

    A. A university that makes you pay the entire tuition by the first day of the term.
    B. A magazine that persuades you to buy a one-year subscription.
    C. A symphony orchestra that sells you a season ticket.
    D. All of the above are selling short.
    E. None of the above is selling short

15. The word "futures", as used in commodity markets, refers to

    A. goods whose production has not yet occurred.
    B. goods that have been ordered but not yet delivered.
    C. contracts to deliver (or accept delivery of) goods in the future at prices agreed upon now.
    D. goods whose commercial value has yet to be demonstrated.

16. Speculators who anticipate a future price higher than the current price will tend to act in ways that

    A. raise the current price and lower the future price.
    B. raise both the current price and the future price.
    C. lower the current price and raise the future price.
    D. lower both the current price and the future price.

17. Speculators who are correct in their reading of the future take actions whose effects are to

    A. reduce uncertainty for others.
    B. increase fluctuations in prices.
    C. cause shortages.
    D. cause surpluses.
    E. increase scarcity.

18. Lower current prices caused by the transactions of speculators

    A. harm producers of the good in which the speculators have traded.
    B. encourage users of the product in which the speculators have traded to defer some of their purchases until a later date.
    C. have both of the effects above.
    D. have neither of the effects above.

19. Speculators who act on the basis of erroneous forecasts harm

    A. themselves and society.
    B. themselves but not society.
    C. society but not themselves.
    D. no one.

20. Full disclosure by sellers and buyers in all transactions is

    A. an ambiguous concept.
    B. both desirable and currently required by law.
    C. desirable but not required by law.
    D. efficient.
    E. possible if sellers and buyers are honest.

21. A legal requirement that people reveal everything they know prior to any transaction would

    A. destroy much of the incentive to acquire valuable information.
    B. prevent fraudulent trading.
    C. put all traders on an equal footing.
    D. result in more wealth-enhancing trades.

22. Fiduciary obligations are

    A. debts incurred through speculation.
    B. moral and legal duties taken on by contract or agreement.
    C. obligations to tell the truth under all circumstances.
    D. promises that cannot be legally enforced.

23. The text recommends that illegal insider trading be defined to include trading

    A. on the basis of information not available to everyone.
    B. that benefits one party more than the other.
    C. that confers no net benefits on society.
    D. that violates fiduciary obligations.

24. The easiest way to assign liability for unanticipated damages in a fair and efficient way is to assign it

    A. by advance agreement between the parties entering a transaction.
    B. to the party that caused the damages.
    C. to the party that suffered least from the damages.
    D. to the party with greater wealth.

25. The legal doctrine of *caveat emptor* means that sellers cannot be held responsible for

    A. anything they do.
    B. lying.
    C. product qualities that they have not specifically guaranteed.
    D. adhering to the law if they are ignorant of the law.
    E. *nolo contendere*.

26. Buyers gain when the law or the courts assign responsibility for assuring buyer satisfaction to

    A. sellers.
    B. buyers.
    C. the party to a transaction who can provide such assurance at the lowest cost.
    D. government.

27. If the law required automobile manufacturers to compensate fully anyone injured in an accident while driving or riding in one of their cars,

    A. automobile buyers would be better off.
    B. automobiles would become larger, heavier, and slower.
    C. accidents would no longer occur.
    D. automobiles would sell at lower prices.

28. If sellers are required to compensate buyers for any deficiencies in a product of which buyers were ignorant when they purchased the product, sellers will

    A. stop advertising.
    B. tend to tell buyers many things the buyers already know or don't want to know.
    C. inform buyers fully about all qualities of the product.
    D. be worse off.

29. If economics professors could be sued for negligent practice by students to whom they gave credit in introductory economics courses despite their failure to learn, we could be most confident that

    A. teaching would improve.
    B. exams would become more difficult.
    C. grades would rise.
    D. economics professors would be sued regularly.

30. Evidence on whether people want the risk of death or injury to themselves reduced regardless of the cost is provided by the way people
    A. complain about unsafe products.
    B. vote on such issues as nuclear safety.
    C. behave when driving cars.
    D. purchase life insurance.

31. How does advertising affect the expected marginal benefits of additional search?
    A. Because advertising provides more information to customers more quickly, customers find that after comparatively little search, the expected benefits of additional search decline quickly.
    B. It rotates the expected marginal benefits of search curve counter clockwise.
    C. Advertising lowers the expected marginal benefits of search because it isn't always truthful.
    D. It has no effect on the expected marginal benefits of search. It raises the expected marginal costs of additional search.
    E. It has no effect on the expected marginal benefits of search. It lowers the expected marginal costs of additional search.

32. By providing centralized, easily accessible information about job opportunities, how does the federal department, Human Resources Development Canada affect the expected benefits of additional search for jobs by people who are unemployed?
    A. Because the department provides more information to job seekers more quickly, job seekers find that after comparatively little search, the expected benefits of additional search decline quickly.
    B. It rotates the expected marginal benefits of search curve counter clockwise.
    C. It lowers the expected marginal benefits of search because government bureaucrats are not always truthful.
    D. It has no effect on the expected marginal benefits of search. It raises the expected marginal costs of additional search.
    E. It has no effect on the expected marginal benefits of search. It lowers the expected marginal costs of additional search

33. What happens to the profits of a firm if the price of one of their inputs unexpectedly rises and they *have not hedged* against this possibility by buying contracts for this input in the futures market?
    A. Their profits increase.
    B. Their profits remain unchanged from what they would have been if the price of the input had remained constant.
    C. Their profits decline.
    D. There is not enough information provided to answer this question.

34. What happens to the profits of a firm if the price of one of their inputs unexpectedly rises and they *have hedged* against this possibility by buying contracts for this input in the futures market?
    A. Their profits increase.
    B. Their profits remain unchanged from what they would have been if the price of the input had remained constant.
    C. Their profits decline.
    D. There is not enough information provided to answer this question.

D. Answers to the Review Questions in Chapter 10

1. A	2. B	3. C	4. B	5. B	6. C	7. B
8. C	9. C	10. A	11. C	12. B	13. A	14. D
15. C	16. A	17. A	18. D	19. A	20. A	21. A
22. B	23. D	24. A	25. C	26. C	27. B	28. B
29. B	30. C	31. A	32. A	33. C	34. B	

E. Speculators and the Movement of Goods through Time

Assume that the demand and supply curves for soybeans in Canada are as shown in Figure 10.1. A price of $6 per bushel will be consistent with the intentions of both demanders and suppliers and six million bushels of soybeans will be grown and exchanged. At any higher price, growers will want to supply (1) (more / less) than demanders will want to purchase, and so the price will (2) (rise / fall). At any price lower than $6, growers will want to supply (3) (more / less) than demanders will want to purchase and the price will (4) (rise / fall).

Now assume that speculators conclude that a drought is going to reduce next year's crop to four million bushels. Growers will still want to supply six million bushels in expectation of a price of $6; but the speculators are predicting that drought will prevent them from fulfilling their intention. If this drought effect occurred without warning, the price of soybeans would be $6 this year but would rise to

(5)$ _10_ after next year's harvest. Speculation, however, will narrow this difference.

Speculators will begin (6) (buying / selling) soybean futures, which are contracts to deliver and accept soybeans next year at a price agreed upon today. This means the speculators will be able to purchase soybeans for delivery next year, when they expect the price to be $10, at the currently anticipated price of $6. The ability to purchase for $6 a good expected to be worth $10 is a "good deal," and the price of a "good deal" rises through competitive bidding until it is no longer a good deal. This means that the price of soybean futures, which is the price at which delivery next year is promised, will rise until it approaches

(7) _the price expected_ to prevail next year

Figure 10.1
Soybeans in Canada

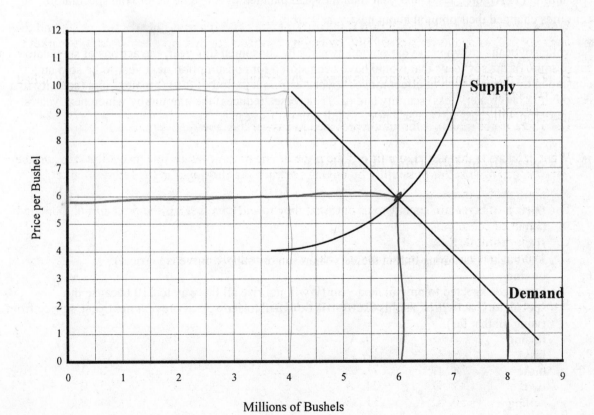

Millions of Bushels

People who handle actual soybeans (growers, processors, exporters, and elevator operators) use the price of soybean futures (the contracts to deliver soybeans) as the best available prediction of the future price of soybeans. A rising price for futures tells them that knowledgeable people think soybeans will have a higher price next year than it has this year. This information encourages people to withhold soybeans from sale this year in order to have more available for sale next year when they expect to receive more from selling them. This decision has the effect of (8) (raising / lowering) the current price, which in turn induces users to consume (9) (more / less) in the current period, thereby making (10) (more / less) available for consumption next year when soybeans are expected to be scarcer. This increased availability will make next year's price lower than it otherwise would have been.

In this way the actions of speculators cause goods to be transported forward in time from a period of less scarcity to a period of greater scarcity. These actions also cause price fluctuations to be less than they would otherwise be. Can the actions of speculators cause goods to be transported backward in time when goods are expected to be less scarce in the future than they are now?

Assume speculators conclude that a bumper harvest is going to increase next year's crop of soybeans to eight million bushels. If this occurred without warning, the price of soybeans would be $6 this year but

would fall to (11) _2_ dollar(s) next year. Speculators will begin (12) (buying / selling) soybean futures, which will cause the price of soybean futures to (13) (rise / fall). This will indicate to holders of actual soybeans that next year's price will be (14) (higher / lower) than this year's price. People storing soybeans for sale later will consequently decide to store (15) (more / less) for sale later and sell (16) (more/less) soybeans now. This action will (17) (raise / lower) the current price of soybeans, which in turn will induce users to consume (18) (more / less) in the current period and to make plans for consuming (19) (more / less) next year than they had planned to consume before the speculators' activities changed their opinion about next year's crop.

So while soybeans grown next year obviously can't be consumed this year, the actions of speculators can cause some of the soybeans that would have been stored for consumption next year to be sold and consumed this year, which in effect moves soybeans from a period of (20) (greater / less) scarcity to a period of (21) (greater / less) scarcity and (22) (increases/reduces) the amount by which next year's bumper crop will cause next year's price to fall below this year's.

F. Answers to the Questions in Section E

1. more
2. fall
3. less
4. rise
5. $10/bushel (assuming that in the very short run the supply curve is vertical).
6. buying
7. the price expected to prevail next year (it will not rise all the way to $10 because the speculators' activities, as this exercise is designed to show, will prevent next year's price from rising all that far).
8. raising
9. less
10. more
11. two
12. selling
13. fall

14.   lower
15.   less
16.   more
17.   lower
18.   more
19.   less
20.   less
21.   greater
22.   reduces

G. Questions to Think about

1.   Should people be allowed to profit from "inside" information? How would you distinguish inside information from legitimate information?

2.   What do you make of the fact that Canadian laws are far more severe on people who disseminate misleading information about mouthwashes than they are concerning people who publish blatantly false information during a political campaign?

H. Answers to Questions in Section G

1.   A member of the highway commission who buys land in the path of a new super highway before the public learns about the route the highway will take profits from inside information. This type of transaction is almost always illegal. But what about a map printer who infers the location of the new highway from some printing work the commission had him do? What about someone who just pays close attention to everything and figures out on her own where and when the highway is going to be constructed? The line between a fair advantage and an unfair advantage is often extremely hard to discern and defend. Remember that we would all be losers if no one at all ever took advantage of information not generally available.

2.   Does it imply that we think less harm is done by deceiving a voter than a gargler? Or does it imply that we think it's harder to pin down falsehood in political statements than in commercial claims? There are other possibilities. Those who make the laws engage in political campaigning but rarely sell mouthwash. Does that explain the difference?

Chapter 11 _____

Price Searching

A. Multiple-Choice Questions on the Principal Ideas of Chapter 11

1. A seller maximizes net revenue by selling

    A. as many units as possible.
    B. all units and only those units for which people are willing to pay a price that exceeds the cost of producing them.
    C. all units and only those units whose marginal revenue equals their marginal cost.
    D. all units and only those units from whose sale the marginal revenue is greater than the marginal cost.

2. The popular cost-plus-markup theory of prices, which assumes that business firms set prices by adding a standard percentage markup to externally determined costs, is inadequate

    A. because it fails to explain variations in percentage markups within and among firms.
    B. because it falsely implies that firms can and will consistently raise their prices by the same percentage that their costs rise.
    C. because it implicitly assumes firms do not try to set prices that maximize net revenue.
    D. for all of the reasons above.

3. Marginal revenue is

    A. revenue earned by increasing the margin between average unit cost and price.
    B. revenue on which a seller is not dependent for survival.
    C. the additional revenue obtained as the result of a decision.
    D. revenue earned in the stock market by investing borrowed funds.

4. Marginal revenue will be equal to price for a seller who is

    A. a price taker.
    B. a price searcher.
    C. a price searcher able to confine price reductions to those units that would not be sold except at lower prices.
    D. either a price taker or a price searcher able to sell each unit at the price buyers are willing to pay rather than do without the unit.

5. A. V. Rice owns four lithographs by the famed artist Chartreuse Boudoir that he wants to sell in order to obtain cash. He could sell one of the lithographs for $ 10 000, two of them if he lowered his price to $8000, three by setting the price at $6000, and all four only if he reduced the price to $4500. In order to decide how many to sell, he ought to know the expected marginal revenue from selling one, two, three, or four of the lithographs. The marginal revenue would be (successively)

    A. $10 000, $8000, $6000, and $4500.
    B. $10 000, $16 000, $18 000, and $18 000.
    C. $10 000, $6000, $2000, and $0.
    D. $10 000, $18 000, $24 000, and $28 500.

6. A. V. Rice enjoys owning the lithographs of Chartreuse Boudoir and values each one at $5000 for his own collection. If he must charge a single, uniform price, how many should he sell?

    A. one
    B. two
    C. three
    D. four
    E. not enough information is provided to answer this question.

7. If A. V. Rice could get in touch with the prospective buyers who contribute to the demand curve and charge each one the maximum that buyer is willing to pay for a Boudoir lithograph, he would want to sell

    A. one.
    B. two.
    C. three.
    D. four.
    E. not enough information is provided to answer this question.

8. If A. V. Rice bought these four lithographs from different dealers over the course of several years at prices of $4000, $6000, $9000, and $3000, he would be selling below cost any lithograph offered at a price less than (hint: think about what is meant by "cost")

    A. $9000 for the first, $6000 for the second, $4000 for the third, and $3000 for the fourth.
    B. $3000 for the first, $5000 for the second, $7000 for the third, and $9000 for the fourth.
    C. $5500.
    D. $5000.
    E. $3000.

B. Answers to, and Explanations of, Multiple-Choice Questions on the Principal Ideas of Chapter 11

1. **D**. The rule that specifies equality between marginal cost and marginal revenue as the condition for maximum net revenue actually means that selling should continue so long as marginal revenue is greater than marginal cost. In other words, keep selling *up to* the point at which marginal revenue equals marginal cost.

2. **D**. The best antidote for someone susceptible to the cost-plus-markup theory is to pay close attention to the enormous variety of percentage markups that sellers use and to note that the size of the markup changes as circumstances vary.

3. **C**. *Marginal* in this context is another word for *additional* or *incremental*. The marginal revenue from a decision or course of action is the difference between the revenue that comes to the decision maker if the action is taken and the revenue that comes in if it is not taken.

4. **D**. This answer combines the options A and C. Marginal revenue is always equal to price for price takers because they can sell additional units without lowering their price. The addition to revenue from selling another unit will therefore be the price of that unit. But price searchers must, by definition, lower their price to make additional sales. If they must also offer that reduced price to the buyers who are willing to pay more, the expected gain from selling another unit must be offset by the loss from selling previous units at a lower price. Option C points out that a price searcher's marginal revenue curve and demand curve would be identical if the price searcher could lower the price on only those units that wouldn't be sold without the price reduction. Option D restates this same condition in a different way.

5. **C**. Option A gives the demand schedule, option B the total revenue schedule, and option C the differences between total revenue as Mr. Rice moves from no sales to selling four lithographs.

Option D shows the total revenue he would obtain if he could sell each lithograph at the maximum price successive buyers are willing to pay.

6.   **B.** Selling the second lithograph adds $6000 to his revenue; selling the third adds $2000. But since it costs Mr. Rice $5000 worth of satisfaction to give up a lithograph, the third is not a profitable one to sell. Marginal revenue exceeds marginal cost for two lithographs, and so two should be sold.

7.   **C.** Under these circumstances, marginal revenue would be the same as price. And so for all but the fourth lithograph, marginal revenue would exceed marginal cost.

8.   **D.** The cost of an action is the value of the opportunity forgone through taking that action. What Rice originally paid is irrelevant. The opportunity cost is the cost of giving up ownership, which question 6 says is $5000.

C. A Step-by-Step Review of Chapter 11

1.   The logical principle for maximization can be stated as follows:
   A.   Do it if it feels good.
   B.   Do it if the benefit from doing it is greater than the cost of doing it.
   C.   Do it unless it's illegal, immoral, or fattening.
   D.   Do it whenever the marginal benefit equals the marginal cost.

2.   When the cost of producing a good increases, the firm producing it
   A.   can raise its price by the amount of the cost increase.
   B.   can raise its price by the same percentage as the cost increase.
   C.   may not be able to raise its price at all.
   D.   will not be able to increase its net revenue by raising its price.

3.   The percentage markups that sellers use
   A.   are between 10 and 15 percent.
   B.   are the same on all products of a single firm.
   C.   differ between products but are the same on average for all firms.
   D.   tend to be rules of thumb based on their estimates or guesses about marginal cost and marginal revenue for particular goods.

4.   Sellers who lower their prices and consequently sell a larger quantity earn more
   A.   gross (or total) revenue as a result.
   B.   net revenue (revenue minus cost) as a result.
   C.   gross revenue only if the demand is elastic and may even then earn less net revenue.
   D.   net and gross revenue if the demand is inelastic.

5.   If total revenue from the sale of a good declines when the seller lowers its price, the demand for that good TR↓ P↓
   A.   is inelastic, which means that marginal revenue is negative.
   B.   must not obey the law of demand.
   C.   is elastic, which means that marginal revenue is zero.
   D.   must have changed when the price was lowered.

6.   If additional units of a firm's output can be sold only by lowering the price to all buyers, we know that
   A.   the demand for that good is elastic.
   B.   the demand for that good is inelastic.
   C.   the marginal revenue curve for that good lies below the demand curve.
   D.   the marginal revenue is negative.

7. Net revenue is maximized by selling every unit for which marginal revenue

    A. exceeds marginal cost.
    B. is equal to marginal cost.
    C. is less than marginal cost.
    D. is greater than zero.

8. The more successful a seller is in inducing buyers to pay the maximum price they would be willing to pay rather than do without the good, the

    A. closer will the seller's marginal revenue curve come to the demand curve.
    B. greater will be the demand for the good.
    C. more inelastic will be the demand for the good.
    D. more elastic will be the demand for the good.

9. Many universities provide financial aid only to students who persuade the university of their financial "need" primarily in order to

    A. diversify their student body.
    B. improve the welfare of the society.
    C. increase their net income through price discrimination.
    D. improve their athletic teams.

10. Price discrimination in the form of financial aid

    A. keeps low-income students from being able to attend university.
    B. keeps down the number of students who are able to attend university.
    C. increases the number of students who are able to attend university.
    D. increases the enrolment at universities that don't price discriminate.

11. Theatre owners often set lower ticket prices for students than for adults primarily because

    A. the demand for theatre entertainment is more elastic in the case of students.
    B. students eat more popcorn.
    C. they want to get students hooked on the movie-going habit.
    D. students otherwise couldn't afford movies.

12. Theatre owners sometimes consider suspending their discounts while showing an extremely popular movie because

    A. it's bad for people to get something good at too low a price.
    B. the demand for tickets increases when popular movies are running, which raises the cost of admitting people when seating capacity is limited.
    C. popular movies usually contain sex and violence, which theatre owners don't wish to subsidize through discounts.
    D. people judge quality by price.

13. An 11-year-old child who gets into a sold-out showing by purchasing a $1.00 ticket when the regular price is $7.50 adds $1.00 to the theatre owner's

    A. net revenue.
    B. total revenue and costs the owner $7.50.
    C. net costs.
    D. total costs.

14. An 11-year-old child who gets to watch a movie in an almost empty theatre by paying $1.00 when the regular price is $7.50 adds $1.00 to the theatre owner's

    A. net revenue.
    B. total revenue and costs the owner $7.50.
    C. net costs.
    D. total costs.

15. In order to be successful in increasing net revenue by charging buyers different prices, a seller must
   A. have no information about demand.
   B. obtain a license from the government.
   C. be utterly without a sense of social responsibility.
   D. be able to prevent buyers from exchanging among themselves.

16. If a restaurant offers its dinners at $13 each, but on Monday through Thursday offers a second dinner for only $1, the restaurant management
   A. must have surplus food left over from the weekend.
   B. thinks people are more likely to eat two dinners on weekday nights than on weekends.
   C. hopes to attract couples on uncrowded weeknights when it can provide dinners at a cost below $7 each.
   D. must pay its employees only from Monday through Thursday.

17. You go into the local hardware store to buy a hammer and find that the store is running a special on quality hammers: $14 each, two for $20. You are likely to buy two rather than one if a second hammer is worth more to you than
   A. $14
   B. $10
   C. $6
   D. a screwdriver

18. The hardware store doesn't simply sell hammers at $10 each because
   A. that would be less than marginal cost.
   B. it wants to get $14 from those customers who value a second hammer at less than $6.
   C. "two for $20" will sell more hammers than "$10 each."
   D. it has too little information about the demand for hammers.

19. A price searcher will determine the best price or set of prices to charge by
   A. adding a constant percentage markup to marginal cost.
   B. examining marginal revenue and marginal cost curves.
   C. estimating the probable consequences of alternative policies.
   D. adding overhead costs to marginal costs.

20. A price searcher who determines selling prices by adding some standard percentage to marginal cost
   A. cannot be maximizing net revenue.
   B. maximizes net revenue when the markup is 100 percent or more.
   C. necessarily maximizes net revenue.
   D. may be maximizing net revenue subject to the limited information available.

D. Answers to the Review Questions in Chapter 11

1. B	5. A	9. C	13. B	17. C
2. C	6. C	10. C	14. A	18. B
3. D	7. A	11. A	15. D	19. C
4. C	8. A	12. B	16. C	20. D

E. Marginal Revenue And Its Friends: Graphic Exercises

1. Figure 11.4 in the textbook describes a simple technique that can be used to obtain quickly the marginal-revenue curve corresponding to any straight-line demand curve. You can try your hand on the figure on the next page, following the directions provided.

Figure 11.1
Deriving a Marginal Revenue Curve

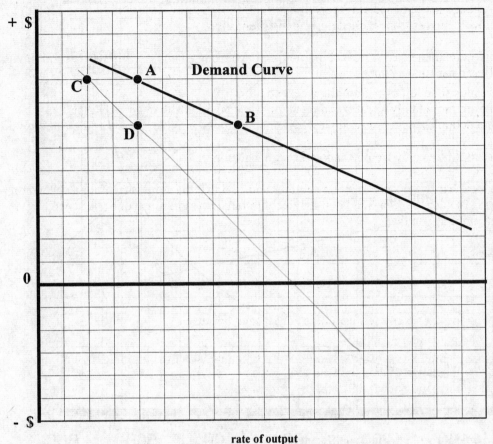

Select any two points on the demand curve, such as points A and B.

Draw perpendicular lines across to the price axis from these points. Then bisect the perpendicular lines to find points C and D.

Connect points C and D with a straight line that lies directly *under* (rather than to the left of) the demand curve.

This line is the marginal revenue curve corresponding to the demand curve. Note that marginal revenue is related to *quantity* and only indirectly to price. The curve shows the addition to revenue that comes from selling an additional quantity. The demand curve shows the price at which that additional quantity can be sold.

Figure 11.2

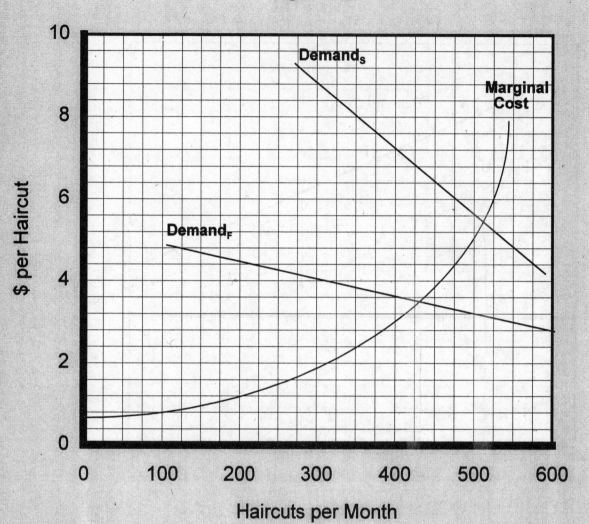

2. Figaro is the only barber in Seville, and his twin brother Samuel is the only barber in Seaford. The opportunity cost to each of supplying haircuts happens to be the same. The marginal-cost curve on the graph in Figure 11.2 shows the cost to each in dollar equivalents of providing an additional haircut at rates up to about 500 per month.

    The demand for haircuts differs between Seville and Seaford. Samuel faces the demand curve labeled S; Figaro the demand curve labeled F.

    a. Assuming that Figaro and Samuel both want to maximize the net benefit accruing to them from cutting hair, how many haircuts should each one provide per month?

    b. What price should each one set?

    c. Many people in Seaford cut their own hair rather than pay Samuel's price. The graph shows that a number of them would be willing to pay Samuel in excess of $2 more than his cost to give them a haircut. Why then don't Samuel and these people manage to effect a satisfactory exchange?

    d. Can you think of a pricing scheme that would benefit both Samuel and these self- barbering citizens of Seaford?

3. Return to question E.5 in Chapter 8 of this study guide and calculate the price Tom Sawyer would want to charge.

F. Answers to Questions in Section E

1. Practice reading the marginal revenue curve below. At quantity q, marginal revenue is D. The quantity q can be sold, according to the demand curve, when the price is at A.

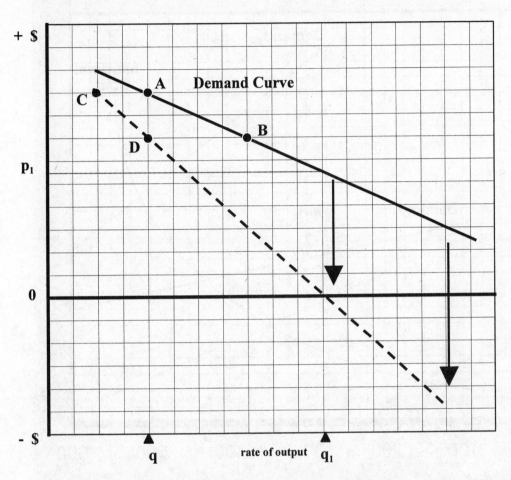

At quantity q_1 marginal revenue is zero. If you put this all together with what you learned in Chapter 3 about price elasticity of demand, you will realize that demand is unit elastic at price p_1, elastic above p_1, and inelastic below p_1.

2. The marginal revenue curves corresponding to the two demand curves are drawn in the above graph. They both intersect the marginal cost curve at 350 haircuts per month. Consult the graph while reflecting on the answers to questions a through d.

   a. Each barber should provide 350 haircuts because up to that amount, the marginal revenue for each of them exceeds the marginal cost. Beyond a rate of 350 haircuts per month, marginal cost is greater than marginal revenue for each barber.

   b. Figaro can sell 350 haircuts per month by charging $3.80. Samuel can sell 350 haircuts by charging $8.00.

   c. The difference between consumer demand and Samuel's marginal cost shows the potential gain that could be realized through further production and exchange. But Samuel would have to lower his price to realize the gain on any haircuts beyond 350, and the marginal revenue curve shows that lowering the price to all his customers would not be advantageous to him. Could Samuel reduce his price only for those who won't patronize him unless he does? Perhaps. But effective price discrimination itself entails costs. In this case Samuel would have to acquire information on the varying amounts people will pay for haircuts and charge different prices without antagonizing his customers too much. The cost of doing all this could easily exceed the prospective benefit from doing it.

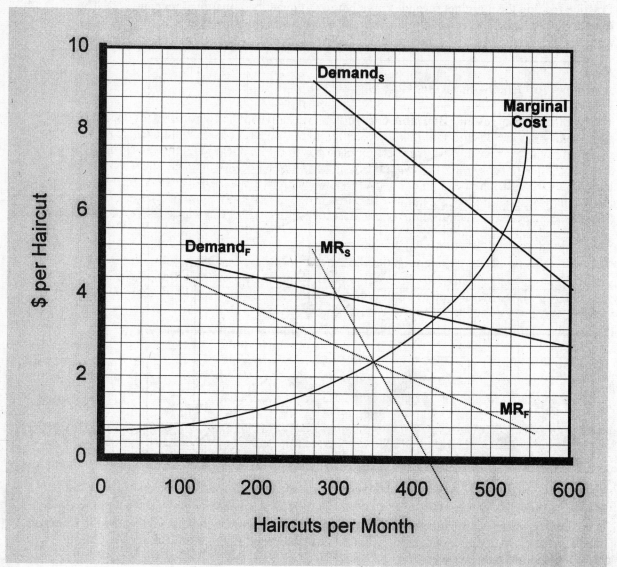

d.   Over the years, Samuel might come to learn who some of the people are who would come to him for haircuts at lower prices. And he might start offering them discounts based ostensibly on some personal characteristic of which he is aware: fellow church member, military veteran, senior citizen, student, neighbour, etc.

3.   The marginal revenue Tom expects from raking is $7 for the first yard, $5 for the second, $3 for the third, and $1 for the fourth. Given his marginal opportunity cost, Tom will want to rake the first two yards and will be indifferent about doing the third. So he will either set his price at $6 and rake two or at $5 and rake three.

G. Questions to Think about

1.   When a large corporation (Chrysler Canada? Eaton's? Canadian Air? a large hog-farming operation?) is threatened with bankruptcy, should the government provide financial assistance in order to prevent a loss of output, jobs, and income? Many advocates of aid in such cases seem to

assume that bankruptcy would terminate all the activities of the firm. Why is this assumption almost surely wrong?

2. If price discrimination enables sellers to earn more net revenue and enables some buyers to purchase who otherwise would not do so, why don't *all* sellers use price discrimination more consistently?

H. Answers to Questions in Section G

1. The fact that the net revenue of a large corporation is negative in the aggregate does not mean that marginal cost is greater than marginal revenue for all of its operations. It could even be the case that marginal revenue exceeds marginal costs for each one of the its operations, and the financial losses are entirely due to sunk costs, outlays that are owed as a result of past actions. That might lead to bankruptcy, but it would be in no one's interest in such cases to shut down a single operation. The loss of output, jobs, and income that would ensue from the financial failure of a large corporation (like those suggested in the question) is greatly exaggerated by those in whose interest it is to secure government assistance.

2. Once you become aware of the rationale for price discrimination (and the conditions that must prevail before it can be practiced), you will probably begin to discover that it occurs more widely than you had realized. But the cost of devising, administering, and enforcing a successful system of price discrimination is always positive and often prohibitive.

Chapter 12

Interdependence, Game Theory, and Markets

A. Multiple-Choice Questions on the Principal Ideas of Chapter 12

1. When business persons make decisions about the price to charge, if they wish maximize their net revenues, they should set a price that
   A. at least covers their costs.
   B. is determined by their expectations of future events.
   C. is based on their astrological sign.
   D. reflects what their customers tell them is appropriate.

2. Pricing policy in business firms can never yield certain results because
   A. it is based on expectations about how others in the economy will behave.
   B. it depends on businesses' estimates of probabilities about future events.
   C. businesses must make decisions based on incomplete information.
   D. A, B, and C above.
   E. None of the above.

3. What is the nature of the basic prisoners' dilemma game?
   A. The prisoners cannot decide whether to riot.
   B. The prisoners cannot decide whether to confess.
   C. The prisoners cannot decide whether to go on a hunger strike.
   D. The prisoners cannot decide what meals to order for dinner.

4. In the payoff matrix of the prisoners' dilemma game, what numbers are shown in the cells of the matrix?
   A. the expected net returns to each player.
   B. the expected net returns to the winning player.
   C. the expected net returns to the losing player.
   D. the sum of the expected net returns to the players.
   E. the difference between the expected net returns to the two players.

5. What determines which strategy players will choose in the prisoners' dilemma?
   I.   the expected length of the dilemma lag
   II. the expected length of the detection lag
   III. the expected length of the retaliation lag
   IV. the expected size of the retaliation

   A. I, II, and III
   B. I, III, and IV
   C. I, II, and IV
   D. II, III, and IV
   E. I, II, III, and IV

6. Why do businesses that offer you a special, low price, sometimes ask you not to tell their rivals about their low price?
   A. They are trying to practice price discrimination.
   B. They are trying to lengthen the detection lag.
   C. They are trying to avoid playing the prisoners' dilemma game.
   D. They don't understand the importance of information transmission.

7. Why do gasoline stations start price wars?
   A. They don't expect to start a price war when they lower their price; they lower their price so they can steal customers from their rivals.
   B. The government requires them to cut their prices every once in awhile to share their profits with their customers.
   C. When the price of crude oil falls, the companies pass along the savings to their customers.
   D. They realize that their rivals will match their price cuts, but they expect the benefits of the strategy to outweigh the costs.

B. Answers to, and Explanations of, the Multiple-Choice Questions on the Principal Ideas of Chapter 12

1. **B.** Customers cannot be relied on to give advice to firms that will help the firms maximize net revenues. Rather, firms must forecast their costs and the demand for their output. These forecasts are fraught with possible errors. Also, in the short run, it may be the case that the firm maximizes its net revenues even if it doesn't cover all its historical costs. Decisions must be forward-looking.

2. **D.** All decisions are forward-looking in the sense that they are based on *expected* net benefits. But people's expectations are not always correct because we cannot know perfectly what will happen in the future. Acquiring information about the future is costly; sometimes we make mistakes; and sometimes we don't analyze the information correctly. Consequently, all economic decisions are based on probabilities and contain some random elements.

3. **B.** While the prisoners' dilemma game can be, and has been, applied to many different situations, its original representation is of two prisoners who are faced with the problem of deciding whether to confess to a serious crime.

4. **A.** The number in the upper right portion of each cell of the payoff matrix is the expected net payoff to the person whose strategies are listed at the top of the payoff matrix. The number in the lower left portion of each cell is the expected net payoff to the person whose strategies are listed along the left side of the payoff matrix.

5. **D.** There are many determinants of players' strategies in the prisoners' dilemma game. We summarize the possible determinants by grouping them into three categories: the expected length of the detection lag, the expected length of the retaliation lag, and the expected size of the retaliation if and when it ever materializes.

6. **B.** They may not ask you to tell other *customers* about special low price when they are trying to practice price discrimination. But when they ask you not to tell their rivals about their special low price, it is most often because they are trying to avoid setting off a price war. If you expect to do considerable repeat business with this firm, you might honour their request: if you don't honour it — i.e. if you blab about the low price to rivals — and the original firm finds out about it, you may not be offered the special low price again in the future.

7. **D.** Oil companies and gas station operators know that the detection lag is short, as is the retaliation lag — other gas stations can meet or beat their low prices in a matter of minutes. So they really don't expect to steal market share from their rivals by cutting prices. More often, gasoline price wars occur

because oil companies expect the lower prices to induce customers to buy more gasoline in general, thereby temporarily solving costly storage problems for the firms.

C. A Step-by-Step Review of Chapter 12

1. Game theory gained added prestige in economics with the 1994 awarding of the Nobel Prize in Economics to
   A. Paul Samuelson.
   B. Milton Friedman.
   C. John Harsanyi, John Nash, and Renhard Selton.
   D. Paul Heyne and John Palmer.
   E. Larry, Moe, and Curly.

2. The reason that game theory has become so important, not just in economics, is that
   A. it is the one remaining area of social science in which mathematical analysis can help to shed some light on the questions of human behaviour.
   B. people tend to make most decisions in a light-hearted fashion, as if they were just playing a game.
   C. people's decisions are usually interdependent.
   D. economists are usually willing to sell out their partners in crime.
   E. after all, life is just a game.

3. Why can't we say anything about the demand curve facing a firm unless we make an assumption about the interaction between that firm and others in the same industry?
   A. Firms try to hide their intentions from economic analysts.
   B. Any price and output combination chosen by one firm will have an impact on the decisions of other firms in the industry, and their expected reactions will in turn have feedback effects on the original firm.
   C. Firms that are interdependent behave as if they are price takers.
   D. Business decisions must be based on marginal cost and marginal revenue considerations.

4. In a standard prisoners' dilemma game, what are the possible strategies that the prisoners can play?
   A. cut prices or don't cut prices
   B. cheat on a tacit price-fixing agreement or don't cheat
   C. confess to a crime or don't confess
   D. launch a new advertising campaign or stick with the old one
   E. begin a new research and development program or stick with the old products

5. How many possible outcomes are there in the basic prisoners' dilemma game?
   A. one
   B. two
   C. three
   D. four
   E. an infinite number

6. What must each player estimate before making a choice of strategies in the prisoners' dilemma game?
   A. the length of time it will take before their rival finds out which strategy they have adopted
   B. the length of time it will take before their rival is able to respond to their own strategy
   C. the type of response their rival might adopt
   D. A, B, and C above
   E. none of the above

7. What will be the likely outcome of the prisoners' dilemma game if both prisoners expect the detection lag to be quite long?

   A. Neither will confess.
   B. One will confess and the other will not.
   C. Both will confess.
   D. Both will be more likely to confess.
   E. Nothing. The expected length of the detection lag has no effect on their decisions.

8. Even if one prisoner is not inclined to confess to the crime, that prisoner will be more likely to confess if

   A. there is a short detection lag.
   B. she believes the other prisoner is likely to confess.
   C. there is a short retaliation lag.
   D. she expects to lose her life if she confesses.
   E. None of the above.

9. When are people more likely to break the law? When the probability of being caught is

   A. low and the expected size of the punishment is also low.
   B. low, but the expected size of the punishment is high.
   C. high, but the expected size of the punishment is low.
   D. high and the expected size of the punishment is also high.

10. What does a straight-forward application of the prisoners' dilemma predict about pricing strategies?

    A. Rivals each have a strong incentive to cut prices because they expect the other firm to cut prices.
    B. Some rivals will cut prices; others won't.
    C. Both firms will raise prices.
    D. Because the detection and retaliation lags are very long, firms will be reluctant to cut prices.
    E. Because the detection and retaliation lags are short, firms will be reluctant to cut prices.

11. Why do we observe price competition in the real world when the basic prisoners' dilemma model implies that rivals would not likely engage in price competition?

    A. When there are many rivals in an industry, the expected temporary gain from cutting prices is large.
    B. Each firm anticipates that someone somewhere in a large industry will cut prices.
    C. No decision maker expects the other firms to retaliate by more than matching a price cut.
    D. In some industries, firms often offer secret discounts or "off-list" prices to some customers, hoping to keep the detection lag long.
    E. All of the above.

12. Suppose the member of a cartel or price-fixing group would like to cheat on its agreement with the other members of the cartel. What is it likely to do?

    A. Raise its price and reduce its output.
    B. Lower its price and reduce its output.
    C. Raise its price and increase its output.
    D. Lower its price and increase its output.
    E. None of the above.

13. Suppose that two different sporting goods suppliers are the only producers of hockey pucks. What will likely happen if they expect to bid against each other only once for a long-term contract to supply hockey pucks to the National Hockey League?
    A. They will cooperate in their pricing policies because the NHL will encourage them to do so.
    B. They will charge a high price because the NHL has a lot of money.
    C. They will expect the detection and retaliation lags to be short, and so they will cooperate and charge a high price.
    D. They will expect that the size of retaliation, if they cut prices, will be high, and so they will set a cooperative price.
    E. They will expect the retaliation lag to be very long, and so they will cut the price.

14. Suppose these same two firms of Question 13 above expect, instead, to bid against each other annually to supply hockey pucks to many different hockey leagues, discount stores, and sporting goods retail chains?

    A. They will cooperate in their pricing policies because the NHL and the other customers will encourage them to do so.
    B. They will charge a high price because the NHL and the other firms have a lot of money.
    C. They will expect the detection and retaliation lags to be short, and so they will cooperate and charge a high price.
    D. They will expect that the size of retaliation, if they cut prices, will be high, and so they will set a cooperative price.
    E. They will expect the retaliation lag to be very long, and so they will cut the price.

15. Many large firms advertise "We will match any price by our competitors, or we'll give the product to you free!" Why would they advertise such a policy?
    A. They are too lazy and too cheap to determine appropriate prices on their own.
    B. They are letting their rivals know that price competition will not pay off for them.
    C. They are trying to break down the pricing discipline within the industry.
    D. They are trying to coordinate price reductions in the industry.
    E. They like giving away "free" stuff.

16. Why do firms in some industries frequently engage in *non-price competition* even when they don't change their prices very often?
    A. The detection lag is shorter for non-price competition than it is for price competition.
    B. The retaliation lag is shorter for non-price competition than it is for price competition.
    C. The expected size of the retaliation is smaller for non-price competition than it is for price competition.
    D. All of the above.
    E. None of the above.

D. Answers to the Review Questions in Chapter 12

1. C	5. D	9. A	13. E
2. C	6. D	10. E	14. C
3. B	7. D	11. E	15. B
4. C	8. B	12. D	16. E

E. The Prisoners' Dilemma: A Numerical Example

Bill and Monica have recently been arrested. They are placed in separate rooms and are told they have the following options: if neither of you confesses to this crime for which you have been arrested, we will still be able to convict for a minor misdemeanour and you will have to pay a $500 fine. If, however, you confess, you will not be charged with any crime and you will have no criminal record, but the other person will have to spend a year in jail. And if you *both* confess, you will each have to serve a 30-day jail sentence. In the space below, identify the strategies and complete the payoff matrix for this game.

Figure 12.1 Payoff Matrix for Bill and Monica

		Bill's Choices	
		Strategy A: Confess	**Strategy B:** Don't Confess
Monica's Choices	**Strategy A:** Confess	30 Days in Jail / 30 Days in Jail	No Record (Punishment) / 1 year in Jail
	Strategy B: Don't Confess	1 year in Jail / No Record (Punishment)	$500 Fine / $500 Fine

A. If Bill and Monica are able to communicate the entire time and expect to maintain an ongoing relationship, which strategy/strategies will they be likely to adopt?

B. Suppose that Bill and Monica are unable to communicate with each other during the interrogations, and that Bill would like to continue their friendship after the ordeal is over. Suppose further that Monica would *not* like to continue the relationship, and Bill doesn't know this. Which strategy/strategies will they be likely to adopt?

C. Suppose that Bill and Monica are unable to communicate with each other during the interrogations, and that Bill would like to continue their friendship after the ordeal is over. Suppose further that Monica would not like to continue the relationship and that Bill is aware of her preferences. Which strategy/strategies will they be likely to adopt?

D. Suppose that Bill and Monica never expect to see each other again. Which strategy/strategies will they be likely to adopt?

Answers on the other Page →

F. Answers to Questions in Section E

Figure 12.2 Payoff Matrix for Bill and Monica

		Bill's Choices	
		Strategy A: Confess	***Strategy B:*** Don't Confess
Monica's Choices	***Strategy A:*** Confess	30 days in jail 30 days in jail	1 year in jail no punishment
	Strategy B: Don't Confess	no punishment 1 year in jail	$500 fine $500 fine

A. Since they can communicate and since they expect to maintain a relationship after the ordeal, the detection and retaliation lags are fairly short, and there is some potential for retaliation. Consequently, they are less likely to confess in this scenario than they would be in the others.

B. Bill will expect the same situation as in scenario A above, but knowing this, Monica will find it to her advantage to confess. They will end up in the upper right-hand cell of the above payoff matrix.

C. Here, even though Bill would like to continue the friendship, he anticipates that Monica will find it to her advantage to confess. Knowing that she will likely confess, he realizes that he will be better off doing only 30 days instead of a year in jail, and so he confesses too. They end up in the upper left-hand cell of the payoff matrix.

D. They will both be likely to confess and end up doing 30 days jail time each.

G. Applying the Prisoners' Dilemma to Business Decision-Making

The OK Tire Company and Alright Tires are the only two sellers of tires in the town of Zenith. The owner of OK and the owner of Alright would like to collude to keep prices high, but they know that explicit, overt collusion is illegal and would get them bad publicity as well. Over the years, however, they have evolved a tacit working arrangement that pretty much approximates what they would decide if they just sat down and talked about keeping prices high. Each owner knows that if s/he cut the price of the tires, the other would match the price cut, and their profits would fall from roughly 15% on invested capital to only about 10% on their invested capital. They both proudly advertise that they will match the other's prices, and this strategy has emphasized to each of them that the expected payoffs from price cutting are likely to be minimal and probably negative after a very short period of time. At the same time, each owner expects that cutting the price could increase their profits to 25% if the other firm didn't go along with the price cut; and if the other firm cut its price, it would earn 25% and their own firm would earn only 6%.

In Figure 12.3 on the next page, complete their strategies and fill in the correct payoffs in the payoff matrix.

Figure 12.3 The Payoff Matrix for OK Tires and Alright Tires

Strategies for OK Tires

		Strategy A: Cut Price	Strategy B: Don't Cut
Strategies for Alright Tires	**Strategy A:** Cut Price	10% / 10%	6% / 25%
	Strategy B: Don't Cut	25% / 6%	15% / 15%

Called a cell in the payoff matrix.

A. Using terms discussed in this chapter, why don't OK and Alright engage in price competition?

B. Would you expect each owner to offer some secret, unadvertised price cuts to his or her best friends, fellow church members, neighbours, etc.? Why or why not? Under what conditions?

C. Would you expect the beneficiaries of secret price cut offers to go to the other retailer and say, "The other dealer offered me a discount off their best price. What can you do for me?"

D. Even though OK and Alright seem to have reached some sort of agreement on pricing, they still compete in many ways. Why don't they reach agreements on these other forms of competition?

E. If OK and Alright can work out, over time, a tacit agreement on prices, why is it so difficult for a pricing agreement to evolve when there are more firms involved in the industry?

F. Using the data in the payoff matrix, explain why the two firms might compete vigorously in their attempts to get new brands of tires that they can offer to their customers.

H. Answers to Questions in Section G

Figure 12.4 The Payoff Matrix for OK Tires and Alright Tires

	Strategies for OK Tires	
	Strategy A: Cut Prices	**Strategy B:** Don't Cut Prices
Strategy A: Cut Prices	10% / 10%	6% / 25%
Strategy B: Don't Cut Prices	25% / 6%	15% / 15%

(Strategies for Alright Tires — row labels)

A. The detection and retaliation lags are very short; hence, the expected net benefits of cutting prices are probably negative.

B. Yes, for two reasons. (1) They might be attempting to engage in price discrimination. (2) alternatively, they might be hoping to practice some secret price cutting with customers who would not tell the other seller about the price cut. If they are successful, they can reduce prices for some customers without setting off a price war. Of course, after not too long, both owners will expect that the other owner is doing this as well. Also, not all beneficiaries of secret price cuts are tight-lipped. Some tell their friends who in turn expect to be able to negotiate lower prices from both dealers.

C. They might, but not if the owner has selected them with care. The owner will likely offer the secret price cuts primarily to those who expect to maintain an ongoing relationship with owner over time [called a "repeated play" in game theory]. Sometimes, the ongoing relationship need not be a buyer-seller relationship — it might be as members of the same service club or church. But the ongoing relationship means that the buyer is less likely to talk about the price cut if the seller asks him not to.

D. Competition and rivalry exist in other ways because the expected detection and retaliation lags are longer. To that extent, the expected net benefits to either firm from engaging in non-price competition are more likely to be positive.

E. The more firms there are in an industry, the greater the potential payoffs to each firm from cutting its price. Also with more firms it is sometimes more difficult for the other firms to know for sure who, if anyone, is secretly cutting prices.

F. If one dealer is able to secure an exclusive franchise to sell a very popular brand of tire, its profits might skyrocket, perhaps to 25%, while the rival's profits sag to only 6%.

I. Question to Think about

In 1945, when no other country had nuclear weapons, the United States dropped atomic bombs on Japan. Following that experience, increasing numbers of countries developed nuclear weapon capabilities and the world's stockpile of nuclear armaments increased dramatically. And yet none of these weapons has been used since then. Why not?

J. Discussion of the Question in Section I

When the United States dropped the atom bombs at the end of World War II, the detection lag was very short, but the expected net benefits of doing so were nevertheless very large. The expected length of the retaliation lag was very long because the Japanese airforce and navy had already been virtually decimated and the Japanese researchers were not known to be anywhere close to developing nuclear weapons. These same considerations led the U.S. to estimate that the expected size of the retaliation, if any, would be small.

Since then, however, countries have been reluctant to use nuclear weapons. They have set up elaborate radar and other sensing systems to anticipate a nuclear attack before it happens. These systems reduce the detection lag and permit the target country to launch retaliatory strikes before being destroyed, themselves. Consequently, the expected detection and retaliatory lags are short. Also, depending on the target country, the nuclear arms race ensured that if a country could retaliate, it would likely be able to do so with immense power. The strong likelihood that two countries would end up destroying each other (and most of the rest of the world along with them) has kept the major powers from initiating nuclear attacks on each other.

Chapter 13 _____

Competition and Government Policies

A. Multiple-Choice Questions on the Principal Ideas of Chapter 13

1. Sellers are able to eliminate the constraints that competition imposes upon them if they can
   - A. prevent substitutes for their goods from being offered at attractive prices.
   - B. lower their prices below the full cost of production.
   - C. become large enough to attain a monopoly position.
   - D. persuade buyers that their product is distinctly superior to the customary alternatives.

2. Competition gives sellers increased incentives to
   - A. lower the wages of employees.
   - B. reduce the quality of their products.
   - C. make their products appear more attractive to potential buyers.
   - D. make use of unethical selling practices.

3. Agreements among competing sellers _not_ to lower their prices aren't likely to be effective unless the sellers can
   - A. agree on a division of the market.
   - B. prevent new firms from entering the industry.
   - C. prevent other, already existing, firms from offering close substitutes at lower prices.
   - D. do all of the above.

4. The principal advantage that sellers find in using government to reduce competition is that
   - A. government has the unique power to impose additional costs on the actions of competing sellers.
   - B. it costs the sellers nothing to obtain assistance from government.
   - C. government can find ways to reduce competition that are fair to everyone.
   - D. government will reduce competition only when this is in the public interest.

5. The assertion that some firm is "selling below cost"
   - A. is most likely to be made as an accusation by a competing seller.
   - B. has no clear meaning until we are told what action it is whose cost is not being covered by the price.
   - C. usually acquires credibility only through some arbitrary allocation of sunk costs or joint costs.
   - D. All of the above are true.

6. Predatory price cutting is not likely to be a successful competitive tactic for sellers unless
   - A. the predator is able to raise prices substantially after destroying rival sellers.
   - B. the predator is able to prevent new rivals from appearing in response to its substantially higher prices.
   - C. the resources of the rivals that the predator drives out of business are destroyed or dispersed.
   - D. all of the above occur.

7. Legislation designed to prevent any firm from capturing an additional share of the market and thereby taking business away from other firms

    A. increases the range of alternatives available to consumers.
    B. keeps prices lower than they otherwise would be.
    C. assures the preservation of competition.
    D. does all of the above.
    E. does none of the above.

8. Firms selling in price-searchers' markets usually

    A. refrain from producing goods at a cost that is above the price that buyers are willing to pay.
    B. are free from the constraints that competition imposes.
    C. will never sell at the same prices as their competitors unless they are engaged in collusive pricing.
    D. sell fewer goods if they are allowed to charge different prices to different consumers.

B. Answers to, and Explanations of, Multiple-Choice Questions on the Principal Ideas of Chapter 13

1. **A**. Competition always consists of the offering by others of substitute goods and can therefore be eliminated only by preventing others from supplying attractive alternatives. Lowering prices is more likely to be a response to competitive pressure than a way of eliminating it. A firm that grows large does not thereby acquire a monopoly position or eliminate competition. Persuading buyers that its product is superior to alternatives is what every seller obviously must do in order to sell, and success in doing so should be regarded as a successful response to competition rather than an elimination of competition.

2. **C**. The question is always how sellers can best go about making their products appear more attractive. Reducing quality is certainly not an assured formula and neither is the use of unethical selling practices. Both these techniques are especially liable to make a seller's product less rather than more attractive in the long run. While competition gives sellers an incentive to control their costs, including labour costs, it doesn't necessarily give them an incentive to reduce wages. Lower wages don't entail lower production costs if they make it harder for a firm to attract and retain productive employees.

3. **D**. Agreements among sellers to maintain their prices at some level substantially above marginal cost would be unstable even if they were not illegal. Products have so many different dimensions through which sellers can engage in costly (to them) competition that a clear division of the market will be an essential supplement to any price-fixing agreement. But the problem presented by firms that are not parties to the agreement will still remain. How will the cartel prevent new entrants to its industry and the improvement of substitute products? Both responses become more probable the more effectively price is held above marginal cost.

4. **A**. Government is uniquely able to exclude competitors by imposing special costs on them because government is the one social institution with a generally acknowledged right to use coercion. This implies that sellers will compete against one another to secure the beneficial assistance of government, a competition that ordinarily will be costly to them (because of lobbying expenditures). It is not a competition whose outcome is guaranteed to be "fair to everyone" or "in the public interest" (Chapter 17 looks more closely at these questions.)

5. **D**. Who except a competing seller would have any interest in complaining? But complainants conveniently lose sight of the fact that only actions have costs. This neglect usually enables them to overlook the relevant action, whose cost the seller is almost certainly covering, and to pad their definition of cost with a lot of expenses unrelated to the seller's decision.

6. **D.** Substantially higher prices for an extended period of time would be required for predators to gain from predatory price cutting. But will the predator be able to exclude new rivals, especially if the resources of the firms driven out of business by the predator are still available?

7. **E.** Competition is not preserved by preventing it, even if this is done in the name of preserving competitors. When sellers are prevented from competing, buyers tend to receive poorer choices and pay higher prices.

8. **A.** The output restriction that is characteristic of price-searchers' markets diminishes when sellers practice price discrimination. Identical prices are not a proof of collusion; they may merely be the consequence of competition, from which price searchers are by no means protected simply because they have some power to choose the prices they will set.

C. A Step-by-Step Review of Chapter 13

1. If there is only one daily newspaper published in a city with a population of 100,000, the owner of the newspaper
    A. is a monopolist.
    B. faces no competition.
    C. has some power to vary the selling price.
    D. has unlimited power to vary the selling price.
    E. all of the above.

2. The owners of the only daily newspaper in a city face competition, which restricts their power to raise prices, from

    A. radio and television stations.
    B. newspapers in other cities.
    C. weekly newspapers.
    D. none of the above, for none of them is a perfect substitute.
    E. all of them, for they are all partial substitutes.

3. The large net revenue that a firm earns from an activity

    A. provides incentive to others to engage in that activity.
    B. serves as a threat to prevent others from engaging in that activity.
    C. leaves less incentive for others to engage in that activity.
    D. is conclusive evidence that the firm is a monopolist.

4. A reduction by Canadian Airlines in economy airfares from Toronto to Calgary will have what effect on the demand for economy space on Air Canada from Toronto to Calgary?

    A. No effect, because the two goods are almost perfect substitutes.
    B. No effect, because only the quantity demanded depends on the price.
    C. The demand will decrease because Canadian flights are a very close substitute for Air Canada flights.
    D. The demand will increase because Air Canada will also be compelled to reduce its fares.

5. If Air Canada responds by lowering its economy airfares on the route, what effect will this have on the demand for economy space on Canadian flights from Toronto to Calgary?

    A. No effect, because only the quantity demanded depends on the price.
    B. No effect, because Canadian initiated the fare reductions.
    C. The demand will decrease because Air Canada flights are a very close substitute for Canadian flights.
    D. The demand will increase because Canadian will be compelled to lower its fares still further.

6. Questions 4 and 5 on the previous page show that the demand curve facing any firm, and hence the pricing policy it chooses,

    A. can be controlled by large firms.
    B. may shift in response to the firm's own pricing policy, making the demand curve quite indeterminate.
    C. are entirely under its own control when there are only a few sellers in a market.
    D. leave no room for competition when oligopoly exists.

7. Sellers who try to maintain or increase the demand for their product in the face of competition by improving the quality of the product

    A. waste resources.
    B. would benefit buyers more if they lowered the price.
    C. generate additional benefits for buyers and additional costs for themselves.
    D. are acting inefficiently.

8. A firm will usually choose to increase its advertising expenditures

    A. when the expected gain in revenue exceeds the expected additional cost of doing so.
    B. only if it is not subject to competition.
    C. only if it is not the sole firm selling its product in a particular market.
    D. so long as doing so is expected to increase sales.

9. A price that has been set by agreement between sellers at a price well above the marginal cost of each seller

    A. is easier to maintain if there are many sellers.
    B. guarantees each seller a large net revenue.
    C. leaves each seller with a strong incentive to sell additional units.
    D. will be maintained by each seller eager to cover overhead expenses.

10. Sellers who conscientiously adhere to an agreement not to compete by lowering the price

    A. have no way of attracting business from other sellers.
    B. will find alternative ways of attracting business from other sellers only so long as they do not entail additional costs.
    C. will want to use alternative ways of attracting business from other sellers so long as the marginal cost of doing so is less than the expected addition to their revenue.
    D. behave more ethically than do sellers who lower their prices.

11. A cartel is

    A. a device for transporting groceries in a supermarket.
    B. an agreement among a group of sellers or buyers designed to control prices by regulating sales.
    C. an international demand curve.
    D. a law prohibiting mergers between competing sellers.

12. Sellers eager to escape competition will receive effective assistance from the government

    A. only if the government completely bans competition.
    B. only if the government totally excludes new entrants.
    C. if the government imposes any additional costs on other sellers.
    D. if the government permits sellers to set their prices without legal restraints

13. A law that prevents firms from taking any actions that might reduce the number of their competitors

    A. preserves competition.
    B. increases competition.
    C. restricts competition.
    D. has no effect on competition.

14. Many business firms support legislation to prevent "selling below cost" because they

    A. know that anyone selling below cost is competing unfairly.
    B. know that price competition makes their life more difficult.
    C. want to preserve and extend competition.
    D. believe that fairness is essential to the operation of a free enterprise system.

15. Butcher shops that sell steaks and pot roasts will, in setting prices, distribute the cost of purchasing a side of beef between steaks and pot roasts

    A. equally.
    B. on the basis of weight and volume.
    C. on the basis of the respective demands for steaks and pot roasts.
    D. by adding a standard markup.

16. Selling candy mints at a price below the seller's cost of purchasing them

    A. is a money-losing policy.
    B. probably adds to some sellers' net revenues if we judge by the number of firms that distribute candy mints to customers at no charge.
    C. will not occur if sellers want to maximize net revenue.
    D. proves predatory pricing exists.

17. Predatory price cutting means reducing prices

    A. as part of a marketing strategy.
    B. below cost.
    C. below cost in the hope of driving rival firms out of business.
    D. below cost in the hope of driving rival firms out of business with the intention of raising prices very high after the rivals have disappeared.

18. Minimum price laws designed to prevent "selling below cost"

    A. guarantee fair competition among sellers.
    B. assure the public a continued supply of quality products at reasonable prices.
    C. guarantee higher prices in the vague hope of preventing still higher prices.
    D. protect consumers against unscrupulous sellers.

19. The basic federal law enunciating Canadian policy with respect to competition among business firms is the

    A. Corporation and Labour Union Return Act of 1966.
    B. Mann Act, passed in 1910.
    C. Competition Act, passed in 1986.
    D. McKenzie King Act, passed in 1867.

20. The anti-merger section of the Competition Act prohibits mergers between firms when

    A. one is substantially larger than the other.
    B. the merger cannot be shown to be in the national interest.
    C. the effect of the merger may be a substantial lessening of competition.
    D. their boards of directors have interlocking financial interests.

21. A merger between a firm manufacturing mattresses and a firm manufacturing hardwood flooring is a

    A. diagonal merger.
    B. horizontal merger.
    C. vertical merger.
    D. conglomerate merger.

22. A merger between a firm manufacturing automobiles and one manufacturing sheet steel is a

    A. diagonal merger.
    B. horizontal merger.
    C. vertical merger.   — ➔ *Buyer Seller Relationship.*
    D. conglomerate merger.

23. A merger between two firms manufacturing electrical machinery is a

    A. diagonal merger.
    B. horizontal merger.
    C. vertical merger.
    D. conglomerate merger.

24. Competition occurs between firms when they

    A. are all of similar size.
    B. all charge the same price.
    C. all charge different prices.
    D. attempt to expand their sales.

25. Government actions to increase competition

    A. cannot succeed, because no seller can be compelled to compete.
    B. may entail costs greater than their marginal benefits.
    C. are contrary to the spirit of the Competition Act.
    D. have been completely unsuccessful in Canada over the past century.

D. Answers to the Review Questions of Chapter 13

1. C	6. B	11. B	16. B	21. D
2. E	7. C	12. C	17. D	22. C
3. A	8. A	13. C	18. C	23. B
4. C	9. C	14. B	19. C	24. D
5. C	10. C	15. C	20. C	25. B

E. Price Setting, Collusion, and Competition

The Wobbly Widget Company manufactures and sells widgets in Wingham. The demand curve it faces and its marginal-cost curve are shown in Figure 13.1 on the next page. Use the graph to answer the following questions. Assume fixed costs are equal to zero for this problem.

1. How many widgets will Wobbly want to make and sell per day in Wingham? _____

2. What price will it set in order to sell this number? _____

3. What area on the graph represents the net revenue that Wobbly gains from this marketing policy?

4. Wobbly's profits attract the Wrestful Widget Company into Wingham. Wrestful's marginal costs of making and selling widgets happen to be exactly the same as Wobbly's. Why will Wrestful's entry into the market tend to result in a lower price for widgets in Wingham?

5. If Wobbly and Wrestful agree not to engage in price competition but to divide the market equally, what will happen to the price of widgets, the quantity produced and sold, and the profits of the widget companies?

Wingham Widgets

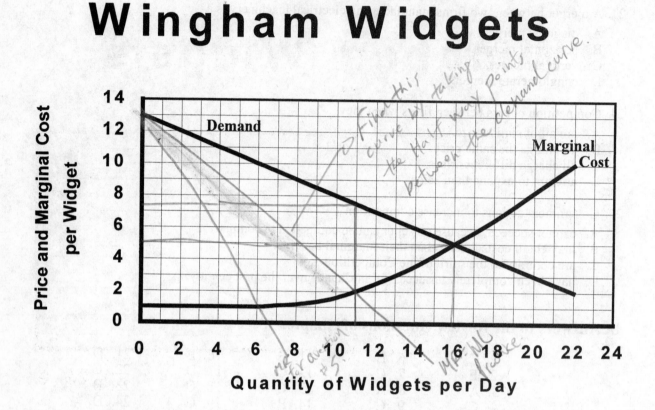

Figure 13.1 Costs and Demand for Widget Production

6. What would it cost Wobbly (or Wrestful) to make and sell one widget in addition to the quantity it is currently selling under this cartel arrangement? What would be its marginal revenue if one of its competitor's customers started to purchase from Wobbly (or Wrestful)?

7. What would be the additional net revenue accruing to Wobbly (or Wrestful) from such a switch in patronage? How much would each firm be willing to pay to induce such a switch if it could be sure that the other firm would not find out and retaliate?

8. If you were a widget sales representative working on commission for one of the firms, would you have any incentive to offer potential customers a secret rebate?

F. Answers to Questions in Section E

1. The marginal-revenue curve intersects marginal cost at 11 units.
2. Eleven units can be sold at a price of $7.50.
3. The area between $7.50 and the marginal cost curve up to the quantity eleven, which is outlined with the heavy, dotted line on the graph on the next page.

4. The simplest and most common way of gaining access to a new market is to offer a price below that being charged by existing sellers. When marginal cost is well below price, this is especially likely to occur. Existing sellers must then decide whether to bank on customer "loyalty" (which includes lack of information about the lower price) or to reduce their own prices. The longer the situation continues, the more likely it is that customers will discover the advantage in shifting to the new seller, and the more likely it is therefore that existing sellers will lower their prices.

Wingham Widgets

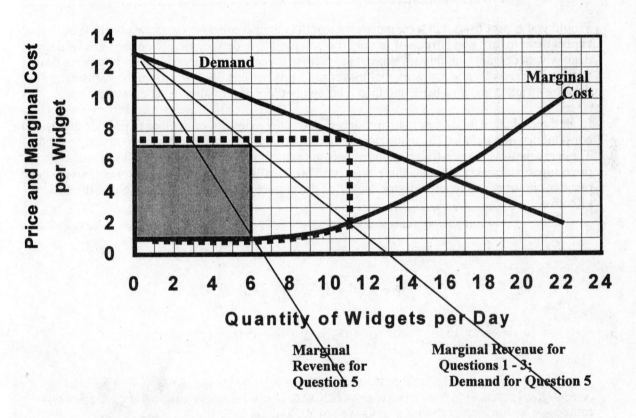

5. Everything depends on how they manage to allocate sales between themselves. If each seller ends up with half of the demand curve (so that Wobbly and Wrestful each face a demand curve identical to Wobbly's marginal-revenue curve before the entry of Wrestful into the market), marginal revenue will equal marginal cost for each firm at a quantity of six widgets per day. Each will be able to sell this quantity at a price of $7. The net revenues of each will be equal to the area between $7 and the marginal-cost curve up to the quantity six: the shaded area in the above graph.

6. Marginal cost is just a bit over $1 for a seventh widget. The additional revenue would be $7 if one of the other firm's customers defected.

7. A gain of almost $6 in net revenue would accrue to the beneficiary of any customer switch. Consequently, this is the maximum amount each firm would be willing to pay to induce a switch if it ruled out the possibility of detection and retaliation.

8. When the firms' top managers agree not to compete, they don't necessarily eliminate the incentive of salespeople on commission to secure additional income by offering price reductions. Salespeople who regard half a commission as better than no commission at all are often the means through which price competition reappears after it has been suppressed by agreement.

G. Questions to Think about

1. If data on Canadian manufacturing show that the larger firms in an industry tend to earn higher rates of return on investment than do the smaller firms, would this be evidence that large firms are able to suppress competition?

2. The standard recital of "basic necessities" always begins with "food, clothing, and shelter." How competitive are the industries that bring us food, clothing, and shelter?

H. Answers to Questions in Section G

1. Would you expect firms that were more efficient than their competitors to grow faster? Would you expect them to earn higher rates of return? It is impossible to decide, merely on the basis of such data, whether bigness confers advantages or whether advantages produce bigness. It appears from much of the recent statistical work that in fact big firms became big and earn high profits because they are efficient and do a better job than their competitors of providing what customers want.

2. In all three of these industries, many producers and sellers vie with each other to provide goods that consumers will purchase. The industries are structured in a way that implies vigorous competition. There are, however, price-fixing arrangements in each industry for which buyers eventually pay: price supports for agricultural commodities, tariffs on textile and apparel imports, restrictive labour practices in the construction industry. Note that government assistance makes all these restrictions effective.

Chapter 14

Profit

A. Multiple-Choice Questions on the Principal Ideas of Chapter 14

1. Calculating a firm's profits over a particular year by subtracting its total costs from its total revenue during the year
   A. will understate profits if sunk costs are included in total costs.
   B. ignores the effects of uncertainty on profits.
   C. ignores the effects of restricted competition on profits.
   D. will overstate profits unless the opportunity costs of all resources employed by the firm are included in total costs.

2. From the perspective of economic theory, interest paid by an enterprise is
   A. no cost at all, because it represents no sacrifice by anyone.
   B. the cost of acquiring present command of resources.
   C. a genuine cost only when it is a contractual obligation.
   D. compensation for the sacrifice made by those who abstained from consumption in order to have money to lend.

3. The interest rate in a society will reflect the
   A. supply of money in that society.
   B. demand for money in that society.
   C. supply of and demand for money in that society.
   D. relative valuation of current command versus future command over goods.

4. The fact that the owners or managers of business firms must make decisions on the basis of expected costs and revenues and that those expectations are never certain
   A. leads to larger profits for those whose predictions turn out to be more nearly accurate than what was commonly predicted at the time they acted.
   B. leads to larger losses for those whose predictions turn out to be less nearly accurate than what was commonly predicted at the time they acted.
   C. produces both of the above results.
   D. cannot affect profits or losses because mistakes average out in the long run.

5. The difference between the entrepreneur and all other participants in a project is that the entrepreneur
   A. accepts responsibility for the outcome.
   B. offers credible guarantees to all the others.
   C. persuades others to give him or her control of the project.
   D. receives the residual, or what is left over after all prior agreements have been honoured.
   E. Each of the above distinguishes the entrepreneur.

6. The property rights of people
   A. must be carefully distinguished from human rights or civil rights.
   B. determine people's incomes but do not affect their decisions.
   C. are rights to control the way in which particular resources will be used.
   D. are the legal rights people have with respect to resources other than their own labour.

7. If the profits and the losses that arise from decisions made on the basis of uncertain expectations accrue primarily to those who made the decisions rather than being shared equally in society,

    A. uncertainty will be substantially increased.
    B. no profits or losses will occur.
    C. information will come to be equally distributed among the members of the society.
    D. decision makers will acquire better information before acting.

8. People search for more efficient ways to combine resources, exercise diligence in performing difficult tasks, and take personal risks in trying to provide what other people want

    A. without regard to the potential profit from their actions.
    B. because they hope to make a profit.
    C. if they have already made an adequate profit.
    D. only when they are sure of making a profit.

9. If we define profit as the income that arises from predicting more correctly than others, we are

    A. denying that people do anything to earn the profits they receive.
    B. rejecting the definition of profit as total revenue minus total cost.
    C. explaining why total revenue is often greater than total cost.
    D. justifying windfall profits.

10. In the absence of uncertainty, profits would be

    A. equal for everyone.
    B. driven toward zero.
    C. much larger.
    D. unearned income.

11. If the government prevents existing sellers in an industry from lowering their prices and excludes competitors, both foreign and domestic, the profits of the firms in the industry will nonetheless decline because

    A. everything declines eventually.
    B. non-price competition will raise the firms' costs.
    C. such a situation is fraught with uncertainty.
    D. there will be no incentive to innovate or provide good service.

12. Discounting is a process that uses the prevailing interest rate to

    A. reduce the prices of goods that people pay for in installments.
    B. determine the present value of amounts expected to be paid or received in the future.
    C. compare the relative value of labour income and income from the sale of non-labour inputs.
    D. correct for inflation.

B. Answers to, and Explanations of Multiple-Choice Questions on the Principal Ideas of Chapter 14

1. **D**. If sunk costs entailed financial outlays, these outlays have to be counted in any calculation of historical costs even though they are not relevant to current supply decisions. Uncertainty and restricted competition will have had their effects on the costs and revenues of past years. The common error is to overstate profits by failing to note what it actually cost the firm, in revenues forgone, to employ certain resources. The neglected resources will usually be assets for which no explicit price was paid because they belonged to the firm's owners.

2. **B**. Because present command of resources is usually more valuable than command of the same resources at a later date, people are willing to pay a premium to obtain resources sooner than they otherwise could. They bid against one another for earlier command of resources, and their bidding establishes the prevailing interest rate. The notion that interest is compensation to lenders for the

"suffering" they incurred by saving their income rather than spending it is favoured by many who want a way to justify the receipt of interest income. But this theory runs quickly into absurdity and fails to explain actual interest rate levels. The only "sacrifices" to which the interest rate corresponds are the opportunities forgone by marginal borrowers and lenders.

3. **D**. Interest is offered and demanded for the loan of money because money offers current command over valuable resources. The annual rate of interest will reflect the net advantage that members of the society think they will enjoy by having current command of resources rather than having command one year from now. Focusing on the supply of and demand for money obscures what's going on and promotes the mistaken belief that interest rates can be reduced by making more money available. If this were the case, interest rates would be very low in most of Latin America. Nominal interest rates are in reality very high in countries that have rapid rates of growth of their money supplies.

4. **C**. If you suspect — but no one else does — that students all over the country will be eager next fall to wear pink and chartreuse jeans, you could make a large profit by producing them now and being ready to supply eager retailers next fall when the fad suddenly erupts. If you are wrong, you will have paid to produce a lot of jeans that cannot be sold at a price that will cover their cost of production. If you are right, but your suspicion is also widely held in the garment industry, so many apparel manufacturers will be ready in the fall with large inventories that you won't be able to make a killing. Beware of option **D** and all other ways of thinking that ignore significant differences by dealing exclusively with averages and the long run.

5. **E**. Others are persuaded to give the entrepreneur control by being offered guarantees in return for the cooperating services they provide. These guarantees do not have to be for specific dollar amounts. It follows that the entrepreneur is responsible for the project and will receive what is left — only what is left but everything that is left — after all others have received their agreed-upon payments.

6. **C**. Option **A** is incorrect because human rights or civil rights are always rights to control particular resources and are, therefore, a form of property rights. Option **B** is wrong because it is their property rights that guide people's decisions. Option **D** incorrectly suggests that all property rights are legal rights and, by excluding labour resources, leaves out the set of property rights that plays the largest part in determining the distribution of income: namely, people's power to use their own skills, knowledge, and aptitudes. Chapter 15 will introduce you to the important concept of human capital.

7. **D**. Spreading the profits or losses around equally won't end profits and losses because it won't reduce uncertainty. It will actually make uncertainty greater by giving people less incentive to acquire information before acting. It isn't information but ignorance that will come to be more equally distributed.

8. **B**. It is not past profit but potential profit, or the hope of a profit, that prompts such activities. People don't act exclusively in the hope of a profit, but they surely don't make their decisions without regard to potential profit. Guarantees aren't required; hope is enough.

9. **C**. We neither justify profit income nor assert that it is unearned by pointing out that total revenue exceeds total cost in so many instances largely because people must act on the basis of predictions rather than certainties.

10. **B**. Competition for profit implies that uncertainty can be the only explanation for a continuing divergence between total revenue and total opportunity cost. If everything were known for certain, competition would lower returns and/or raise costs until all differences had been eliminated.

11. **B**. By propping up the price and keeping out new competitors, the government "guarantees" a profit to the firms already in the industry from each additional item sold, so the firms will want to sell additional units. To do that they will all want to attract additional customers. It will be in each firm's interest to expand its selling activities, and hence its costs, so long as the supported price exceeds the marginal cost of selling.

12. **B**. The higher the rate of interest used in discounting, the lower is the present value of any future amount. If the annual interest rate were 100 percent, then $2 one year from now would be worth only $1 now because $1 now would grow to $2 in a year at that interest rate.

C.   A Step-by-Step Review of Chapter 14

1. The word *profit*
   A. is defined for purposes of economic analysis by the Revenue Canada.
   B. is used incorrectly by most of the public.
   C. is used with a clearly defined technical meaning by all informed persons.
   D. has a wide range of well-established meanings.

2. The most common and intuitive definition of profit is
   A. surplus value.
   B. unearned income.
   C. income received through ownership of property.
   D. total revenue minus total cost.

3. Would the profits of a firm of attorneys increase or decrease if the attorney partners discharged their secretaries and law clerks and did the clerical work themselves?
   A. Increase, because the saving in payroll expenditures would lower the firm's total costs.
   B. Decrease, because the opportunity cost of performing the clerical tasks of the firm would almost surely be higher than the explicit costs of hiring others to do these tasks.
   C. Neither increase nor decrease, because the attorneys would in effect be merely paying themselves the salaries of the secretaries and law clerks.
   D. Increase if the attorneys agreed to do the additional work without pay.

4. "Zalmart can sell clothing at lower prices than Wellers because Zalmart owns their own buildings, but Wellers has to pay rent." This statement is
   A. correct if rent is a sunk cost.
   B. correct in asserting that Zalmart has lower costs but wrong in suggesting that Zalmart will therefore charge lower prices.
   C. misleading in its suggestion that there is no cost to Zalmart of using the building it owns.
   D. incorrect because rent is a sunk cost.

5. From the economic point of view, the interest paid by a corporation to banks or bondholders and the dividends paid to its shareholders
   A. constitute unearned income.
   B. both tend to reflect the opportunity cost of obtaining command of resources.
   C. are quite different because only the interest is a contractual obligation and therefore a true cost.
   D. are both taxable revenue for the corporation.

6. The term *capital* means
   A. liquid funds.
   B. accumulated savings.
   C. produced goods that will be used to produce goods in the future.
   D. money available for lending.

7. Interest is best defined as the
   A. rate charged by banks on loans.
   B. difference in value between present and future goods.
   C. price of money.
   D. addition to principal that lenders require of borrowers, exclusive of usury.

8. Borrowers are willing to pay interest and lenders demand interest because
    A. money is a scarce good.
    B. current command over resources is more valuable than command over the same resources at a future date.
    C. people mistakenly believe that money is real wealth.
    D. lenders have more power than borrowers.

9. In an economy that used no money but relied entirely on barter,
    A. there would be no capital.
    B. the phenomenon of interest could not exist.
    C. interest would exist as the difference in the exchange value between currently available goods and goods available at a future date.
    D. no one would want to borrow.

10. People with a positive rate of time preference
    A. place a higher value on satisfactions to be enjoyed in the near future than on satisfactions expected in the distant future.
    B. are irrational or at least shortsighted.
    C. are unrealistically optimistic about their future prospects.
    D. tend to be very punctual about appointments.

11. The more productive capital goods are in a society, the
    A. lower will the rate of interest tend to be, because capital will consequently be less scarce.
    B. higher will the rate of interest tend to be, because the demand for current command over resources will be greater.
    C. more frequently will interest rates be usurious.
    D. less likely is it that people will be willing to lend or borrow.

12. Someone who borrows money from a consumer finance company at a 24 percent annual rate when the going rate on home mortgages is 8 percent is paying a
    A. loanshark.
    B. usurious rate of interest.
    C. substantial risk premium as part of that 24 percent "rate of interest."
    D. rate of interest that is illegal in most provinces in Canada.

13. When the market price of bonds with a fixed maturity value declines, the rate of interest that purchasers of the bonds will receive
    A. rises.
    B. falls.
    C. does not change.
    D. becomes highly uncertain.

14. The difference between what people expect to occur when they make decisions and what actually occurs
    A. is controlled by multinational corporations.
    B. generates income for some people and reduces the wealth of others.
    C. is irrelevant from the economic point of view because economic theory assumes that people are correctly informed when they make decisions.
    D. creates injustices.

15. An entrepreneur is someone who
    A. buys risky stocks or makes other risky investments.
    B. lends savings to a group or individual that undertakes a risky project.
    C. owns land, machinery, or buildings and allows them to be used in a risky way.
    D. takes the risk of reorganizing a segment of the social world.

16. The entrepreneur receives the residual from a project because he or she
    A. has greater bargaining power than all the other participants in the project.
    B. has guaranteed agreed-upon compensation to all other participants in the project.
    C. is the legally certified owner of the project itself.
    D. is the only one who understands the technical details of the project.
    E. owns all the resources used in the project.

17. Which of the following assertions describes a consequence of property rights, as the term is used in the textbook?
    A. Hazel flies because she can reserve a seat in the forward section of the airplane.
    B. Hartburn registers for one class each year to be eligible for a university library card.
    C. Huffer enjoys blocking traffic by walking slowly through pedestrian crosswalks.
    D. Puffer builds his house out of straw instead of bricks because he doesn't own the land on which it was built.
    E. They all describe consequences of specific property rights.

18. If the laws and customs of a society decree that people who must go out in the rain have a right to take any available umbrella for their use,
    A. fewer umbrellas will be purchased.
    B. more umbrellas will be purchased.
    C. there will be no effect on the number of umbrellas purchased, but existing umbrellas will be used more frequently.
    D. it will rain more often.

19. If a law is passed that prohibits apartment owners from raising rents when the vacancy rate falls below 3 percent but that does not compensate the owners for loss of income when the vacancy rate rises above 10 percent,
    A. fewer apartment units will be constructed.
    B. more apartment units will be constructed in order to get the vacancy rate slightly above 3 percent.
    C. the incomes of apartment owners will decline, but there will be no effect on apartment construction.
    D. the vacancy rate will steadily increase.

20. When the profits or losses that arise as a result of uncertainty regularly accrue to the people whose decisions led to those profits or losses,
    A. people take all sorts of absurd risks because they are eager to make a profit.
    B. people exercise more care when making decisions.
    C. income is distributed equally in the long run.
    D. income is distributed justly.

21. The profits that are the result of astute predictions can be clearly distinguished from the profits that are the result of pure luck by
    A. asking the profit recipients.
    B. majority vote.
    C. asking the people who sustained losses.
    D. careful empirical studies.
    E. no currently known procedure.

22. The income or addition to wealth that arises from predicting more correctly than others is best described as
    A. windfall profit.
    B. unearned income.
    C. profit.
    D. surplus value.

23. The certainty that the total revenue from a particular set of actions will be greater than the total cost to be incurred by those actions
    A. will generally exceed the certainty of death and taxes.
    B. will lead to an elimination of the difference between revenue and cost through increased competition.
    C. will lead to an increase in wealth for everyone involved.
    D. will produce windfall profits.

24. The price of an urban lot comes closest to reflecting
    A. the value of the lot as assessed for tax purposes.
    B. the present value of expected net benefits from ownership of the lot.
    C. what the current owner paid for the lot plus improvements since it was purchased.
    D. the average price of lots of the same size in the suburbs.

25. The price of a share of stock comes closest to reflecting
    A. what the share was sold for originally.
    B. the present value of expected net benefits from ownership of the stock share.
    C. what the current owner paid for the share plus retained per-share earnings since it was purchased.
    D. the cost of production of the corporation's assets.

26. The price of a residential or commercial building comes closest to reflecting
    A. the present value of expected net benefits from ownership of the building.
    B. what the current owner paid for the building plus improvements minus depreciation since it was purchased.
    C. the building's cost of construction.
    D. what it would cost to construct a similar building.

27. The annual cost of owning a valuable pearl that one finds by sheer luck is approximately equal to
    A. the cost of insurance and security precautions.
    B. the cost of purchasing a comparable pearl divided by the number of years its value is expected to last.
    C. the market price of the pearl times the prevailing rate of interest.
    D. zero, because the pearl was acquired at no cost.
    E. answers A plus C above.

28. Someone receiving $80 per year in income from a $1000 investment is receiving
    A. a pittance.
    B. an 8 percent return on investment.
    C. enough to live comfortably.
    D. unearned income.

29. Someone who wants to earn a return of at least 8 percent on investment and is offered an opportunity to purchase an asset that will pay $80 per year should *not* offer to purchase that asset for
    A. more than $640 for the asset.
    B. more than $1,000 for the asset.
    C. anything at all for the asset.
    D. for the asset until one year later.

30. If this same person is determined to accept no less than a 12 percent return on investments made, the maximum price offered should be
    A. $667.
    B. $800.
    C. $960.
    D. $1400.
    E. $1500.

31. Who receives the bulk of the profit from a federal government decision to raise the support price paid for wheat?

    A. All wheat farmers
    B. No one, because the support price removes uncertainty from the situation
    C. Only those wheat farmers who continue to grow wheat
    D. Those who owned wheat land when the government's intention to raise the support price first became known

32. When the Canadian Radio-Television Telecommunications Commission assigns valuable broadcast rights to the one applicant it deems the most qualified owner, profit from ownership of the broadcast rights
    A. goes to the government.
    B. goes to the general public, whose interest is thereby served.
    C. is reduced considerably by costly efforts to appear qualified.
    D. is maximized because uncertainty is minimized.

D. Answers to the Review Questions in Chapter 14

1. D	5. B	9. C	13. A	17. E	21. E	25. B	29. B
2. D	6. C	10. A	14. B	18. A	22. C	26. A	30. A
3. B	7. B	11. B	15. D	19. A	23. B	27. E	31. D
4. C	8. B	12. C	16. B	20. B	24. B	28. B	32. C

E. Future Amounts, Present Values, and Discounting

Use the tables at the end of Chapter 14 to answer the following questions.

1. Goldie Lox is 35 years old. She just inherited $10,000 from the estate of her great-uncle and has decided to put the money aside for her retirement. How much will she have at age 65 if she invests the $10 000 at 6 percent? At 9 percent? At 12 percent?

2. At age 65, Ms. Lox purchases a lifetime annuity with the accumulated proceeds. This will be an annual sum, paid at the end of each year, for as long as she lives. The life insurance company estimates her life expectancy at an additional 15 years and consequently agrees to provide her with the annual amounts that a 15-year annuity would yield, but for the duration of her life. (If she dies before age 80, the insurance company gains; if she lives beyond 80, it loses.)

    a. How large an annuity could she purchase at a 6 percent interest rate with the sum accumulated from having her inheritance invested for 30 years at 6 percent?
    b. How large an annuity could she purchase at 9 percent with the proceeds from 30 years of investment at 9 percent?
    c. How large an annuity could she purchase at 12 percent with the sum accumulated over 30 years at 12 percent?

3. If Goldie Lox had purchased a 30-year annuity at 9 percent when she received her $10 000 inheritance, how large an income would it have yielded her each year up to the age of 65?

4. (This is a tough one to solve with just the tables given to you at the end of Chapter 14. See what you can do with it.) Suppose that Goldie Lox inherits nothing but nonetheless decides at age 35 that she would like to have $500 000 on which to retire at age 65. How much would she have to save each month for the next 30 years in order to have $500 000 at retirement? Assume that she sets the amount aside each month and then invests it at the end of each year for an 8 percent return.

F. Answers to Questions in Section E

1   According to Table 14.1, $1 invested at 6 percent grows to $5.7435 in 30 years. $10 000 will therefore become $51 435 at 6 percent. At 9 percent she would have $132 677 at age 65. At 12 percent she would have $299 599.

2.

   a.   According to Table 14.3, a $1 annuity for each of the next 15 years has a present value of $9.7122 when discounted at 6 percent. This tells us that if the insurance company uses a 6 percent interest rate in selling annuities, it will ask $9.7122 now for each $1 it promises to pay per year for each of the next 15 years (ignoring administrative and transaction costs). Ms. Lox has $57 435 to spend on her annuity (from question 1), which is 5914 times as much as $9.7122. She can therefore purchase an annuity 5914 times as large as a $1 annuity, or an annuity of $5914 per year.

   b.   A $1 annuity for 15 years has a present value of $8.0607 when discounted at 9 percent. Therefore, $132 677 (from question 1) will enable her to purchase a $16 460 annuity ($132 677 divided by $8.0607 = $16 460) at 9 percent.

   c.   When the relevant interest rates are 12 percent, she can obtain an annuity that pays $43 988 per year ($299 599 divided by $6.8109 = $43 988).

3.   According to Table 14.3, $10.2737 will enable one to purchase, at 9 percent, a 30-year annuity of $1. Therefore, $10 000 will purchase a 30-year annuity of $973.76: ($10 000 divided by 10.2737 = $973.76).

4.   Begin by asking what would be the present value of $500 000 to be received 30 years from now when discounted at 8 percent. From Table 14.2 we calculate that it would be $500 000 times .0994, which is $49 700.

   The next step is to ask what annual sum, received or paid(!) at the end of each of the next 30 years, has a present value of $49 700 when discounted at 8 percent. Table 14.3 informs us that a 30-year annuity of $1 has a present value of $11.2578 when discounted at 8 percent. Dividing 11.2518 into $49 700 gives us $4,414.72. So if the rate of return is 8 percent, $4,414.72 is the amount that would have to be saved and invested at the end of each of the next 30 years to accumulate a sum of $500 000 after 30 years. Divide that annual amount by 12, and we learn that the amount Goldie would have to lay aside each month is $367.89.

   If we again use 8 percent as the discount rate, Goldie could buy a 15-year annuity of just over $62 000.

G. Questions to Think about

1.   What influence do the profits earned by pharmaceutical companies have on the amount they will spend searching for new drugs?

2.   When is a restriction on competition acceptable, and when is it not?

H. Answers to Questions in Section G

1. If pharmaceutical companies did not live in fear of hostile government actions, past profits earned would affect their search for new drugs only insofar as they were a predictive indicator of future profits from investments in drug research. It is *expected* returns that guide decisions. Will the fear of hostile legislative measures induce drug companies to spend more on research than they otherwise would in the hope of blunting hostility? Or will it induce them to spend less in the belief that they will have to shoulder all the costs of the research but will not be allowed to enjoy all the profits from a successful discovery?

2. Acceptable to whom? Potential competitors will find all restrictions unacceptable. Historically, Canada has endorsed many restrictions in the form of special privileges granted. A prime example is the granting of patent monopolies to inventors for a limited period on the grounds that such a restriction benefits society in the long run. We probably cannot do anything at all to reduce some restrictions on competition, such as those resulting from the special talents some people have, so it would probably be wise to accept them. Of course, we could, as the text says, make Stompin' Tom Connors wear bedroom slippers while performing. But for most people the goal of better music (in his fans' eyes and ears, at least) would take precedence over the goal of giving all competitors an identical chance for success.

Chapter 15

The Distribution of Income

1. The distribution of income among families and individuals in Canada
   A. is significantly affected by the choices of consumers, workers, and owners of productive resources.
   B. is *not* the product of decisions by income receivers.
   C. is entirely the result of decisions by income payers.
   D. has been rigidly fixed in the 20th century by the balance of power between corporations and labour unions.

2. Most of the income that Canadians receive annually derives from
   A. the ownership of human capital.
   B. rent, interest, and profits of incorporated and unincorporated enterprises.
   C. the ownership of stocks, bonds, and commercial real estate.
   D. transfer payments made by federal, state, and municipal governments.

3. Use of the concept of *human capital* by economists implies that
   A. all productive resources are the result of human effort and initiative.
   B. people acquire abilities that enable them to increase their future income.
   C. the rights of capital are as important as the rights of humans.
   D. human beings can be regarded as commodities for analytical purposes.

4. The concept of property rights as used in economic analysis attributes the ownership of resources to those who
   A. have legal title to the resources.
   B. can transfer title by selling or giving the resources to others.
   C. have historically had possession of the resources.
   D. are able to control the resources so as to obtain the benefit from their use.

5. People who discount the future at a high rate will, relative to those who discount at a low rate, tend to
   A. receive higher annual incomes in the later years of their lives.
   B. acquire more education early in life.
   C. save a larger percentage of their income.
   D. do all of the above.
   E. do none of the above.

6. The demand for the services of particular productive resources
   A. generally obeys the law of demand: a larger quantity of any specific resource will be demanded the lower its price.
   B. is derived from the demand for the goods these services are capable of producing.
   C. depends on the price and availability of other resources that compete with them.
   D. is described by all of the conditions above.

7. A machine will be more efficient than a human being and will therefore tend to be used in place of a person if
    A. the ratio of the anticipated marginal revenue to anticipated marginal cost is higher for the machine than for the person.
    B. the machine can produce a larger physical quantity of goods than can the person in the same period of time.
    C. the anticipated marginal revenue from the machine's use exceeds the anticipated marginal revenue from hiring a person.
    D. any of the above is true.

8. Those who obtain income by selling the services of the resources they own
    A. must usually compete against others selling similar services.
    B. must usually compete against both buyers and sellers of those services.
    C. can eliminate competition by persuading all who sell the same services to agree on a common price.
    D. must usually compete against the buyers of those services.

9. The ability of the federal government to regulate the distribution of income among families and individuals is
    A. enormous, as shown by the redistribution that has occurred from the rich to the poor since World War II.
    B. largely limited to what can be accomplished through revisions in the rules of the game.
    C. unlimited because government is sovereign.
    D. virtually unlimited because few people would be willing to emigrate merely in order to escape taxation.

B. Answers to, and Explanations of, Multiple-Choice Questions on the Principal Ideas of Chapter 15

1. **A.** The choices of many different people interact to establish the demand curves and supply curves that ultimately shape the distribution of income. A decision to acquire a particular skill will affect the income a person receives, but only in conjunction with other people's decisions to supply particular services and other people's demands for the products of various resources.

2. **A.** The major portion by far of the income received by Canadians is a return to labour services. But labour services are very far indeed from being a homogeneous commodity, and the differences in the value that people assign to other people's services accounts for most of the inequality in Canada's distribution of income. The term *human capital* refers finally to the acquired portion of these perceived differences.

3. **B.** Because capital means produced productive resources, use of the term *human capital* implies that people act in ways that "produce" enhanced ability to earn income. This does not mean, however, that effort and initiative account for everything, which is an absurd notion on its face.

4. **D.** If we want to use the concept of property rights to predict or explain how resources will be used, we must consider the actual property rights as resting with those who are able to manage the resources for their own benefit.

5. **E.** A high rate of time preference implies that people will prefer current income to education and current consumption to saving, as a consequence of which their incomes will on average tend to be lower in the later years of their lives.

6. **D.** The demand for any resource depends, among other things, on the conditions of demand and supply for competing resources and competing products. This means there are substitutes for the services of a particular resource, which in turn means that less will be demanded at higher prices.

7. **A**. High cost can cancel out the effects of high productivity as measured in units of physical output, just as low price can compensate for low physical-output productivity.

8. **A**. Sellers compete with other sellers, buyers with other buyers. Sellers don't want to eliminate competition among buyers or see the number of buyers reduced. Nor can they eliminate all competition merely by eliminating price competition.

9. **B**. Taxes and subsidies designed to redistribute income will change the marginal benefits and costs of engaging in any taxed activity and in occupying any subsidized status. That is why redistributive programs at the federal level don't achieve the results they were designed to achieve.

C. A Step-by-Step Review of Chapter 15

1. Economic theory examines the forces determining the distribution of income on the assumption that the distribution of income

    A. is impersonally determined.
    B. determines supply and demand but is not itself determined by the forces of supply and demand.
    C. is shaped by decisions based on the expected costs and benefits of alternative courses of action.
    D. depends not on past occurrences but on free choice.

2. The assumption of economic theory that income is the product of constrained choices implies that

    A. people are forced to accept the income that is offered to them.
    B. people can make their income as high (or as low) as they want it to be.
    C. people receive the income they deserve.
    D. people's estimates of future costs and benefits affect their incomes.

3. People receive income in exchange for the supply of productive services, meaning services

    A. that add to the society's stock of material goods.
    B. that increase the aggregate welfare of society.
    C. that require a painful sacrifice on the part of the supplier.
    D. for which others are willing to pay.

4. Most of the income that Canadians receive annually derives from the ownership of capital in the form of

    A. acquired knowledge and skills.
    B. real estate.
    C. stocks and bonds.
    D. money.

5. Most of the income that Canadians receive annually comes in the form of

    A. wages and salaries.
    B. profits.
    C. interest.
    D. rent.

6. Which of the following would be most effective, in the short run, in reducing the inequality of money income between families in Canada?

    A. Confiscating all privately owned land and real estate
    B. Equalizing all employee compensation
    C. Distributing after-tax corporate profits equally among all citizens
    D. Imposing a 100 percent inheritance tax

7. The term *capital* refers to

    A. all privately owned financial assets.
    B. any resources that people did not create by their decisions.
    C. all productive resources.
    D. productive resources that were themselves produced.

8. The term *human capital* refers to

    A. human beings owned by other human beings.
    B. capital owned by individuals rather than corporations.
    C. acquired knowledge, skills, or other abilities that enable people to increase their incomes.
    D. contracts for the supply of labour services.

9. People can be said to invest in human capital if they

    A. take steps to acquire attributes that will increase their future earnings.
    B. buy stock in corporations that pursue humane policies.
    C. invest in companies in the service industries rather than in agriculture, manufacturing, or construction.
    D. sign contracts that obligate others to provide labour services.

10. The value of a lawyer's services, once admitted to practice, depends chiefly on

    A. how hard the lawyer worked to acquire the necessary knowledge and skills.
    B. how much the lawyer paid, in income forgone as well as tuition, to acquire the law degree.
    C. the perceived knowledge and skills of the lawyer, however he or she came to acquire them.
    D. the labour time put into the provision of services.

11. According to the concept of property rights used in the text, the owners of a house have been deprived of property rights if a law is passed that

    A. confiscates the house without compensation to the owners.
    B. prohibits them from selling the house.
    C. sets a low legal ceiling on the rent they may ask for renting the house to someone else.
    D. grants a zoning variance that permits the people next door to operate a kennel.
    E. does any of the above.

12. A municipal rent-control ordinance

    A. does not affect property rights.
    B. transfers some of the property rights of apartment owners to tenants.
    C. reduces the income of apartment owners for the benefit of tenants but without transferring any property rights.
    D. transfers property rights from apartment owners to the people of the city.

13. Do motorists on super highways have the right to drive five kilometres per hour faster than the posted speed limit?

    A. No, because the posted speed limit establishes their rights
    B. They do not have the legal right but they do have the actual right because no one is likely to interfere with them if they do so.
    C. Yes, because speed limits violate the moral rights of citizens
    D. Yes, because standardized speed limits are absurd on super highways

14. Do ordinary citizens of large cities have the right to stroll unaccompanied through unlit and unguarded sections of a city park at 2 a.m.?

    A. No, because they do not own the park
    B. Only if there is no ordinance prohibiting it
    C. They have the legal and moral right but no actual right on which they can depend.
    D. Yes, because it would be morally wrong as well as illegal for anyone to mug an innocent stroller

15. As a consequence of the property rights discussed in the preceding two questions, we would expect to observe
    A. few motorists exceeding the posted speed limits on super highways and few night time strollers in urban parks.
    B. few motorists exceeding the posted speed limits on interstate highways but many night time strollers in urban parks.
    C. many motorists exceeding the posted speed limits on interstate highways and many night time strollers in urban parks.
    D. many motorists exceeding the posted speed limits on interstate highways but few night time strollers in urban parks.

16. Casanova spends much of his income each month on expensive clothes. Casablanca puts every dollar he can spare into common stocks. We can infer from this that Casablanca
    A. has a higher rate of time preference and will be wealthier than Casanova in later life.
    B. has a lower rate of time preference and will be wealthier than Casanova in later life.
    C. doesn't know how to have a good time.
    D. is a more rational person than Casanova.

17. Policies that make the returns from current investment less certain induce people to
    A. invest more in order to guarantee their future income.
    B. discount future returns at a lower rate of interest.
    C. reduce their current consumption in order to achieve greater security in the future.
    D. do all of the above.
    E. do the opposite of each action described above.

18. The demand for the services of specific productive resources is
    A. close to perfectly inelastic because employers cannot operate without such services.
    B. close to perfectly inelastic because the input requirements for a production process are dictated by technological considerations.
    C. more elastic the better the substitutes for those resources.
    D. less elastic than the demand for productive resources in general.

19. An increase in the legal minimum wage
    A. makes poor people better off by compelling employers to pay them more.
    B. does not make anyone better off because employers won't hire people if they have to pay them more than the expected value of their services.
    C. makes some workers better off by eliminating competition from other workers willing to work for very low wages.
    D. makes everyone better off by increasing the purchasing power of those most likely to spend.

20. Does the introduction of machinery make workers better off or worse off?
    A. Better off if it increases the demand for labour
    B. Better off, because it increases total output
    C. Worse off, because it reduces the demand for workers
    D. It makes some whose efforts the machinery complements better off and makes some whose services it displaces worse off.

21. When the wages of carpenters rise relative to other wages and prices, the quantity of carpenters' services demanded decreases

    A. because employers look for ways to substitute other inputs for the services of carpenters in order to keep their costs down.
    B. because customers will buy smaller quantities of goods produced by carpenters insofar as the higher wages lead to higher prices.
    C. for both of the reasons above: substitution for carpenters can occur in both production and consumption.
    D. because carpenters can now earn more while working less.

22. The owner of a dairy farm can obtain income from the resources owned because

    A. human labour is required to operate a dairy farm.
    B. cows produce milk.
    C. there is a demand for milk
    D. cows produce milk for which there is a demand.

23. The relative price of oil rose rapidly during the 1970s because of

    A. increased competition between oil producers and oil users.
    B. decreased competition between oil producers and oil users.
    C. continuing competition among oil users and decreased competition among oil producers.
    D. inflation.

24. A labour union will be able to increase the income of its individual members if it can

    A. persuade more people to join the union.
    B. eliminate some of the competition its members face from other workers.
    C. help its members compete more effectively against large corporate employers.
    D. reduce competition among employers for labour services.

25. The various junior hockey leagues in Canada, by enforcing strict limits on the value of the inducements that their teams may offer to young players,

    A. protects the moral standards of young athletes who might otherwise be tempted to choose to play hockey rather than attend some educational institution.
    B. prevents competition for athletes from transferring sports revenue from the teams to the athletes.
    C. makes young athletes better off by preserving their amateur status.
    D. protects the integrity of the game, at least at the junior levels.

26. The wage that an employer must pay to obtain an employee's services is determined primarily by the

    A. other opportunities available to the employee.
    B. amount of income the employee must have to live and support dependants.
    C. average wage level in the economy at the time.
    D. relative bargaining power of the employer and the employee.

27. The percentages of total money income received by the lowest fifth through the highest fifth of all households in Canada

    A. have been fairly constant since 1980 because children almost always stay in the economic class that their parents occupied.
    B. have been fairly constant since 1980 because individual families tend to remain throughout their "lifetimes" in one economic class.
    C. show that since 1980 the poor have been getting steadily poorer and the rich steadily richer.
    D. have changed considerably in the direction of greater equality if we take account of taxes and in-kind transfers and calculate on a per capita basis.

28. If each person in Canada received the same income over the course of a lifetime as every other person, family incomes as measured at any one time would
    A. necessarily be the same.
    B. be unequal because families would still contain different numbers of income recipients.
    C. be unequal because people usually receive different incomes at different ages.
    D. be unequal because families contain different numbers of income recipients and because people usually receive different incomes at different ages.

29. What is the marginal tax rate on someone who pays $1000 in income tax when his income is $20 000 and $2000 in income tax when his income rises to $25 000?
    A. 5 percent   B. 6.67 percent   C. 8 percent   D. 20 percent   E. 40 percent

30. Unpredictable changes in property rights caused by legislative action or judicial decisions tend to
    A. have no effect on the economy because people obviously cannot predict the unpredictable.
    B. turn many potentially correct decisions into wrong ones that people will then try to correct.
    C. encourage people to adopt a long-run point of view because the immediate future is so uncertain.
    D. encourage people to plan more carefully and to make more adequate provision for their future.

D. Answers to the Review Questions in Chapter 15

1. C	6. B	11. E	16. B	21. C	26. A
2. D	7. D	12. B	17. E	22. D	27. D
3. D	8. C	13. B	18. C	23. C	28. D
4. A	9. A	14. C	19. C	24. B	29. D
5. A	10. C	15. D	20. D	25. B	30. B

E. Time Preference and the Value of Lifetime Income Streams

The graph in Figure 15.1 on the next page portrays two contrasting lifetime income profiles. Profile **A** shows the annual income up to age 65 of a person who quits school on his 16th birthday to take a job paying $15 000 per year. His annual income rises fairly rapidly at first, then more slowly, until it peaks at about age 55 at $35 000.

Profile **B** shows the annual income of someone who finishes high school, goes to university, and then acquires two years of graduate professional education. His income is increasingly negative up to age 24, reflecting the expenses of his education. His first job pays $30,000 a year. His salary rises steadily after that to a top level of $100 000 at about age 55.

If we assume that the person who received the income of profile **A** *could* have received profile **B** by continuing in school and "investing in human capital," can we say that he made a mistake? It turns out that we can't even say the income shown by profile **A** is less, in the relevant sense, than is the income shown by profile **B**. Profile **A** was "chosen" by a decision at age 16. The question is whether the lifetime income shown by curve **B** is more than the lifetime income shown by curve **A** when it is *anticipated* at age 16 *and discounted* at an appropriate rate of interest — as all future income must be.

Figure 15.1

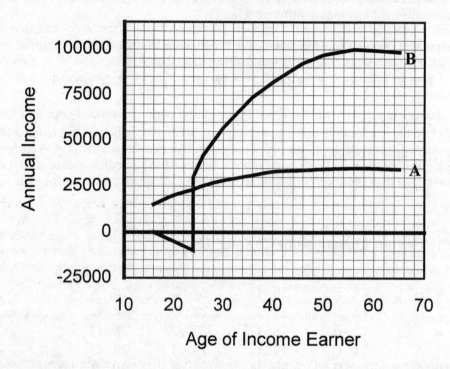

To show the effect that different rates of time preference can have on decisions affecting lifetime income, compare the cases of Mr. Ant and Mr. Grasshopper. Each can choose to receive either no income for 10 years and $100 000 for each of the next 20 years after that; or $30 000 for each of the next 30 years. Obviously $100 000 times 20 is more than $30 000 times 30 — more than twice as much, in fact. But let's suppose that Mr. Ant discounts future income at 4 percent and Mr. Grasshopper discounts at 15 percent. Calculate the present value to each of them of the two alternative future income streams.

F. Answers to Questions in Section E

The easiest way to calculate the present value of $100 000 for 20 years *beginning 10 years from now* is to calculate the present value of $100 000 for 30 years and subtract the present value of $100 000 for the first ten of those years. Using Table 14.3, we learn that at a discount rate of 4 percent, this income stream has a present value of $918 110. For someone who discounts at 15 percent, however, its present value is only $154 720.

The present value of $30 000 for each of the next 30 years is $518 760 for someone discounting at 4 percent and $196 980 for someone who discounts at 15 percent.

Mr. Ant consequently finds the option of no income for 10 years and $100,000 for the next 20 years worth about 75 percent more than the alternative, whereas Mr. Grasshopper places a 25 percent higher valuation on $30,000 for each of the next 30 years.

The next time you observe yourself or someone else making what appears to be a short-sighted decision, ask yourself whether a low or a high discount rate is implied by such a decision.

G. Questions to Think about

1. One common way of thinking about the income of a society is to divide it into wages and profits. This classification is often accompanied by the assumption that profits accrue largely to the wealthy and wages largely to the poor and members of the middle class. How adequate is this approach to the issues of income distribution?

2. Many Canadians apparently believe, and Canadian government policy certainly assumes at many points, that low-income people should be assisted at the expense of higher-income people. Example: subsidies from tax revenues to help low-income families meet their heating bills when fuel oil prices rise. How would you draw the line between those whose incomes are low enough for a subsidy and those whose incomes are not?

H. Answers to Questions in Section G

1. Most of the income of physicians, professional entertainers and athletes, corporate executives, and other wealthy people in Canada derives directly from the sale of their labour services. We could, if we wished, think of these people's large incomes more as profits than wages; but precisely how will we make that distinction? What comes first to most people's minds when they hear the word profits is the net revenue of corporations. If after-tax corporate profits in the first half of the 1990s had been distributed equally among all individuals in Canada, each person's annual income would have increased by less than $1900. Where does that income go at the present time? A large and growing part of all corporate stock belongs to such institutions as pension funds, universities, and even labour unions.

2. Wherever you draw the line, you will probably discover that it is above the income that the vast majority of Canadian families received only half a century ago. If you reflect on this, you will discover that "low income" is a relative notion and not an indicator of poverty in the sense of destitution: having too little food, clothing, and shelter to sustain life and physical health. Unless income is equally distributed (which is even harder to define), there must necessarily be some lower-income families. Will lower-income families always be considered poor families? How much inequality is acceptable? Does the social significance of income differences increase as the differences themselves shrink? If you were looking for an answer, you have found only further questions. Moreover, most of the redistribution that the federal government actually accomplishes transfers income to middle- and upper-income people. The "welfare state" for those who are not poor is about five times as large as the welfare state for the poor.

Chapter 16

Externalities and Conflicting Rights

A. Multiple-Choice Questions on the Principal Ideas of Chapter 16

1. An externality in economic theory is a cost or benefit produced by an action that
   A. does not influence the decisions of the actor (decision maker).
   B. the actor is not aware of.
   C. is a cost or benefit to someone other than the actor.
   D. makes everyone worse off than if the action were not taken.

2. Externalities would not exist if
   A. everyone adhered to the golden rule: Behave toward others as you want them to behave toward you.
   B. everyone obeyed the laws regardless of whether or not anyone was watching.
   C. people were not selfish.
   D. transaction costs were zero.

3. Ownership rights or property rights have the effect of
   A. determining only who will receive the benefits from the use of particular resources.
   B. determining only who will be responsible for controlling particular resources so that they yield benefits.
   C. determining both the distribution of benefits and the assignment of responsibilities associated with the use of particular resources.
   D. encouraging people to use particular resources without regard for long-run consequences.

4. The sound of jet engines is not an externality for airport baggage handlers because
   A. they have been paid to subject themselves to the noise.
   B. the sound level is below the tolerable decibel level established by the government.
   C. they wear noise-reducing ear muffs while working.
   D. the sound of the engines does not do them significant physiological damage.

5. The advantage of viewing negative externalities as the consequence of conflicting expectations among people, or conflicting property-rights claims, is that this perspective
   A. points up the impossibility of completely eliminating negative externalities in an urban society.
   B. enables us to eliminate all negative externalities through precisely drawn legislation.
   C. shows why negative externalities cannot be eliminated or even reduced without the intervention of government.
   D. demonstrates the impossibility of reducing negative externalities without turning private property rights into public property rights.

6. Vaguely defined property rights
   A. create fewer negative externalities by inducing people to behave more cautiously.
   B. cause negative externalities to decline because no one knows who has which rights.
   C. reduce negative externalities by inducing people more often to secure other people's consent before acting.
   D. result in more negative externalities by making successful negotiation more difficult.

7. The advantage of resolving conflicts over property rights through adjudication rather than turning to legislation is that adjudication

    A. can create clearly defined rights, and legislation cannot.
    B. better maintains the continuity of expectations and thereby reduces uncertainty.
    C. has no costs of its own, whereas legislators and their staffs command large salaries.
    D. can give all parties what they want, whereas legislation inevitably harms one side or the other.

8. Legislation aimed at establishing exactly who has which property rights

    A. must be used when the primary social concern is efficiency rather than equity or justice.
    B. eliminates the role that negotiation plays in reducing problems caused by negative externalities.
    C. will tend to displace adjudication when disagreement over property rights has been created by a radical change in circumstances.
    D. is a more evolutionary approach to externality problems than adjudication is.

9. The creation through legislation of new "rules of the game" in response to the sudden appearance of negative externalities

    A. is more likely to promote efficiency if the rules establish grounds for voluntary exchange among the affected parties.
    B. must aim at efficiency rather than fairness because fairness depends on people's subjective preferences.
    C. will not work if polluting parties are permitted to exchange "rights to pollute" among themselves.
    D. is a way of dealing with negative externalities without redistributing wealth among the members of a society.

B.   Answers to, and Explanations of, Multiple-Choice Questions on the Principal Ideas of Chapter 16

1. **A.** The crucial characteristic of an externality is that it does not influence the decisions of the person who produces it. Whether the producers know about the spillover benefits or costs makes no essential difference: They could know but not care. The mere fact that costs fall upon or benefits accrue to people other than the actor in no way distinguishes an externality. Actors often pay people to accept the costs they generate (to clean up after them, for example, or simply to work on their behalf); and anyone who "goes into business" intends to generate benefits for others — in order to sell those benefits. Such costs and benefits are not externalities. And if externalities made everyone worse off, no one would create them.

2. **D.** Kindness and consideration toward others and respect for the law will tend to reduce externalities. But it is important to see that externalities are not exclusively and perhaps not even primarily the consequence of moral failings. They are the consequence of transaction costs that make it impossible or at least too costly to arrange the world so that actors take into account all the costs and all the benefits that their decisions generate.

3. **C.** We tend to think of ownership as something that entails benefits and to forget that ownership also assigns responsibility. Those who own a resource have an incentive to generate benefits from it and to hold down the costs associated with its use.

4. **A.** Noise does not have to be above some legally or physiologically tolerable level to be unpleasant. Wearing ear muffs can reduce the unpleasantness, but only by introducing an unpleasantness of another sort. The sound is not an externality for the baggage handlers because their employers (who generate the noise) are taking it into account and paying the baggage handlers to accept it.

5. **A.** The complete elimination of negative externalities would require at minimum the complete reconciliation of all the different notions people have about what they are entitled to. That is difficult enough with just Robinson Crusoe and Friday on an island; it's inconceivable in an urban society.

That doesn't guarantee, of course, that voters won't expect government to accomplish the job anyway.

6. **D**. Negotiation or voluntary exchange cannot proceed effectively unless the negotiating parties know what they have to offer and can count on the other party's having a similar knowledge. When property rights are not clearly defined, the parties won't have that knowledge. People will consequently be less successful in arranging compromises to reduce the costs they impose on one another.

7. **B**. Legislation and adjudication are both capable of defining rights clearly. Both procedures have costs of their own. And neither is more capable than the other of satisfying everyone. But adjudication has the advantage that its outcomes tend to be more predictable. Unexpected changes in property rights create windfall profits and losses by increasing the uncertainty that decision makers face.

8. **C**. When a new situation arises for which there is no adequate precedent, long-established rules may not provide adequate guidelines. When circumstances have changed radically, newly devised rules or newly defined property rights may do a better job than adjudication of preserving the continuity of expectations, keeping uncertainty to a minimum, promoting efficiency, and providing solutions regarded as fair. But negotiation will continue to be an important procedure for reducing negative externalities.

9. **A**. This picks up on the last sentence of the preceding answer. A great deal of knowledge that will not be available to legislators can be used to reduce negative externalities after legislation has established new property rights. Detailed restrictions may prevent people from making mutually advantageous arrangements that achieve desired goals at less cost. Any legislation that reassigns property rights will redistribute wealth. Option B is wrong because efficiency as well as fairness depends, in part, upon subjective preferences.

C. A Step-by-Step Review of Chapter 16

1. Economists apply the term *externalities* to
    A. the consequences of actions, whether harmful or beneficial, that are not taken into account by the actor in making decisions.
    B. the superficial consequences as distinct from the underlying causes of a situation.
    C. economic factors that are beyond control because they are not the result of anyone's decision.
    D. any production beyond that required to sustain economic growth.

2. A motorist who decides to enter a busy highway during the morning rush hour
    A. adds to congestion but does not generate an externality because the congestion slows everyone down.
    B. adds to congestion but does not generate an externality if it is legal to enter the highway at this point and this time.
    C. does not generate an externality because one additional motorist has no discernible impact on the traffic flow.
    D. generates an externality insofar as that decision took no account of the additional congestion it would create for other motorists.

3. Transaction costs are responsible for externalities, both negative and positive, because transaction costs
    A. are not taxed.
    B. are not paid for out of taxes.
    C. are usually sunk costs rather than marginal costs.
    D. effectively rule out the possibility of social arrangements that would induce actors to take full account of all costs and all benefits from their action.

4. In an urban society it is

    A. essential that everyone consents to everything that other people want to do.
    B. essential that all externality problems be eventually eliminated.
    C. absurd to believe that everyone's expectations can be made completely compatible with the expectations of everyone else.
    D. relatively easy to control externality problems because they are entirely a human creation.

5. The text maintains that such civic virtues as empathy, courtesy, and tolerance

    A. cannot reduce negative externalities because people act in their own interest.
    B. cannot reduce negative externalities unless people stop acting in their own interest.
    C. can make it easier for a society to reduce negative externalities by modifying people's conception of what is in their own interest.
    D. are important to sociologists but unimportant in the economic way of thinking.

6. Ownership is an assignment of

    A. rights and privileges.
    B. obligations and responsibilities.
    C. both privileges and responsibilities.
    D. unearned income.

7. The property rights that people actually possess are

    A. the rights written into the Charter of Rights.
    B. the rights they can exercise regardless of what other people may do.
    C. heavily dependent on the cooperation of other people.
    D. the rights they are willing to extend to others.

8. Private property entails

    A. rights without responsibilities.
    B. an unlimited right of property owners to do as they please with their own property.
    C. the right of property owner to do as they please with their own property within some limits set by the rights and obligations of others.
    D. chaos and anarchy in a social setting.

9. The assignment of property rights promotes social cooperation most effectively when people

    A. do whatever they wish without considering anyone else's preferences.
    B. know exactly what their rights are and are confident that they will continue to enjoy those rights in the future.
    C. know that they can lose their rights if their actions offend the majority of people in society.
    D. do not know exactly what their rights are and therefore behave cautiously and conservatively.

10. Negotiation is most effective in reducing the burden of the costs that people inflict upon one another when

    A. social decisions are made democratically.
    B. property rights are clearly defined and enforced.
    C. property rights are held in common.
    D. people don't assume that they have any rights of their own.

11. Adjudication of conflicting property rights claims

    A. eliminates negative externalities directly.
    B. increases negative externalities by coercing people.
    C. makes it easier for people to negotiate arrangements that reduce negative externalities.
    D. cannot reduce negative externalities because people don't agree on who has the power to adjudicate.

12. In taking a disagreement to court to have it adjudicated, the contending parties are asking the court to
    A. decide on the most efficient way to allocate resources.
    B. discover who in fact possesses which rights.
    C. decide who is more deserving of the contested rights.
    D. create new kinds of property rights.

13. Adjudicatory procedures that try to resolve disagreements over property rights by extending past precedents
    A. benefit only the wealthy.
    B. prevent all social change.
    C. make it easier for people to engage in long-term planning.
    D. create extensive windfall profits and losses.

14. Legislation or the creation of new rules to resolve property rights disagreements
    A. is the only procedure for controlling negative externalities when interests conflict.
    B. cannot contribute to the reduction of negative externalities because legislation entails coercion.
    C. can reduce negative externalities by clarifying property rights in a previously uncertain situation.
    D. cannot resolve negative externalities caused by technological change.

15. Legislation that tries to reduce air pollution by setting some maximum level for emissions from each source
    A. will reduce air pollution more quickly than will other methods.
    B. is the fairest approach because the cost of reducing emissions is typically very different from one source to another.
    C. will usually fail to produce the desired reduction in air pollution at the lowest cost.
    D. will achieve the largest but not the most efficient reduction in air pollution.

16. The legislation of uniform physical restrictions on the emission of undesirable particles into the air or water is the
    A. command-and-control approach.
    B. efficient approach.
    C. fair or equitable approach.
    D. political approach.

17. Economists tend to view a legislated tax on polluting activities as an attempt, through taxation, to
    A. achieve a fairer distribution of the benefits of industrialization.
    B. induce polluters to pay attention to the costs they are ignoring.
    C. raise revenue without reducing efficiency.
    D. stop pollution.

18. A legislated tax on polluters based on the units of pollutant emitted
    A. will benefit the wealthy members of society exclusively.
    B. will not reduce pollution from large firms that can afford to pay the tax.
    C. will not reduce pollution because it grants a license to pollute to anyone willing to pay the tax.
    D. will reduce the pollution coming from those who find the tax more costly than pollution reduction.

19. A society secures an improvement in environmental quality at the lowest cost when pollution is reduced by
    A. large firms.
    B. small firms.
    C. firms that are heavy polluters.
    D. firms that have the greatest comparative efficiency in pollution reduction.

20. Suppose that Firm A is ordered by Environment Canada to reduce its smokestack emissions until the air in the region reaches a specified quality. Firm A instead persuades other firms, through monetary inducements, to reduce their emissions by enough to achieve the Environment Canada target. This action by Firm A

    A. defeats the purpose of the Environment Canada directive.
    B. achieves the Environment Canada directive at a lower cost.
    C. proves that the air-quality target should have been made even more stringent.
    D. shifts the cost of improving air quality from Firm A to the other firms.

21. Should Environment Canada require the steel mills in the Hamilton area of Ontario to reduce their smokestack emissions? If we know that the total benefits from previous Environment Canada regulations imposed on metal operations throughout Canada are over twice the total costs of meeting the regulations, we know

    A. that the new regulations would add at least twice as much to benefits as to costs.
    B. that the benefits of the new regulations are likely to be larger than the costs.
    C. nothing about the benefits-to-costs ratio of the proposed regulations.
    D. everything we must know to reach an efficient solution.

22. The bubble concept as explained in the textbook

    A. assumes that pollution increases steadily until it reaches a maximum.
    B. assumes that at some point pollution will destroy the very processes that are creating it.
    C. prohibits all trade-offs among pollution sources.
    D. tries to control the total amount of pollution in an area rather than controlling the emissions at each and every point.

D. Answers to the Review Questions in Chapter 16

1. A	5. C	9. B	13. C	17. B	20. B
2. D	6. C	10. B	14. C	18. D	21. C
3. D	7. C	11. C	15. C	19. D	22. D
4. C	8. C	12. B	16. A		

E. Marginal Costs and Environmental Regulations

The table below reproduces the data on page 297 of the textbook.

	Units of Yuck Emitted Monthly	Cost of Eliminating Yuck, per Unit
Factory A	15 000	$1
Factory B	30 000	2
Factory C	45 000	3

1. What is the lowest tax per unit that would reduce yuck emissions from their present level of 90 000 per month to 75 000 per month?

2. What is the lowest tax per unit that would reduce emissions to 45 000 per month?

3. What is the lowest tax per unit that would eliminate emissions altogether?

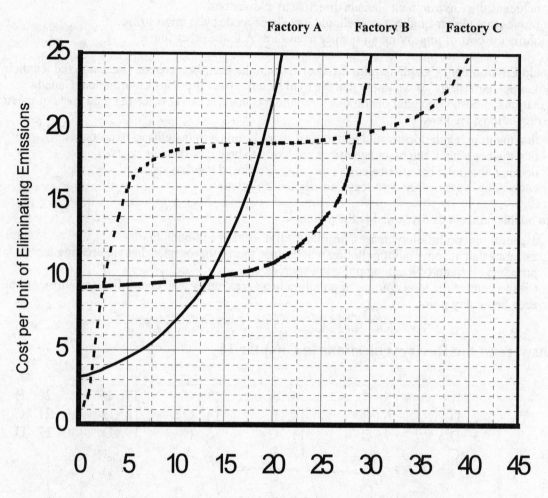

Figure 16.1

It would be most unusual if any source could reduce emissions from the current level to zero at a *constant* cost per unit. In many cases, initial reductions can be achieved at a quite low cost whereas the cost of eliminating the last units is very high. The graph in Figure 16.1 above presents a more plausible picture than does the simplified table on the previous page. According to the graph, pollution reduction efforts are subject to diminishing returns, or increasing marginal costs.

4. Under the circumstances depicted by the graph, what tax rate per unit would reduce emissions from 90 000 to 70 000 per month?

5. What tax rate would reduce emissions by 40 000 per month?

6. Compare the cost of reducing emissions to 50 000 through imposing a tax with the cost of reducing emissions to 50 000 by ordering Factory C to eliminate all its emissions. Why is the former so much less costly?

F. Answers to Questions in Section E

1. $1.01

2. $2.01

3. $3.01

4. The tax rate that would come close is about $9.40. At that rate it will pay Factory A to eliminate a bit more than 12 500 units of pollution per month; it will pay Factory B to eliminate a little less than 5000 units per month; and it will pay Factory C to eliminate about 2500 units per month. All units beyond these cost the yuck emitters more to eliminate than the tax they must pay, so they will choose to pay the tax. The graph below tries to portray these results.

5. An $11.90-per-unit tax would come close to hitting the target. Factory A would want to eliminate a bit less than 15 000 units of yuck; Factory B would want to reduce its emissions by almost 22 500; and Factory C would eliminate more than 2500 units of yuck.

6. The total cost of reducing the emissions in any particular way will be the sum of all the marginal costs incurred in the process, or the areas under the appropriate marginal cost curves. Once Factory C has reduced its emissions by about 31 000, it costs more than $20 per unit for that factory to reduce them further. The taxation system is less costly because it does not require some to do at high cost what others can do at lower cost. The tax paid then compensates the community for the yuck that Factory C is still emitting.

Pollution Cleanup

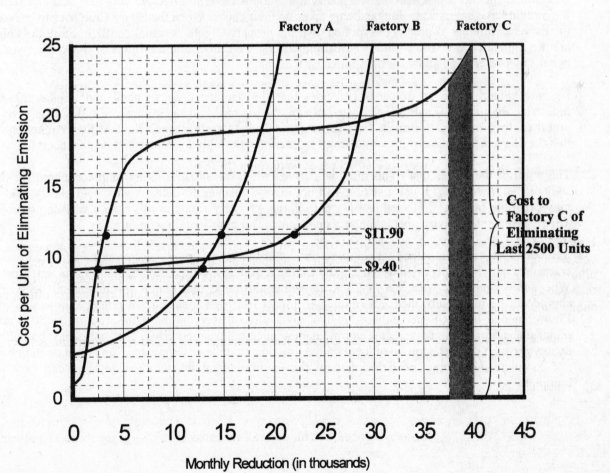

G. Questions to Think about

1. If we view pollution as a negative externality, do we thereby exclude from consideration actions that damage the environment but without imposing costs on human beings? What about pollution activities that impose all their costs on animals or even nonliving entities such as streams and mountains? Do only human beings have rights?

2. Does environmental legislation actually *clarify* property rights, as the text suggests? Hasn't environmental legislation in fact created vast new uncertainty over what property rights particular parties have?

H. Answers to Questions in Section G

1. By treating pollution as a cost to humans, we do seem to exclude from that category a great deal of clear environmental damage. Whether the exclusion is arbitrary is another matter. This approach emphasizes the nature of the problem for public policy and calls attention to the necessary conditions for a solution. People complain about a lot of activities that don't entail environmental damage (e.g., a neighbour who keeps used tires in his front yard), and they do not complain about a lot of other activities that do cause environmental damage (e.g., hiking in some wilderness areas tends to damage a very fragile environment). A policy problem arises only when people complain, when they protest and say, "You have no right to do that."

   The text tries to focus on this problem and its solution. It could be argued, of course, that plant life and animal life have some rights too, or, more plausibly, that human beings have obligations to plant and animal life. As a practical matter, plants and animals have no effective way to assert any rights they might have unless some human being takes up their cause. When the Sierra Club tries to prevent the harvest of timber to protect the spotted owl, the property rights in actual conflict before the court are the rights of those who would benefit from cutting the timber and the rights of those who would benefit by preserving habitat for the spotted owl.

   If some person or group of persons decides that the damage done to plant and animal life by industrial dumping offends them, even though the damage occurs entirely on the firm's own premises, they may try to stop it. They can do so only by asserting some right. If they cannot show that they have a legitimate right, any attempt to intervene through the courts will be unsuccessful.

2. The point of the text is that rights must be *defined* when the situation is too unprecedented for the rights to be *discovered*. But legislation will not always manage to define rights with clarity; and it may be in the interest of elected legislators to define property rights in as vague a way as possible. The requirement of environmental impact statements is an excellent illustration.

   Reluctant to take a clear stand on complex and contested issues, where any clear stand would make enemies, many legislative bodies have opted for the requirement of environmental impact statements. Who could find fault with that? Isn't it altogether desirable that major developmental decisions should not be made until their environmental impact has been assessed? In practice, however, the Environmental-Impact-Statement requirement gives almost everyone a vague property right in any major decision and thereby creates enormous new uncertainties and costs. Decisions may be halted by anyone who doesn't approve of them on the grounds that the environmental impact statement was not complete. Of course, no description of the environmental impact of a decision can ever be complete.

Chapter 17

Markets and Government

A. Multiple-Choice Questions on the Principal Ideas of Chapter 17

1. Economic theory assumes that elected and appointed government officials

   A. place their personal or private welfare ahead of the public interest.
   B. place the public interest ahead of any personal or private interests of their own.
   C. are free to pursue the public interest because they aren't constrained by competition.
   D. respond to the anticipated costs and benefits to themselves of decisions contemplated.

2. The most significant difference between government and other institutions in a society is that government

   A. possesses a generally conceded and exclusive right to coerce adults.
   B. must assume the responsibility for making all the rules under which the other institutions function.
   C. is the court of last resort, the ultimate authority beyond which there can be no appeal.
   D. fulfills all three of the above functions.

3. The use of coercion can enable the members of a society to cooperate more effectively

   A. by reducing the cost of arranging the exchanges they would like to make.
   B. by compelling all the beneficiaries of an action to contribute their share of its cost.
   C. by making goods available that cannot be supplied exclusively to those who pay for the goods.
   D. in each of the ways mentioned above.

4. The limitations on purely voluntary exchange created by positive externalities

   A. make it impossible for government to use coercion to supplement the voluntary efforts of people to cooperate.
   B. function also to distort the actions of government.
   C. do not affect the actions of government because government uses coercion.
   D. almost guarantee that coercive action by a democratically elected government will make most citizens better off than they would be otherwise.

5. People who expend more effort investigating cars before buying one than investigating political candidates before voting for one are saying, in effect, that

   A. their well-being depends more on a good car than on a good politician.
   B. the well-being of the larger society is less important to them than their own private well-being.
   C. any effort which they expend investigating cars will probably make more difference to their welfare than effort they expend investigating political candidates.
   D. all of the above are the case.

6. The interests of producers tend to be better represented in lobbying efforts before legislatures than are the interests of consumers because
    A. producers usually have larger incomes than do consumers.
    B. the interests of consumers are automatically cared for when the interests of the producers are attended to.
    C. producers usually have a much stronger interest in the outcome of a particular issue than do consumers.
    D. there are usually more producers than consumers affected by the outcome of a particular issue.

B.   Answers to, and Explanations of, Multiple-Choice Questions on the Principal Ideas of Chapter 17

1. **D**. It can be, and often is, in the perceived private interest of a government official to serve the public interest with dedication and great personal sacrifice. Economic theory does not claim that no one cares about the public interest, but only that elected and appointed officials will pursue it more single-mindedly (whatever *it* happens to be!) when it is in their personal interest to do so. They all pay attention to the expected impact of their actions on their own positions. The fact that they must often compete against others for their jobs or for budget allocations will under some circumstances induce them to serve the public interest more effectively. But under other circumstances it will induce them to sacrifice the public interest in order to improve reelection prospects or to secure a larger appropriation.

2. **A**. Option B is wrong because government's rule making is itself based on already existing rules — not only on constitutional rules where a constitution exists but also on the rules regarding rights and justice which are presupposed in any law-making process. Option **C** is wrong for a similar reason; some governments are put out of office, peacefully or violently, by what proves to be a more ultimate, and certainly stronger, authority. It is the right to coerce that distinguishes the institution of government.

3. **D**. Coercion is sometimes effective in reducing transaction costs, which are the costs of arranging mutually beneficial exchanges. Relying entirely on voluntary cooperation sometimes makes it so costly to exclude free riders (people who want to consume a good without contributing toward its production) that the good won't be produced in the absence of coercion.

4. **B**. The coercive actions of government arise ultimately out of voluntary actions undertaken by people: citizens, elected officials, government employees. The problems created by free riders affect the formation and administration of government policies. This does not inevitably render government action ineffective, but it does distort those actions and make them less likely to reflect majority opinion than we casually assume.

5. **C**. Many people who genuinely believe that the choice of a politician is more important to them than the choice of a new car also know that the effort they personally expend investigating the qualifications of political candidates will almost surely have no effect on the outcome of the election.

6. **C**. The amount of time, money, or other resources that people will be willing to invest in efforts to affect the outcome of an issue depends very much on the size of the benefit they anticipate as a consequence of their own (costly) action. Producers expect large benefits from a few issues; consumers expect small benefits from many issues. On any single issue, therefore, and consequently on every single issue, the affected producers are more likely to make their views known and to press them insistently.

C. A Step-by-Step Review of Chapter 17

1. The text maintains that elected and appointed government officials
   A. can always be bribed.
   B. have no genuine concern for the public interest.
   C. have a greater concern for the public interest than do business executives.
   D. discern the public interest in the light of private or personal interests.

2. The text maintains that competition exists in government
   A. only because we have a federal system with different governments at the provincial level.
   B. only when government engages in business activities.
   C. only during election campaigns.
   D. between people, parties, policy advocates, and program defenders.

3. Economic theory becomes more capable of explaining or predicting government policies the more that
   A. government officials learn about economic theory.
   B. participants in the political process are guided by calculation rather than caprice.
   C. monetary benefits enter into the decisions of policymakers.
   D. those policies aim at controlling the economy.

4. The assertion that elected and appointed government officials act on the basis of prevailing property rights means that
   A. government officials must be required to get rid of all investments during their tenure.
   B. the expectations they associate with their positions guide their decisions.
   C. they do not take any actions that alter property rights.
   D. they are governed by the wishes of the majority that prevailed at the last election.

5. What is the relationship between government and coercion?
   A. Only government practices coercion.
   B. Government is the institution in a society to which most people assign an exclusive right to use coercion.
   C. Government induces people to cooperate exclusively through coercion or the threat of coercion.
   D. Government does not practice coercion if the government is genuinely democratic.

6. How does the text distinguish between coercion and persuasion?
   A. Coercion uses force; persuasion uses reasoning.
   B. Coercion uses violence; persuasion is peaceful.
   C. Coercion cannot make everyone better off, but persuasion can.
   D. Coercion is evil, and persuasion is good.
   E. Coercion induces cooperation by threatening to reduce options, persuasion by promising to expand options.

7. Is coercion capable of expanding the freedom of all the people in a society?
   A. Yes, but only if it is approved in a voters' referendum
   B. No, because coercion is a limitation of freedom
   C. Yes, because it can sometimes expand everyone's options by denying a few particular options to anyone
   D. No, because coercion would not be necessary if everyone wanted it

8. Transaction costs refer to the costs   *Between Persuaders & Suppliers.*
   A. of arranging a satisfactory exchange.
   B. created by middlemen.
   C. of actions that create nothing of value to any of the participants in a voluntary exchange.
   D. of buying on credit.

9. Because transaction costs are deadweight costs, or costs to one party that are not benefits to the other, they

    A. reduce the amount of voluntary exchange that occurs.
    B. make voluntary exchange impossible.
    C. give an advantage to the party that doesn't have to bear them.
    D. increase as the rate of interest increases.

10. A free rider in economic theory is someone who

    A. uses a bus transfer after it has expired.
    B. doesn't have to pay transaction costs.
    C. can obtain a desired good without paying for it and therefore has no incentive to contribute to the costs of making it available.
    D. can produce a good at zero marginal cost.

11. Police protection is a good usually provided by government because

    A. police officers must sometimes use force.
    B. everyone benefits equally from the good.
    C. it is a good that is hard to finance through voluntary contributions.
    D. police officers are representatives of the state.

12. The funds to pay for police protection are usually raised through taxation because

    A. police protection is hard to provide exclusively to those who pay for it.
    B. people would not voluntarily pay salaries to officials who might arrest them.
    C. police protection is a basic necessity.
    D. goods financed through taxation can be guaranteed to all.

13. The fact that everyone wants a particular good produced and is willing, if necessary, to pay a proportionate cost of its production

    A. guarantees that the good will be produced.
    B. means coercion will never have to be used in supplying the good.
    C. does not assure that anyone will in fact contribute toward paying for its production.
    D. guarantees that it will be supplied in adequate quantities.

14. Governments usually provide national defense from tax funds because

    A. everyone wants national defense.
    B. national defense benefits everyone.
    C. more security is better than less.
    D. it is hard to supply national defense exclusively to those who volunteer to pay for it.

15. A judicial system for resolving disputes among the members of a society creates benefits even for people who never use it because

    A. the social contract entitles everyone to share in the benefits from goods produced by government.
    B. people are compelled to obey court decisions whether they want to or not.
    C. judicial decisions generate uniform rules that everyone can count on.
    D. silence implies consent.

16. Positive externalities create a case for financing education to some extent from tax revenues insofar as

    A. people tend to ignore the benefits their education confers on others in deciding how much education to obtain.
    B. education is not a good that the consumer is capable of evaluating.
    C. everyone is entitled to an education as a matter of right.
    D. teachers are also voters.

17. The argument for using coercion rather than relying entirely upon voluntary philanthropy to assist very poor people is that

    A. people must often be compelled to do what they know is right.

    B. people may be willing to contribute only if they are assured that others are also contributing their appropriate share.

    C. poor people are free riders in the technical sense of economic theory.

    D. poor people must be prevented from rebelling.

18. Government certification of the weights and measures used in business can be justified on the grounds that

    A. no business operated for profit would have any interest in weighing and measuring accurately.

    B. people cannot be trusted.

    C. it reduces total transaction costs below what they would be if all individual buyers or sellers had to check for themselves.

    D. government officials, unlike private parties selling for profit, have no incentive to cheat.

19. The impediments that transaction costs and positive externalities place in the way of social cooperation through voluntary exchange

    A. make it expensive for free riders to support themselves at government expense.

    B. can be entirely removed by government.

    C. can best be removed by a democratically controlled government.

    D. are also impediments to the effective working of democratically controlled governments.

20. Citizens typically cast their ballots without acquiring adequate information about the candidates or the issues because they

    A. know that the outcome of the election will make little difference to them personally.

    B. are apathetic and uncaring.

    C. believe that the information they acquire will have no effect on the outcome of the election.

    D. think that no one can be trusted to supply accurate information.

21. Legislators usually acquire more information on an issue before voting on it than do ordinary citizens

    A. because their individual votes are much more likely to affect the outcome.

    B. because they are provided with information-gathering resources at public expense.

    C. because constituents hold them accountable for their actions.

    D. for all of the above reasons.

22. An interest in being reelected encourages legislators to support policies that

    A. confer long-run benefits.

    B. entail short-run costs.

    C. confer short-run benefits with deferred costs.

    D. benefit all the people.

23. If a city council holds hearings on a proposed law that would require all restaurants to provide segregated tables for nonsmokers, the people most likely to be well represented at the hearings are

    A. smokers.

    B. nonsmokers.

    C. restaurant owners.

    D. manufacturers of tables.

24. Suppose the federal cabinet conducts hearings to decide whether federal loan guarantees ought to be extended to the Palmer-Heyne Tricycle Manufacturing Corporation to save it from bankruptcy. The union representing employees of the firm is likely to be well represented at these hearings because the union

    A. represents all working people.
    B. would be harmed by any government action that strengthened the economy.
    C. and its members have a large stake in the issue.
    D. does not want government to strengthen the corporation against which it must bargain.

25. The millions of taxpayers who must pay for a federal government bail-out of the Palmer-Heyne Tricycle Manufacturing Corporation will not be well represented at the hearings on the issue, because

    A. they do not gain or lose, no matter how the issue is decided.
    B. no hearing room is large enough to hold all the taxpayers who would want to appear and testify.
    C. no single taxpayer has a large enough stake in the issue to justify the cost of attending the hearings.
    D. they know that what's good for Palmer-Heyne is good for Canada.

26. The existence of positive externalities in the democratic political process makes it more likely that government policies will

    A. *not* produce budget deficits.
    B. be conducted openly and above board, or in a positive and external way.
    C. lean toward programs that help a few people a great deal but cost a lot of people only a little.
    D. be the policies that the majority prefers.

27. For many years, especially during major wars, many countries have been able to institute a system for drafting young men into the armed forces because

    A. the public feared the menace of Communism.
    B. patriotism has declined and so volunteers have not been available.
    C. young men were not willing to risk their lives.
    D. many people adversely affected found it more to their advantage to use some personal escape route than to attack the system directly.
    E. young women began to insist that they be made eligible for the draft as well.

28. Legislators are not likely to substitute money transfers to low-income people for all the other benefits now extended in kind because

    A. this would create welfare dependency among low-income people.
    B. low-income people prefer in-kind transfers.
    C. low-income people do not know how to manage money.
    D. special interest groups obtain large benefits from the system of in-kind transfers.

29. Members of the bureaucracy within Health Canada will tend to require more testing of proposed new drugs than is best from the point of view of people who use the drugs, because these bureaucrats

    A. identify themselves with the drug industry.
    B. have the technical knowledge to decide what is best for the users of drugs.
    C. are blamed if new drugs turn out to have damaging side effects but are not blamed for the lives lost or discomfort suffered because new drugs were not available sooner.
    D. pay for the testing from their own budget and consequently can do as they please.

30. "The prisoners' dilemma" is a concept that helps us understand why

    A. crime does not pay.
    B. majority rule produces outcomes in the public interest.
    C. punishment does not always deter criminal behaviour.
    D. social behaviour sometimes fails to produce results that everyone in the society genuinely desires.

31. The "dilemma" in the prisoners' dilemma is that, under certain circumstances,
    A. individuals who pursue their private interests end up promoting the public interest.
    B. it is in each person's interest to choose in a way that produces results in no one's interest.
    C. people deliberately act in ways that are contrary to their own best interests.
    D. selfish emotions turn out to be stronger than rational thought.

32. Even though the prisoners' dilemma predicts that people can be expected to leave a considerable amount of litter around, we frequently observe that people bear some personal costs to avoid littering. Why?
    A. The expected marginal benefits of littering outweigh the expected marginal costs.
    B. They put their trash in proper receptacles only when they think someone is observing them.
    C. They derive personal benefits from not littering that are not offset by the costs of properly disposing of their trash.
    D. They know that littering is against the law.

D. Answers to the Review Questions in Chapter 17

1. D	5. B	9. A	13. C	17. B	21. D	25. C	29. C
2. D	6. E	10. C	14. D	18. C	22. C	26. C	30. D
3. B	7. C	11. C	15. C	19. D	23. C	27. D	31. B
4. B	8. A	12. A	16. A	20. C	24. C	28. D	32. C

E. Property Rights, Positive Externalities, Free Riders, Transaction Costs, and Coercion

Beauregard Veene lives in the Mu Mu Fraternity house with 29 other young men, all of sterling character. He tells a friend: "Call me tonight at the frat house between seven and ten. You may have to let the phone ring a long time. But don't give up. I'll be there." When the friend phones (at seventeen minutes past eight), 30 fraternity brothers, including Beau Veene, ignore it and continue whatever they're doing. After the phone has rung six times, everyone begins wondering, "When will somebody answer that blasted phone?" They are all still wondering as it rings for the sixtieth time.

1. Who benefits when the phone is answered?

2. Who incurs a cost when the phone is answered?

3. Will a fraternity brother whose study area is right next to the phone have a stronger incentive than others to answer when it rings?

4. Beau will be harmed if someone calling for him hangs up in disgust after a while, and the harm will exceed (in his estimate) the cost of getting up to answer. Does this mean he will answer when the phone rings for him?

5. Because members of Mu Mu are missing important calls from people who hang up before the phone is answered, the officers call a meeting to deal with the problem. Everyone wants the problem solved. Who will want to attend the meeting?

6. The members who come to the meeting vote to assess each resident $2 per month and to pay a $60 monthly salary to an officially designated phone answerer. Some members (who missed the meeting) protest that they almost never get calls and therefore should pay less than those who get called all the time. Could the Mu Mu membership work out a system of assessments based on the number of calls each member receives?

7. Where in the tale of Beau Veene and Mu Mu do you find positive externalities, free riders, difficulty in excluding nonpayers, transaction costs, the use of coercion, and the importance of property rights?

F. Answers to Questions in Section E

1. Everyone benefits because the ringing stops. Beau (and whomever else some other call is for) receives a substantial additional benefit in the form of valued information from his friend.

2. The person who interrupts his work to answer incurs a cost. Even if the interruption is less costly to each member than the continued ringing, each member hopes that someone else will accept that cost and pick up the phone.

3. Yes, most likely he will have a stronger incentive, but he will also have a stronger incentive to take the phone off the hook when no one is looking.

4. How confident is Beau that this particular ring is for him? A one-thirtieth probability of a large benefit becomes a much smaller benefit.

5. Those who love to go to meetings to hear themselves talk and whose faithful attendance induces other members to find excuses for missing will want to attend. ("After all, what difference will it make if I'm not there?")

6. The phone answerer could keep track of incoming calls and present each member with a bill at the end of the month. Notice, though, how transaction costs would expand: record keeping, billing, disagreements, and additional uncertainty for all parties.

7. You ought to find them throughout this Beau Veene tale. Did you wonder about the property rights of the Mu Mu member who lives by the phone and takes it off the hook surreptitiously? Did you consider the difficulties inherent in a system of "taking turns"? Of refusing to answer incoming calls for people who themselves don't answer the phone when it is their turn? Did you see how the organization of coercion in order to overcome free-rider problems runs into transaction costs and free-rider problems of its own? Did you reflect on the fact that people typically benefit in different amounts from goods supplied through coerced levies? Do you see why so many fraternity members choose to pay for a private phone despite their (alleged) poverty? Is this wasteful and inefficient? If you think it is, you're probably pretending that transaction costs don't exist. Or are you assuming that they ought not exist? And that people ought not behave like free riders?

G. Questions to Think about

1. Consider the following hypothetical situation: suppose a federal cabinet minister told a group of reporters that the federal government intended to focus the spending of discretionary federal funds on communities where the government "has confidence in the local procedures." Suppose the minister followed this statement by saying that their confidence in your local mayor had recently "gone down a great deal." Upon further investigation, some reporters discover that your town received $386 million from the federal government in the previous fiscal year, $135 million of which was discretionary and thus could have been withheld. The mayor of your town, it should be noted, had recently surprised government officials by announcing her support for the opposition party despite having earlier made statements interpreted as favouring re-election of members of the present government.

    How does this story illustrate the existence of property rights in government and their role in guiding the behaviour of government officials?

2. Would you expect the free-rider problems created by positive externalities to be more or less important in small towns than in large cities?

H. Answers to Questions in Section G

1. Insofar as government officials are allowed any discretion in the allocation of tax-financed benefits, they will have some power to allocate the benefits in ways that best promote their own interests, whatever these are. This is probably a principal reason why political parties so seldom deny renomination to an incumbent member who wants to be renominated: an incumbent has substantial property rights in the power to grant or withhold significant benefits.

    The mayor of your town may also important property rights. Among other rights, she could expect to be able to influence party workers, using the power and influence of her office in ways that could significantly affect the outcome of the local riding's nomination process.

2. The question is designed to get you thinking about the many procedures that we can and do use to induce others to internalize externalities when we are well acquainted with those people. Most people have "less responsibility," that is, they generate more external costs and generate fewer benefits that will accrue to others, when "no one knows them." The well-known social pressure that exists in a small town does not exist in anything like the same degree in a large city. As a consequence, people who live in small towns will often choose to act in highly considerate ways. If they move to a large city, however, substantial transaction costs may have to be incurred to induce them to behave in an equally "public-spirited" manner.

Chapter 18

Inflation, Recession, and Unemployment: An Introduction

A. Multiple-Choice Questions on the Principal Ideas of Chapter 18

1. It is misleading to speak of inflation as "an increase in the cost of living" because
   A. inflation is basically an increase in the value or price of money.
   B. inflation is really only an increase in the average money cost of living.
   C. all prices do not increase at the same rate during an inflation.
   D. the cost of living is a biological fact unaffected by inflation.

2. Inflation imposes real costs upon at least some members of a society in which it occurs
   A. because it fosters resentment and thereby promotes social conflict.
   B. because it redistributes wealth and income.
   C. because it induces people to use up scarce resources in efforts to protect themselves.
   D. for all of the reasons above.

3. A recession is most adequately defined as a period during which
   A. the percentage of the population employed is declining.
   B. unintended or unexpected declines occur in employment, output, and income.
   C. the price level is declining.
   D. the rate of output of goods produced for sale to others is declining.

4. The unemployment rate as calculated by Statistics Canada is a highly subjective ratio because
   A. both the numerator and the denominator depend on people's assessment of the relative value to themselves of alternative opportunities.
   B. Statistics Canada calculates the ratio from interview data obtained from less than one-fifth of 1 percent of all the households in the nation.
   C. unemployed is a loaded word that many people don't like to apply to themselves.
   D. it is based on payment of unemployment compensation, and not all unemployed workers are eligible for unemployment compensation.

5. When we compare Canadian experience in the 1960s with that of the 1980s and 1990s, we find that in the latter period on average
   A. the unemployment rate was lower and the employment rate was higher.
   B. both the unemployment rate and the employment rate were significantly higher.
   C. both the unemployment rate and the employment rate were lower.
   D. the unemployment rate was higher and the employment rate was lower.

6. When the economy unexpectedly goes into a recession, the unemployment rate goes up because on average
   A. People are still expecting good times, economically, and search longer, looking for better jobs than are available.
   B. People are expecting bad times, economically, and search longer, looking for better jobs than are available.
   C. People are still expecting good times, economically, and search less, looking for worse jobs than are available.
   D. People are expecting bad times, economically, and search less, looking for worse jobs than are available.

B. Answers to, and Explanations of, Multiple-Choice Questions on the Principal Ideas of Chapter 18

1. **B**. Inflation is a decrease in the value or price or purchasing power of money. More money must be given up, as a consequence of inflation, to obtain food, clothing, shelter, and other goods. But this increase in the *money* cost of living is an increase in the *real* cost of living only for someone whose money income rises less rapidly than the rate of inflation. Because all prices (including wages) usually do not increase at the same rate as a result of inflation, some people will experience a rise in their cost of living. But the cost of living will fall during inflations for those who find the prices of the goods and services they sell increasing more rapidly than the average prices of the goods they buy.

2. **D**. Inflation introduces new and additional uncertainties for decision makers, who understandably want to protect themselves against losses of wealth or income. The private and political actions people take to defend their interests entail *real* costs.

3. **B**. The proportion of the population that is employed would decline if more people chose leisure in preference to more money income. The output of goods produced for sale would also probably decline under such circumstances. A recession is a decline in employment and output that does not fulfil, but rather frustrates, people's intentions. A fall in the price level is a deflation, but not necessarily a recession.

4. **A**. People choose whether to enter the labour force and whether to accept job offers by estimating the expected value to themselves of the various options available. The total unemployed and the total in the civilian labour force are therefore both subjective numbers, in the sense that people's choices change over time in response to changes in incentives. Those who erroneously believe that one cannot say anything with confidence about 30 million people by talking to only 55,000 households will have to study the theory of statistics; they will learn that the Statistics Canada sample is in fact extremely large. Unemployed is indeed a loaded word, and for that reason the household interviewers do not ask people to say whether or not they're unemployed. The widespread notion that unemployment data are derived from a count of those receiving unemployment compensation is incorrect.

5. **B**. In the 1980s and 1990s, a significantly larger percentage of the noninstitutional population wanted employment badly enough to either accept a job or actively look for one. This produced a higher employment rate. But when compared with the 1960s, a higher percentage of those who wanted employment in the 1980s and 1990s were looking rather than working, which produced a higher unemployment rate at the same time.

6. **A**. When a recession happens, it is because economic times are worse than people expect and their plans are frustrated. People searching for jobs expect, on average, to find better jobs than are available, and since they can't find what they like right away, they keep searching longer, until their expectations get in line with the new reality. When more people, on average, search longer, the overall unemployment rate will increase.

C. A Step-by-Step Review of Chapter 18

1. Inflation means that people

    A. have less money to spend.
    B. have fewer goods available to consume.
    C. must pay more money for the goods they purchase.
    D. must work harder to obtain the money they spend.

2. In an economy where all exchange occurs through barter arrangements, inflation

    A. would be almost impossible to stop once it had begun.
    B. could not occur.
    C. would occur if every seller demanded a higher price.
    D. would redistribute income.

3. The problems that inflation creates for the members of a society are caused primarily by

    A. greed on the part of sellers.
    B. uncertainty regarding the rate at which different prices are increasing or will increase.
    C. the inability of most people to afford the higher prices.
    D. greed on the part of union leaders.

4. Which of the following is an effect of *deflation*?

    A. It benefits low-income people.
    B. It causes problems for much the same reason as inflation does.
    C. It lowers the cost of living.
    D. solves the problems caused by earlier periods of inflation.

5. Disinflation is

    A. a slowing in the rate of inflation.
    B. an inflation not related to the value of money.
    C. the absence of inflation.
    D. the opposite of inflation.
    E. synonymous with "deflation".

6. A financial institution that wants a 4 percent *real* rate of return on its loans and expects a 2 percent annual inflation rate should make risk-free loans at a *nominal* interest rate of approximately

    A. 2 percent.
    B. 4 percent.
    C. 6 percent.
    D. 8 percent.

7. If the financial institution of the preceding question extends a 10-year loan at this interest rate, and then the inflation rate increases suddenly and unexpectedly to 6 percent per year, the institution will receive on its loan a real return of

    A. minus 2 percent.
    B. 0 percent.
    C. 6 percent.
    D. 10 percent.

8. Inflation redistributes income and wealth to people who

    A. receive incomes that are fixed by long-term contracts.
    B. sell commodities rather than labour.
    C. can increase the prices of the goods they sell more rapidly than the prices of the goods they buy are rising.
    D. are holding large amounts of money.

9. People who benefit from inflation are most often strongly opposed to inflation because

    A. they are trying to obtain sympathy from others.
    B. inflation is unfair to others.
    C. they don't realize they are benefiting from inflation.
    D. they know that no one can really gain from inflation.

10. The fact that inflation is often referred to as a "change in the length of the yardstick which we use to measure relative values" means that inflation

    A. has no effects in Canada because we use metres, not yards, to measure distance.
    B. has no net effects on the economy.
    C. causes the cost of comparing relative values to increase.
    D. enables people to predict more accurately.

11. Inflation tends to make the members of society

    A. more satisfied with their positions because they believe others are doing worse.
    B. more satisfied with their positions because they are earning more dollars as a result of inflation.
    C. less satisfied with their positions because they believe they are being defrauded by inflation.
    D. less satisfied with their positions because the cost of living has gone up.

12. Which of the following is most likely to be harmed by an *unexpected* disinflation?

    A. Creditors who have made long-term loans
    B. Creditors who have made short-term loans
    C. People who have borrowed heavily to purchase real estate
    D. Those who purchase entirely with cash rather than credit

13. A recession is a slowdown in the rate of increase in employment, output, and income that is

    A. large.
    B. prolonged.
    C. both large and prolonged.
    D. unintended.

14. The amount of unemployment that policymakers should *not* worry about because it constitutes no social problem is

    A. 2 percent of the labour force.
    B. 4 percent of the labour force.
    C. the amount that is due to people's choices among available alternatives.
    D. not any single amount that can be clearly measured.

15. The noninstitutional population does *not* include those members of the population who are

    A. under 15.
    B. attending school full-time.
    C. over 65.
    D. either under 15 or over 65 or attending school full-time.

16. The seasonal adjustment factor causes the number of people reported as unemployed after seasonal adjustment during the month of June to be

    A. constant from year to year.
    B. lower than the unadjusted figures.
    C. higher than the unadjusted figures.
    D. almost totally meaningless.

17. A person who refuses an offer of employment in order to keep looking for a better job is counted by Statistics Canada as
    A. not in the labour force.
    B. unemployed.
    C. a discouraged worker.
    D. eligible for unemployment compensation.

18. People who are not currently employed, but say they want a job, are counted as unemployed only if they
    A. have previously held a job.
    B. are actively seeking employment.
    C. are willing to accept a reasonable offer.
    D. are between 15 and 65 years of age.

19. The labour force participation rate in Canada over the past 15 years has
    A. declined as the work ethic has eroded.
    B. declined as rising incomes have encouraged people to choose more leisure.
    C. increased as much higher percentages of women have entered the labour force.
    D. increased as inflation-adjusted wage rates have fallen.

20. The teen-age unemployment rate in Canada is much higher than the unemployment rate among people over age 25 largely because
    A. most teenagers are attending school.
    B. most teenagers would like to have income from employment but also can survive comfortably without it.
    C. there are few jobs for teenagers.
    D. teenagers are lazy.

21. Unemployment in the Canadian economy when the economy is *not* in a recession is typically
    A. zero.
    B. not a social problem of any sort.
    C. the same for people regardless of age, race, or sex.
    D. lower than during recessions.
    E. unrelated to the generosity of Canada's unemployment and social programs.

22. Which of the following is *least* likely to lead to a rise in the unemployment rate?
    A. A higher rate of labour force participation
    B. An aging of the population that reduces the percentage of the population under 20 years of age
    C. More families with multiple earners
    D. More generous unemployment compensation benefits

23. When more people search longer for jobs, what happens to the unemployment rate?
    A. It declines because people who are engaged in job search are not included in the unemployment rate.
    B. It rises because people who are engaged in job search are always unemployed.
    C. It declines because there will, on average, tend to be fewer people unemployed while they are searching.
    D. It rises because on average more people will be remain out of work while they engage in job search.
    E. Nothing.

24. Why might people this year, on average, choose to search for a job for a shorter period of time than people did last year?
    (A.) If the demand for labour picks up unexpectedly, they will get better job offers than they expected, take the offers, and cut short their job search.
    B. If the demand for labour slacks off unexpectedly, they will get better job offers than they expected, take the offers, and cut short their job search.
    C. If the demand for labour falls off unexpectedly, they will get worse job offers than they expected, take the offers, and cut short their job search.
    D. If the demand for labour suddenly increases, they will get worse job offers than they expected, take the offers, and cut short their job search.

D. Answers to the Review Questions in Chapter 18

1. C	5. A	9. C	13. D	17. B	21. D
2. B	6. C	10. C	14. D	18. B	22. B
3. B	7. B	11. C	15. A	19. C	23. D
4. B	8. C	12. C	16. B	20. B	24. A

E. Employment and Inflation: Measures and Effects

1. Use the data provided below and the official Statistics Canada definitions to calculate each of the following:

Noninstitutional population	_____ million
Labour force	_____ million
Unemployment rate	_____ percent
Employment rate	_____ percent
Not in the labour force	_____ million

   Data:
   Total population   26 million
   Population under 15 years of age or in an institution   6.5 million
   Employed   12 million
   Unemployed   1 million

2. Suppose a lender wants a 4 percent per year real after-tax return on his investment. At what interest rate must he lend if his interest income is subject to a marginal tax rate on interest income of 25 percent?

   At what interest rate must he lend if, in addition, he expects a 5 percent rate of inflation over the period of the loan?

   At what interest rate must he lend if he expects an inflation rate of 8 percent?

3. Consider the data in Table 18.1 on the following page. The employees become unemployed in different months and remain unemployed for four months, searching for a new job, and then become employed again. What will happen to these data if the economy were to implement less generous social programs, thus reducing expected marginal benefits of search? What would happen to the overall unemployment rate in each period if each person were to choose to search one fewer month than before? [**E** means the person is employed; **U** means the person is unemployed and searching.]

Table 18.1   Individual Unemployment Data

Month: Person:	1	2	3	4	5	6	7	8	9	10	11	12
A	E	E	E	E	E	E	E	U	U	U	U	E
B	E	E	E	E	E	E	U	U	U	U	E	E
C	E	E	E	E	E	U	U	U	U	E	E	E
D	E	E	E	E	U	U	U	U	E	E	E	E
E	E	E	E	U	U	U	U	E	E	E	E	E
F	E	E	U	U	U	U	E	E	E	E	E	E
G	E	U	U	U	U	E	E	E	E	E	E	E
Total Unemployed:	0	1	2	3	4	4	4	4	3	2	1	0

F. Answers to Questions in Section E

1. Total population (26m.) minus all those under 15 or in an institution (6.5m.) = the noninstitutional population (19.5m.). The employed (12m.) plus the unemployed (1m.) = the labour force (13m.). The unemployed divided by the labour force defines the unemployment rate (7.7 percent). The employed divided by the noninstitutional population defines the employment rate (61.5 percent). The difference between the noninstitutional population and the labour force is the number "not in the labour force" (6.5m.).

2. With no inflation, he would receive 4 percent after taxes if he lent the money at 5.33 percent, because 5.33 times .75 (his after-tax share) is 4 percent.

    The nominal interest rate that would be required with a 5 percent inflation rate would be more than 5 percent greater because tax rates are levied on nominal as well as real interest income. In other words, he must pay tax on the "illusory" income that is simply a consequence of inflation. His after-tax return would have to be 9 percent if he is to receive a real return of 4 percent after deducting the 5 percent inflation rate. Consequently, he must charge a 12 percent nominal interest rate: twelve percent times .75 is 9 percent; then, subtracting the 5 percent fall in the value of money leaves a real after-tax return of 4 percent. So a 5 percent inflation rate boosts the nominal interest rate in this case by 6.67 percentage points to yield the same after-tax, real rate of return.

    Matters become progressively worse if the inflation rate accelerates. To receive a 4 percent real return he needs a 12 percent after-tax return when the inflation rate is running at 8 percent. So he must lend at 16 percent: with an 8 percent rate of inflation, then, the nominal interest rate must exceed the real interest rate not by 8 percent but by 12 percent, if he is to earn a real, after-tax rate of return equal to 4 percent. This growing wedge is the result of taxing nominal interest income.

3. The unemployment rate declines when people search less, as shown in the table below:

Month: Person:	1	2	3	4	5	6	7	8	9	10	11	12
A	E	E	E	E	E	E	E	U	U	U	E	E
B	E	E	E	E	E	E	U	U	U	E	E	E
C	E	E	E	E	E	U	U	U	E	E	E	E
D	E	E	E	E	U	U	U	E	E	E	E	E
E	E	E	E	U	U	U	E	E	E	E	E	E
F	E	E	U	U	U	E	E	E	E	E	E	E
G	E	U	U	U	E	E	E	E	E	E	E	E
Total Unemployed:	0	1	2	3	3	3	3	3	2	1	0	0

G. Questions to Think about

1. How would you evaluate this position: "The right to work is a basic human right that should be guaranteed to everyone"?

2. What groups in society are most likely to be hurt by inflation? What groups are most likely to be beneficiaries?

H. Answers to Questions in Section G

1. Remember that no one will actually have a right unless someone else accepts the appropriate obligation. Some have suggested that the government ought to function as the employer of last resort, providing jobs for all those who are unable to find jobs in the private sector. This proposal has in fact been endorsed by some leading political figures from all shades of the political spectrum. Where they differ is on the wage rate the government ought to offer when functioning as the employer of last resort. Should it be a wage just below the federal legal minimum wage? Or should it be a wage adequate to support a family? If the government offers a wage adequate to support a family to everyone who cannot find a job in the private sector how many people will the government have to hire? How many people now working at jobs near the minimum wage would continue in those jobs if government guaranteed employment at a higher wage? How many of the millions of adult Canadians not currently in the labour force at all would enter the labour force if employment were guaranteed to everyone at a wage adequate to support a family? The one thing you should learn from this question is never to use the phrase "right to work" without specifying the wage rare at which people are to be provided this right to work. The quantity demanded and the quantity supplied always vary with the price!

2. The standard answer to the first question is people on fixed incomes and creditors. But who are the people in our society on fixed incomes? The elderly? Many social benefits are now indexed, directly or indirectly, to the rate of inflation.

    How about creditors? They receive back, as a result of inflation, dollars of less value than the ones they lent out. This is typically said to constitute a loss. But why then do creditors continue to extend loans in periods of inflation? They learn to anticipate the rate of inflation and add it on to the rate of interest they're demanding. If the rate of inflation subsequently falls below what it had been expected to be, creditors will be gaining from inflation and debtors will start losing. All of this suggests that debtors, who are supposed to be beneficiaries of inflation because they can repay loans with depreciated dollars, will not necessarily benefit if the inflation is correctly anticipated. In general, it is going to be the case that those who predict inflation most successfully will be its beneficiaries, whereas those who do the poorest job of predicting will be hurt the most.

Chapter 19

Production, Prices, and Aggregate Fluctuations

A. Multiple-Choice Questions on the Principal Ideas of Chapter 19

1. Gross domestic product (GDP) is correctly described

    A. as the sum of the purchases in a year of new final goods by consumers, investors, government, and foreigners, minus purchases of imports by residents of Canada.

    B. as the income earned in the course of a year by all the producers of new goods.

    C. as the sum of the successive value added by producers in the course of contributing to the year's output of new goods.

    D. in each of the ways above.

2. If nominal GDP in a particular year is $770 billion while real GDP is $700 billion, we know that since the base year,

    A. real output has fallen 10 percent.

    B. real output has risen 10 percent.

    C. the price level has fallen 10 percent.

    D. the price level has risen 10 percent.

3. Can inflation and recession occur simultaneously in an economy?

    A. No, because prices cannot rise during a recession

    B. No, because recession is caused by too little demand and inflation by too much demand

    C. Yes, and this has happened several times in the Canadian economy since World War II

    D. Yes, but while it is logically possible, it has never actually happened in any major industrialized economy

4. According to national income and product accounting, total expenditure on new final goods equals by definition the gross domestic product;

    A. but total demand, in the sense of what people desire to spend, may be greater or less than total expenditure.

    B. but since total demand is sometimes greater or less than total supply, the accounting definition is incorrect.

    C. therefore, by definition, the total demand for goods always matches the goods supplied.

    D. however, this will not be true during periods of inflation or recession.

B. Answers to, and Explanations of, Multiple-Choice Questions on the Principal Ideas of Chapter 19

1. **D.** In national income accounting, total output and total income are, by definition, equal. And since all output is assumed to have been purchased by someone (producers are treated as if they "purchase" their own unsold output to add to their inventories), total expenditures on new final goods also must equal total output and total income.

2. **D**. The implicit GDP deflator is nominal GDP divided by real GDP and multiplied by 100. In this case it is 110, which indicates that the prices of goods produced in this particular year were 110 percent of what prices had been in the base or reference year.

3. **C**. If it were true that inflation results only from excessive total demand, and recession only from inadequate total demand, then it would be difficult to envision both occurring simultaneously. But since both have occurred simultaneously — most spectacularly in Canada in the early 1970s and again in the early 1980s — the total demand explanation is inadequate.

4. **A**. This point has confused many students of economics. In demand-and-supply analysis, the concepts always refer to intentions. So total demand means the expenditure that households, business firms, and government desire to undertake. If, however, business firms end up "purchasing" products of their own that they had counted on selling to others, they will have made some unintended expenditures; consequently, they will find themselves with larger inventories of finished goods than they want to hold. In response, they may well reduce their output. If households collectively want to buy a quantity of consumer goods greater than that supplied, they necessarily will find themselves at the end possessing fewer goods than they wanted to own. This often results when competition for the scarce goods raises prices such that households spend all the money they intended to spend but, in return, receive a smaller-than-anticipated quantity of real goods.

C.   A Step-by-Step Review of Chapter 19

1. Gross Domestic Product is the sum of annual purchases

    A. of new and used goods.
    B. by all consumers, business firms, government agencies, and foreigners (net of sales to residents of Canada).
    C. of final goods by consumers, investors, government, and foreigners (net of sales to residents of Canada).
    D. described in any of the three ways above.

2. How does a wheat farmer's contribution to national output get counted in the gross domestic product if Statistics Canada measures only the value of final goods, such as loaves of bread?

    A. It is counted separately by Revenue Canada.
    B. It is included in the cost of materials purchased by those who produce and sell loaves of bread.
    C. It is not counted, which results in an underestimation of the GDP.
    D. Wheat is also a final good because it is more ultimate than bread.

3. Total expenditure for new final goods equals total output of new final goods in the income and product accounts

    A. because no one will produce what cannot be sold.
    B. because prices will rise or fall to clear the market.
    C. because unsold goods are assumed to be purchased by the firms that produced them and added to their inventories of finished goods.
    D. only at equilibrium.

4. If economic development in a society causes a steadily rising percentage of the population to enter the labour force, measured gross domestic product will probably rise

    A. at the same rate as the rate of labour force participation.
    B. more rapidly than the actual production of useful goods is rising in the society.
    C. more slowly than the actual production of useful goods in the society.
    D. in proportion to the increase in real welfare.

5. If a city, in response to a rising crime rate, persuades a number of retired police officers to come back on the police department payroll, what effect will the rising crime rate have had on gross domestic product?

    A. No effect
    B. GDP will rise.
    C. GDP will fall.
    D. We cannot predict because criminal activities don't count in GDP.

6. Real GDP is

    A. nominal GDP minus services.
    B. nominal GDP plus capital goods production.
    C. nominal GDP valued at base-year prices.
    D. the material component of ideal GDP.

7. If you knew that nominal GDP increased 10 percent over a certain period while real GDP increased by 20 percent, you would know that

    A. inflation had occurred during this period.
    B. the price level had fallen by close to 10 percent.
    C. welfare had declined over this period.
    D. people were better off at the end than at the beginning of the period.

8. The implicit GDP deflator is

    A. nominal GDP divided by real GDP.
    B. nominal GDP times real GDP.
    C. real GDP divided by nominal GDP.
    D. the zero economic growth society.

9. As a measure of inflation, the principal advantage of the consumer price index over the implicit GDP deflator is that the consumer price index

    A. avoids double counting of goods.
    B. is adjusted to exclude wasteful expenditures.
    C. is calculated and published monthly.
    D. is more comprehensive.

10. Recessions in the Canadian economy show up in economic data as periods of

    A. declining prices.
    B. rising interest rates.
    C. slower growth or decline in nominal GDP.
    D. slower growth or decline in real GDP.

11. The data of Table 19.1 in the textbook show that

    A. inflation accelerates during recessions.
    B. inflation and recession do not occur at the same time.
    C. the inflation rate falls only at the beginning of a recession.
    D. none of the above is necessarily the case.

12. The data of Table 19.1 show that a dollar in 1991 purchased approximately half as many goods as it had purchased in

    A. 1964.   B. 1968.   C. 1972.   D. 1978.   E. 1985.

13. How many years did it take after 1970 for the output of the Canadian economy to double, according to the data of Table 19.1?

    A. 11   B. 18   C. 24   D. 29   E. 32

14. In what three-year period since 1950 has Canada experienced the most inflation?

    A. 1950-52   B. 1969-71   C. 1973-75   D. 1979-81   E. 1994-96

15. In what two-year period since 1950 has the rate of growth in the output of the Canadian economy been the lowest?

    A. 1954-55   B. 1969-70   C. 1974-75   D. 1980-81   E. 1990-91

16. The fear that total output might increase so fast that it will exceed total income

    A. assumes that machines are used extensively to produce output
    B. is based upon a misunderstanding of the relationship between output and income.
    C. is confirmed in every recession.
    D. was confirmed by the Great Depression of the 1930s.

17. Adam Smith and the great majority of economists up until the 1930s believed that concern for the sufficiency of aggregate demand was

    A. appropriate only for the leisure class.
    B. evidence of ignorance about economics.
    C. more important than concern for aggregate supply.
    D. the task of government.

18. The "Great Depression" of the 1930s laid to rest the notion that

    A. the economy's aggregate production is always adequate to satisfy aggregate demand.
    B. aggregate demand will always be large enough to buy whatever is being produced.
    C. inflation and recession cannot occur at the same time.
    D. machines will eventually replace labour in the production process.

D. Answers to the Review Questions in Chapter 19

1. C	4. B	7. B	10. D	13. B	16. B
2. B	5. B	8. A	11. D	14. C	17. B
3. C	6. C	9. C	12. D	15. E	18. B

E. Aggregate Measures And Concepts

1. Fill in the blanks in the table below, using your knowledge of the relationships among nominal gross domestic product, real gross domestic product, and the GDP deflator.

Year	Nominal GDP	Real GDP	GDP Deflator
1	$50 billion	$200 billion	_____
2	$180 billion	_____	75.0
3	_____	$300 billion	100.0
4	$480 billion	_____	150.0

2. The average annual rate of growth in real GDP from 1960 through 1996 was close to 3 percent per year. We can use this information along with the data of Table 19.1 in the textbook to construct a kind of aggregate success indicator for each year. We shall define it as the amount by which the real

growth rate exceeded the average growth rate (a negative number if it fell short of 3.0) minus the rate of inflation for that year. Thus the success indicator for 1960 would be 2.91 (the real GDP growth rate in 1960) minus 3.0 (the average real GDP growth rate) minus 0.84 (the rate of inflation in 1960). For 1960, this measure is -0.93.

By this standard, which were the most successful years from 1950 through 1996? Which were the least successful years?

F.   Answers to Questions in Section E

1.   The GDP deflator in year 1 would be 25.0. Real GDP in year 2 would be $240 billion. Nominal GDP in year 3 would be $300 billion. And real GDP in year 4 would be $320 billion.

2.   The year 1982 occupies the cellar in this list, and the entire period from 1980 through 1982 fared the worst by this measure. The second-worst year was 1974, and the two years 1974-75 also show dismal performances. In both 1974-75 and 1980-82 the Canadian economy suffered recessions with high inflation. The dramatic improvements in the "success indicator" after 1974-75 and again after 1980-82 were the result of a combination of much more rapid economic growth and a sharp fall in the inflation rate. The best years in this period came in the mid-1950s. The only years since then in which the so-called excess growth rate exceeded the rate of inflation were 1962 through 1965, 1984, and 1994.

Calculations of this sort should be used with caution. To begin with, it makes no sense to divide the data into periods of exactly one year running from January 1 to December 31. Remember, too, that the data are often quite rough. Above all, there is no justification for treating 2 percent of additional economic growth as the exact equivalent of 2 percent of additional inflation. The high inflation rates of the early 1980s, moreover, seem to have been more widely anticipated than the generally lower inflation rates of the early 1970s and may therefore have inflicted less real damage. Nonetheless, these calculations prompt a question: What happened after 1966 to make inflation rates so much higher? The explanation cannot be our greater success in dealing with recessions, because recessions after 1980 were, if anything, deeper than those in the 1950s or the 1960s.

A final consideration is that "excess growth rates" may not necessarily be good things for the economy. They may, in fact, be signs that the economy has been subjected to large, unanticipated increases in demand that have thwarted people's expectations. The readjustments to these unanticipated changes may lead to more future problems.

G.   Questions to Think about

1.   According to World Bank data, gross domestic product per capita in Canada is nearly 100 times as large as the per capita GDP of such countries as Bangladesh, Burma, Nepal, and Zaire. Do you believe the average person in these countries is really *that* much worse off than the average Canadian? Could someone even survive in Canada with such a low income? Then how do so many survive in the countries mentioned? Why are these numerical comparisons seriously misleading?

2.   The last section of Chapter 19 suggests that demand-side economics originated in the Great Depression of the 1930s. It actually has a much longer lineage. Adam Smith devoted considerable space as early as 1776 to attacking what he saw as the superficially plausible, but wrong-headed, view that a nation could increase its wealth by promoting the demand for its products. Since this notion is still widely held, you might want to reflect on it. Can a poor nation ever make itself prosperous by increasing the demand for its goods?

H. Answers to Questions in Section G

1. The issue here is not the poverty of the majority in these countries; that poverty is obvious. Rather, the question concerns the validity of comparing the per capita GDP of an industrialized economy (with its well-developed and highly utilized markets) with that of a country in which a far smaller part of people's consumption is obtained through the market. Per capita GDP in Canada was about $33,000 in 1997. However, much of that was unavailable for consumption because GDP includes military goods, investment goods, and so on. Per capita consumption expenditure in Canada usually runs around two-thirds of per capita GDP. So 1 percent of Canadian consumption would be about $220 per year. No one could survive in Canada on that little real income without some forms of assistance. Since this is an average (arithmetic mean), many people in these other countries would have to receive even lower annual incomes. This is impossible. People in these countries do in fact survive. For instance, the population growth rate of Bangladesh--one of the poorest countries--has been about 2.5 percent over the last decade. It follows that real income must be considerably larger than the numbers suggest. Quite likely much of the real output of poorer economies does not flow through markets and, hence, is not measured as a part of GDP.

2. There would be no poor nations in the world if increasing total demand were the necessary *and* sufficient avenue to prosperity because any nation could easily print more money and distribute the money to its citizens. An adequate demand may be *necessary* for economic growth and the maintenance of prosperity; but it cannot be a *sufficient* condition. Adam Smith was surely correct in insisting that the fundamental challenge for a nation in poverty is to increase productive capability. The question remains, however, why so much productive capacity sometimes sits idle in a society despite the fact that the members of the society are eager to obtain more goods and willing to work to obtain them. We will be trying to answer that question in the remainder of the book.

Chapter 20

The Supply of Money

A. Multiple-Choice Questions on the Principal Ideas of Chapter 20

1. Does the use of money increase the wealth of a society?
    A. Yes, because the more money the members of a society own, the more wealth they have
    B. Yes, because money is a form of wealth that can be produced at relatively low cost
    C. Yes, by making it less costly for people to specialize narrowly in the production of goods in whose production they have a comparative advantage
    D. No, because money is not wealth in itself but only represents as much wealth as it will purchase

2. Demand deposits but not savings deposits are included along with currency in the *narrow* definition of the money stock because
    A. people can and regularly do transfer the ownership of demand deposits to others as a way of making payments.
    B. most savings deposits cannot be converted into currency except with some advance notification to the financial institution, even though the institutions rarely enforce this restriction.
    C. every seller will accept demand deposits in payment for a transaction.
    D. demand deposits can be "cashed" or converted into currency.

3. The basic way in which the stock of money increases is through
    A. expanded output, because all output is simultaneously income.
    B. the printing of additional currency by the federal government.
    C. saving by the public, or the decision not to spend some part of income earned.
    D. a net expansion in the volume of loans made by financial institutions.

4. A chartered bank loan increases the stock of money
    A. as soon as the loan is made.
    B. only if the proceeds of the loan are not spent.
    C. only when the proceeds of the loan are withdrawn in currency.
    D. only when the proceeds of the loan are spent.

5. Every dollar added to the total reserves of the monetary system
    A. compels the financial institutions to reduce the value of their loans by one dollar.
    B. enables the financial institutions to expand their loans by one dollar.
    C. compels the financial institutions to reduce their loans by more than a dollar.
    D. enables the financial institutions, taken as a whole, to expand their loans by more than a dollar.

6. A purchase of government bonds from the public by the Bank of Canada
    A. takes reserves out of the monetary system.
    B. reduces the money stock by the amount of the purchase.
    C. increases the money stock directly and simultaneously increases the reserves of financial institutions.
    D. has the effect of pulling wealth and therefore money out of the private sector.

7. The legal requirement that chartered banks hold reserves equal to some fraction of their deposit liabilities

    A. acts as a constraint on bank lending.
    B. prevents runs on banks by depositors who fear that the banks may not have assets equal to their liabilities.
    C. is without significance because banks are not required to meet their liabilities on demand by depositors.
    D. is a substitute for the gold standard system under which banks were required to hold gold reserves.
    E. has been abandoned in Canada.

B. Answers to, and Explanations of, Multiple-Choice Questions on the Principal Ideas of Chapter 20

1. **C.** Money is wealth for a society insofar as it facilitates exchange and specialization. But beyond some point the creation of more money will merely result in a decline in the value of money.

2. **A.** Most transactions in the Canadian economy, measured in dollar value, are handled by writing cheques. This amounts to transferring ownership of some portion of a chequable deposit to someone else. Cheques are more often deposited than "cashed", or exchanged for currency, but they function as a medium of exchange in either case. Not all sellers are willing to accept cheques as a means of payment. But savings deposits have traditionally only rarely and under special circumstances been used as a medium of exchange. It used to be that you first had to convert them into either a chequable deposit or currency. This distinction is becoming increasingly blurred, however, and so many economists like to pay at least as much attention to the broader definitions of the money supply, such as M2 or M2+. Financial institutions rarely enforce a waiting period before giving you access to your savings deposits, even though the fine print on your savings account contract gives them the right to do so. Nowadays, waiting periods are regularly enforced only in the case of deposits, such as "guaranteed investment certificates", paying higher interest rates.

3. **D.** Expanding output means expanding income, but the flow of income (as Chapter 21 will stress) is not the same thing as the stock of money. The Bank of Canada issues additional currency and retires currency from circulation in response to the public's preference for holding currency relative to other forms of money (most notably, chequing deposits). The act of saving rather than spending money simply keeps financial wealth in the saver's possession rather than transferring it to someone else in exchange for goods or services.

4. **A.** A loan from a financial institution increases the stock of money by the amount of the loan. Whether the loan is taken as currency or as a demand deposit and whether it is held or spent does not have any initial effect on the total stock of money in existence.

5. **D.** A dollar of new reserves enables the monetary system to expand its loans by more than one dollar under a system in which banks may have liabilities equal to some multiple of their reserves.

6. **C.** When the Bank of Canada purchases a government bond, it pays with a cheque drawn on itself. When the seller of the bond deposits the cheque in a financial institution, and that financial institution forwards the cheque to the Bank of Canada, the Bank of Canada credits that institution's reserve account by the amount of the cheque. The seller of the government bond has that much additional money as a deposit, and the financial institution has excess reserves it can use as a basis for making new loans, which will expand the money supply further.

7. **E.** The primary function of reserve requirements in countries that have them is to set limits on the ability of banks to add to the stock of money by extending additional credit to borrowers. In Canada, there are no legal reserve requirements for financial institutions. Instead, the Bank of Canada operates

on its own understanding of what the *desired* reserve ratio is on the part of each of the financial institutions. One reason for this change in Canada is that financial institutions other than chartered banks have not had any legal reserve requirements, and the chartered banks argued they were at a competitive disadvantage as a result.

C. A Step-by-Step Review of Chapter 20

1. Economists today generally agree that

    A. inflation but not recession is linked to the working of the monetary system.
    B. recession but not inflation is linked to the working of the monetary system.
    C. neither inflation nor recession has any connection to the monetary system.
    D. inflation and recession are both linked to the working of the monetary system.

2. The alternative to using money as a medium of exchange is

    A. using chequable deposits.
    B. using currency.
    C. using either chequable deposits or currency.
    D. barter.

3. The most important medium of exchange in current use in Canada is

    A. minted coins.
    B. Bank of Canada Notes.
    C. chequable deposits.
    D. savings deposits.

4. Savings deposits are often counted as part of the money stock because

    A. sellers commonly accept them as a medium of exchange.
    B. they are highly liquid assets.
    C. they cannot be distinguished from demand deposits.
    D. banks hold the savings deposits as currency in their vaults.

5. A liquid asset is an asset that

    A. can be exchanged fairly quickly for other assets at a very low cost.
    B. no one person or institution owns.
    C. circulates through the economy until it reaches the same level everywhere.
    D. has a less certain value than a solid asset.

6. A quick, and usually efficient, way of determining what a particular society uses as money would be to find which asset

    A. is most commonly owned in that society.
    B. the government declares to be money.
    C. the people of that society refer to as money.
    D. is the most liquid in that society.

7. An increase in the demand-deposit liabilities of *chartered banks*, other things remaining equal, causes an increase of

    A. currency but not M1.
    B. M1 but not M2.
    C. M2 but not M1.
    D. both M1 and M2.

8. When the public puts currency into savings deposits in chartered banks
   A. M1 and M2 increase.
   B. M1 and M2 decrease.
   C. M2 increases but M1 does not change.
   D. M1 decreases but M2 does not change.

M1 = demand deposits & currency outside bank
M2 = M1 + everything

9. The average annual rate of increase in M1 and M2 in Canada from 1968 to 1997 was about
   A. 2 percent for M1 and 3.5 percent for M2.
   B. 8 percent for M1 and 10.5 percent for M2.
   C. 10 percent for M1 and 5 percent for M2.
   D. 10 percent for M1 and 20 percent for M2.

10. When financial institutions make loans to their customers, the stock of money
    A. does not change.
    B. increases.
    C. decreases.
    D. fluctuates unpredictably.

11. The ability of financial institutions to expand the stock of money is limited by
    A. the willingness of eligible borrowers to take out loans.
    B. the quantity of reserves held by the financial institutions.
    C. the desired reserve ratios of the financial institutions.
    D. all of the above.

12. Banks extend credit to borrowers by
    A. drawing down the currency in their vaults.
    B. creating new deposits based on the banks' excess reserves.
    C. giving them the chequing deposits of other depositors.
    D. giving them the savings deposits of other depositors.

13. The Bank of Canada can increase the excess reserves of chartered banks by
    A. shifting government deposits from itself to the chartered banks.
    B. extending credit to chartered banks.
    C. purchasing government bonds.
    D. any or all of the above means.

14. The transfer by cheque of a demand deposit into a bank with no excess reserves gives the recipient bank additional liabilities
    A. but not additional assets.
    B. but no additional reserves.
    C. but no excess reserves.
    D. and excess reserves.

15. A dollar of new excess reserves supplied to the monetary system enables the system to create
    A. less than a dollar of new money.
    B. exactly one dollar of new money.
    C. exactly ten dollars of new money.
    D. more than a dollar of new money.
    E. chaos.

16. The principal technique used by the Bank of Canada to adjust the excess reserves of chartered banks in order to control the growth of the money stock is
    A. exhortations and threats, also known as "immoral suasion".
    B. changes in the bank rate.
    C. changes in the legal reserve requirements.
    D. purchases or sales of government bonds.

17. The acquisition by the Bank of Canada of new income-earning assets previously owned by members of the public
    A. decreases chartered bank reserves.
    B. has no effect on chartered bank reserves.
    C. increases chartered bank reserves.
    D. reduces the national debt.

18. The term applied to the Bank of Canada's predominant day-to-day technique for controlling the stock of money is
    A. liquidity operations.
    B. open market operations.
    C. discounting operations.
    D. interest rate operations.
    E. reserve-supplementation operations.

19. If banks were required by law to hold reserves equal to some percentage of their deposits,
    A. banks would have to cut back on the number of security boxes they rent out.
    B. banks would be protected against insolvency because they would not be allowed to extend too many loans.
    C. bank depositors would not be able to obtain their funds when they want them.
    D. the monetary authorities would find it more difficult to control the growth of the money stock.
    E. none of the above.

20. The one essential quality that an asset must have if it is to function as money in a society is
    A. willingness on the part of people to accept it.
    B. backing by gold or some other asset with intrinsic value.
    C. legal tender status.
    D. stable purchasing power.

21. The best argument *for* re-establishing a gold standard in Canada is that
    A. doing so would limit the government's ability to increase the quantity of money in circulation.
    B. gold is durable, divisible, and intrinsically valuable.
    C. other nations will not hold Canadian dollars unless they can be redeemed in gold.
    D. the rest of the world is already on the gold standard.

22. The most cogent argument *against* re-establishing the gold standard in Canada is that
    A. it would impoverish producers of gold.
    B. it would make the prediction of future prices much more difficult.
    C. silver is the metal traditionally preferred in Canada.
    D. the government could easily suspend the gold standard whenever it constrained policy.

D. Answers to the Review Questions in Chapter 20

1. D	5. A	9. B	13. D	17. C	21. A
2. D	6. D	10. B	14. D	18. B	22. D
3. C	7. D	11. D	15. D	19. E	
4. B	8. D	12. B	16. D	20. A	

E. Central and Chartered Bank Actions and the Money Stock

A good way to clarify your understanding of the relationships among Bank of Canada policies, lending done by financial institutions, and changes in the stock of money is to trace their effects on the asset and liability positions of the Bank of Canada and of the monetary system taken as a whole.

Make the appropriate entries to show the effects of the following activities on the balance sheets of the Bank of Canada and on the balance sheets of financial institutions in monetary system. The answers provided on the next page in several instances assume that the financial institutions are satisfied to rest with an increase in their excess reserves. As a further exercise, ask yourself what would happen in each case if the financial institutions strove to have no changes in their excess reserve positions.

1. The Bank of Canada purchases $1 million in treasury bills from members of the nonbank public, paying with cheques drawn on itself. The cheques are deposited in the financial institutions, which, in turn, send the cheques through to the Bank of Canada for clearance.

2. Financial institutions use their new excess reserves as a basis for granting $0.8 million in new loans.

3. The Bank of Canada extends $1 million in new credit to chartered banks.

4. The Bank of Canada purchases a $1 million issue of new treasury bills directly from the federal government and gives the government a corresponding deposit at the Bank of Canada.

5. The federal government spends the proceeds of its new borrowing operation by writing cheques to the nonbank public. These cheques are deposited in chartered banks and trust companies. These financial institutions send them through to the Bank of Canada for clearance.

Bank of Canada		Financial Institutions	
Assets	Liabilities	Assets	Liabilities

F. Answers to Questions in Section E

Bank of Canada		Financial Institutions	
Assets	**Liabilities**	**Assets**	**Liabilities**
(1) +$1 million in treasury bills	(1) +$1million in reserve accounts.	(1) +$1 million in reserve accounts	(1) +$1 million in demand deposits
		(2) +$0.8 million in loans to customers	(2) +$0.8 million in demand deposits
(3) +$1 million in loans to chartered banks	(3) +$1 million in reserve accounts	(3) +$1 million in reserve accounts	(3) +$1 million borrowed from Bank of Canada
(4) +$1 million in treasury bills	(4) +$1 million in federal govt's account		
	(5) +$1 million in reserve accounts -$1 million in federal govt's account	(5) +$1million in reserve accounts	(5) +$1 million in demand deposits

G. Questions to Think about

1. Doesn't the federal government, and through it, the Bank of Canada, have the exclusive right to create money for this country? Why are privately owned institutions like chartered banks, trust companies, and credit unions allowed to create money?

2. What would happen if Parliament, in the next version of the Bank Act, required all chartered banks, trust companies, credit unions, and caisses populaires to hold reserves, either as vault cash or on deposit with the Bank of Canada, equal to 100 percent of their deposit liabilities?

H. Answers to Questions in Section G

1. Some people realized as early as the eighteenth century that banks could create money by making loans, but the process was not well or widely understood. And it was not until past the middle of the nineteenth century that policymakers discovered how deposits that could be transferred by cheque performed the principal functions of money. By the time we had acquired an adequate understanding of the relationship between banking practices and the money supply, the practices were long and well established. Disrupting a functioning system requires the creation of an alternative system, which isn't a simple task, especially if it is to be done in a fair as well as efficient manner.

2. If Parliament took such a politically unlikely step, it would thereby prevent financial institutions from adding to or contracting the money supply in the course of expanding or reducing their lending activities. This would probably result in giving the Bank of Canada more precise control over changes in the size of the money stock. As we shall see in subsequent chapters, the rate of growth of the money stock has important effects on inflation and unemployment, and has also proved extremely difficult to control in recent years. But competent observers disagree on whether the Bank of Canada has failed to manage the money supply effectively for want of the proper system, for lack of the proper understanding, or for lack of the proper desire and determination.

There is yet another issue to be considered. An asset becomes a medium of exchange in a society when members of that society choose to accept and use it as a medium of exchange. If the financial institutions that we think of today were controlled in the manner described, other institutions might find it profitable to try their hand at creating an acceptable medium of exchange. Any hard-to-counterfeit liability of a trusted institution that can be readily exchanged at an easily determined value could evolve into a major component of the society's stock of money. Great West Life Insurance, Canadian Tire, Charles Schwab, or Microsoft might experiment with issuing liabilities that the public would find advantageous to begin using, at least in some transactions, as a medium of exchange. Controlling the supply of money by law is difficult when money is essentially created by the voluntary transactions of issuers and users.

Chapter 21

Demand-Side Economics

A. Multiple-Choice Questions on the Principal Ideas of Chapter 21

1. Did the Great Depression of the 1930s contradict the predictions of economic theorists?

   A. Yes, because until the 1930s most economists had believed that recessions were impossible.
   B. Yes, because until the 1930s most economists had taught that recessions quickly generate forces that give rise to recovery when the decline has run its course.
   C. No, because most economists had long known that government action was required to reverse a recession once it had begun.
   D. No, because most economists had long believed that productive capacity could increase faster than the ability of people to purchase the output increased.

2. Which of the following was a central argument in Keynes's *General Theory of Employment, Interest and Money*?

   A. Competition does not allocate resources efficiently in a modern industrial economy.
   B. Full employment can be maintained even during a major recession if wage rates are lowered far enough.
   C. Modern industrial economies do not tend automatically toward full employment rates of output.
   D. Money does not play an important role in either causing or curing recessions.

3. The dominant opinion among economists before the 1930s was that recovery from recessions occurs automatically because

   A. higher interest rates encourage investment spending.
   B. the ratio of money balances to income and expenditures falls during a recession.
   C. the expectation of falling prices makes consumers and investors more optimistic.
   D. recessions create conditions that make spending increasingly more attractive as the recession continues.

4. In the Keynesian framework, fluctuations in output and income are caused primarily by sharp and sudden changes in

   A. consumer saving.
   B. consumer tastes and preferences.
   C. investment expenditures.
   D. government policies.

5. According to the perspective introduced by Keynes's *General Theory*, an increased desire on the part of the public to save

   A. may discourage investment by reducing the expected demand for new commodities and services.
   B. will produce a higher level of output and income by increasing investment.
   C. will produce a more rapid rate of economic growth by adding to the capital stock.
   D. will release resources from the production of goods for immediate consumption so that they can be used to produce goods that will increase future income.

6. Keynes's contention in *The General Theory* that government intervention might be necessary to maintain full employment or to restore it after a recession was based on the argument that

    A. business firms and consumers are no longer sufficiently eager to maximize their own net advantages.
    B. it might be in no one's interest to spend income at the rate necessary to achieve prosperity.
    C. people are too obsessed with present enjoyment to make adequate provision for the future.
    D. the rate of saving in an advanced industrial society is not adequate to support the necessary rate of investment.

7. An increase in the public's demand for money implies that

    A. people want to hold more currency and maintain larger average balances in their bank accounts.
    B. people want to increase their income without working longer hours.
    C. the price of money has risen.
    D. people are willing to give up leisure to obtain additional income.

8. People <u>add</u> to the quantity of money they hold by

    A. investing in income-earning assets.
    B. depositing currency in their savings accounts.
    C. reducing their expenditures below their income or exchanging other assets for money.
    D. withdrawing currency from their chequing accounts.

9. The quantity of money supplied by the monetary authorities

    A. will be equal to the quantity held by the public.
    B. may be greater than the quantity the public wants to hold.
    C. may be less than the quantity the public wants to hold.
    D. All of the above are true.

10. Increases in the quantity of money supplied eventually increase the quantity of money demanded

    A. because all money supplied must be held by someone.
    B. by causing people to expect the value of money to fall.
    C. by increasing nominal income and expenditures.
    D. by increasing the value of money.

11. The demand for money is stable if the

    A. public holds the same quantity of money regardless of the level of gross domestic product.
    B. size of the money stock is stable over time.
    C. value of money is stable over time.
    D. nominal gross domestic product is some fairly stable multiple of the money stock

B. Answers to, and Explanations of, Multiple-Choice Questions on the Principal Ideas of Chapter 21

1. **B**. Economists had generally maintained up until the experiences of the 1930s that recessions were temporary phenomena. As they ran their course, recessions supposedly created conditions that became increasingly favourable to a recovery. No government action was required, therefore, to restore prosperity, and government intervention was thought more likely to prolong the crisis than to end it. It has sometimes been said that economists before Keynes denied the possibility of recessions. This is an absurd assertion. But economists before and after Keynes, as well as Keynes himself, all denied that productive capacity could increase faster than the ability of people to purchase the production. Aggregate output cannot increase more rapidly than aggregate income or purchasing power, although it may well increase faster for a time than people's willingness to purchase is increasing.

2. **C**. Keynes had no quarrel with the efficiency of the competitive market economy — only with its ability to maintain a consistently high rate of output and employment. He sharply rejected the idea that unemployment was simply a matter of labour surplus that could be eliminated through reduced wage rates. Although his followers tended to deny the importance of money as a stabilizing or destabilizing force in the economy, this was not Keynes's position in *The General Theory* — as the full title of the book itself indicates. Keynes's central argument was that, in industrialized and affluent economies, full-employment rates of production are not guaranteed. Contrary to the teachings of traditional economics, unregulated economic systems do not recover quickly and automatically from recessions.

3. **D**. A recession results from an unexpectedly low rate of spending on newly produced goods. But as the recession continues, interest rates fall, money balances rise relative to income and expenditure levels, and prices decline (making it seem more likely that they will rise in the future rather than decline further). All these circumstances make increased spending a more attractive option for consumers and investors, an option whose attractiveness grows greater the longer the recession continues.

4. **C**. Keynes did not think that the behaviour of consumers or of government was as disruptive as the decisions of investors. The high degree of uncertainty attached to the expected return from investment plus the relative ease with which investment expenditures can be postponed made this component of total spending especially unstable, in Keynes's view.

5. **A**. Keynes disputed the long-accepted proposition that increased saving meant more resources for investment and, consequently, a growth in the capital stock and hence a more rapid rate of growth in output. His emphasis was on the possible failure of demand, which could in turn destroy the incentive to invest. Keynesian analysis focuses on the relationship among intended saving, intended investment, and total output or income. Actual saving and investment are always necessarily equal because any unanticipated change in one will compel a corresponding change in the other. An unanticipated increase in the saving rate, for example, will leave business firms holding larger inventories than they had anticipated, and the unintended addition to their inventories will be an addition to investment that must exactly balance the addition to the rate of saving. But as savers and investors adjust their actions to achieve desired rates of saving and investing, they alter nominal GDP, which in turn alters their "desires," until what savers want to save matches what investors want to invest. This analysis makes no use of relative price changes in explaining how a new "equilibrium" is achieved. Keynes also denied that changes in interest rates were likely to be effective, because saving depended much more on income than on the interest rate and because changing expectations tended to swamp any effect that changing interest rates might have on investment. Much of the empirical work in macroeconomics during the past thirty years has caused economists to shy away from such strong "Keynesian" conclusions. It appears, in fact, that investment *does* respond to interest rate changes; it appears, also, that price changes, changes in expectations, and monetary economics are very important. These results have given rise to "the new classical" or "modern" classical macroeconomics.

6. **B**. While we might all be better off if others spent more and saved less, we could each be worse off if we elected to increase spending and reduce saving. This is a variant of the free-rider problem explained in Chapter 16.

7. **A**. The demand for money is a demand to *hold* money. The desire to hold larger money balances is altogether different from the desire to earn additional income. A rise in the price of money means a rise in the purchasing power or value of money, which we would not associate with an increase in the demand for money.

8. **C**. The stock of money that anyone holds will increase if money flows in (income) at a faster rate than it flows out (expenditures), or if the person "reverses" a previous money expenditure, that is, sells an asset for money.

9. **D**. The quantity of money actually held by the public will necessarily be equal to the quantity supplied. But the quantity the public is actually holding at any time may be more or less than the quantity the public prefers to hold.

10. **C**. When the public is supplied with more money than it wants to hold, people try to reduce their holdings of money by increasing their expenditures for other goods. This will lead to an expansion of nominal gross domestic product. But at higher levels of GDP, the public is willing to hold larger money balances if the demand for money is stable.

11. **D**. A stable demand for money does not imply that the public wants to hold the same quantity of dollars under all circumstances but only that the public wants to hold dollars equal to some stable fraction of income or expenditures. This, in turn, implies that nominal GDP will be some stable multiple of the size of the money stock because the public will increase (or decrease) its spending on new goods when the money stock increases (or decreases) until it reaches the desired ratio of money balances to income or expenditures.

C.   A Step-by Step Review of Chapter 21

1. Real output and income in Canada declined from 1929-33 by approximately

    A. 15 percent.   B. 26 percent.   C. 34 percent.   D. 51 percent.

2. According to the official Statistics Canada income and product accounts, real output and income did not again reach their 1929 levels after falling in the post-1929 recession until

    A. 2 years later.
    B. 5 years later.
    C. 10 years later.
    D. after World War II.

3. From 1931 to 1939 the official unemployment rate in Canada averaged more than

    A. 9 percent   B. 13 percent.   C. 19 percent.   D. 30 percent.

4. The dominant view among economists before the 1930s was that recessions were

    A. the result of a maldistribution of income.
    B. caused by the extensive use of machinery.
    C. a temporary consequence of widespread but erroneous expectations.
    D. caused by labour unions.

5. One of Keynes's objectives in **The General Theory** was to take more adequate account than traditional theory had done of the role played in economic systems by

    A. changing prices.
    B. uncertain expectations.
    C. the maintenance of equilibrium.
    D. economists themselves.

6. Which of the following constitutes investment in the sense intended in Keynesian analysis?

    A. Purchase of a government bond
    B. Purchase of corporate stock
    C. Purchase of an old mansion
    D. All of the above
    E. None of the above

7. Which one of the following is *not* a component of total investment expenditure as measured in the income and product accounts?

   A. Purchases of new buildings
   B. Purchases of new business equipment
   C. Net additions to business inventories
   D. Undistributed corporate profits (retained earnings)

8. Relative to consumer expenditures on new commodities and services, investment spending tends to be

   A. stable because investors are typically wealthier than consumers.
   B. stable because so much of it is done by large companies.
   C. unstable because its timing depends so much upon predictions.
   D. unstable because investors are typically unstable people.

9. According to the dominant view of economists before Keynes, recovery from a recession is stimulated by

   A. large money balances and prices that are expected to fall.
   B. large money balances and low prices that are expected to rise.
   C. low money balances and prices that are expected to fall.
   D. low money balances and low prices that are expected to rise.

10. According to the dominant view of economists before Keynes, recovery from a recession is stimulated by

    A. the attractiveness of high interest rates to banks during a recession.
    B. the high interest rates that result from banks' refusals to lend during a recession.
    C. the low interest rates that result from a reduced demand for credit in a recession.
    D. government control over interest rates.

11. Keynes doubted the capacity of modern industrial economies to recover quickly from recessions

    A. because he believed that errors were often cumulative rather than self-correcting.
    B. because he believed that prices and wages were resistant to downward pressure.
    C. because he believed recessions undermine the confidence of potential investors.
    D. for all of the reasons above.
    E. for none of the reasons above.

12. The contention that the monetary authorities were only "pushing on a string" if they attempted to reverse a recession by increasing the reserves of the chartered banks implied that

    A. central banks could not control bank reserves during a recession.
    B. chartered banks would want to hold considerable excess reserves during a recession.
    C. chartered banks would waste money during a recession by lending it to firms that subsequently went bankrupt.
    D. central banks could not affect interest rates during a recession.

13. The classical view of the relationship between saving and investment held that

    A. saving and investment are identical.
    B. a high rate of investment will be the inevitable consequence of a high rate of saving.
    C. a high rate of saving is made possible by a low rate of investment.
    D. saving and investment are unrelated to each other.

14. The view associated with Keynesian analysis of the saving and investment relationship is that

    A. saving and investment are identical.
    B. a high rate of investment will be the inevitable consequence of a high rate of saving.
    C. a high rate of saving may undermine the incentive to invest.
    D. saving and investment are unrelated to each other.

15. The so-called *paradox of thrift* implies that
    A. the truest spendthrift is a person who saves.
    B. an individual who decides to spend more may as a consequence end up saving more.
    C. a society of people that decides to spend more may as a consequence end up saving more collectively.
    D. investment makes people worse off in the long run.

16. Keynes expressed his fear in *The General Theory* that in wealthy, industrialized societies, the public might chronically prove unwilling to
    A. save as much as it invested.
    B. want to save as much as it wanted to invest.
    C. invest as much as it saved.
    D. want to invest as much as it wanted to save.

17. *Supply-side economists* both before Keynes and after Keynes argued that a greater eagerness to save on the part of the public would lead to
    A. a high rate of investment and faster economic growth.
    B. a recession.
    C. an insufficient level of aggregate demand.
    D. inflation.

18. The concept of a demand for money refers to the quantity of money people want to
    A. A. consume.   B. hold.   C. purchase.   D. use.

19. Money and income differ, in that money is a
    A. necessary means for obtaining income.
    B. stock at a particular time, whereas income is a flow over a period of time.
    C. flow over a period of time, whereas income is a stock at a particular time.
    D. form of income but not the only possible form.

20. Someone who takes a second job thereby demonstrates an increased demand for
    A. income.
    B. money.
    C. both money and income.
    D. money balances.

21. Someone who decides to postpone the purchase of new furniture to see if prices are going to fall is probably demonstrating an increased demand for
    A. income.
    B. money.
    C. both money and income.
    D. furniture.

22. Money provides services to people
    A. only when it is earning interest.
    B. only when it is being spent.
    C. only when it is held.
    D. both when it is being spent and when it is held.

23. The act of holding money balances
    A. is wasteful because it deprives others of income.
    B. has no cost, or people wouldn't do it.
    C. must have no cost to the people who decide to do it.
    D. provides the people who do it a service more valuable to them than the cost of doing it.

24. The principal service that the holding of money provides to those who choose to hold it is
    A. the going rate of interest.
    B. power over others.
    C. the flexibility that accompanies liquidity.
    D. a more luxurious mode of living.

25. The quantity of money supplied to the public by the monetary authorities and banking system and the quantity of money actually held by the public
    A. may occasionally be unequal.
    B. will be equal only by rare coincidence.
    C. are equal only when the economy is in equilibrium.
    D. are always and necessarily equal.

26. The quantity of money supplied to the public by the monetary authorities and banking system and the quantity of money balances demanded by the public
    A. are completely unrelated.
    B. are always and necessarily equal.
    C. may differ substantially.
    D. will never be equal because people always want more money than they have.

27. Efforts on the part of the public to reduce its money balances
    A. may cause the quantity of money held by the public to fall below the quantity supplied to it.
    B. will cause the demand for goods other than money to increase.
    C. tend to cause recession or deflation.
    D. will reduce the stock of money.

28. If the monetary authorities increase the stock of money substantially at a time when the public is satisfied with its current holdings of money balances, the public's responses and adjustments will most surely lead to
    A. inflation.
    B. an increase in nominal gross domestic product.
    C. a decrease in nominal gross domestic product.
    D. a recession.

29. An increase in nominal gross domestic product when the demand for money has not changed leads to
    A. no change in the quantity of money balances demanded by the public.
    B. an increase in the quantity of money balances demanded by the public.
    C. a decrease in the quantity of money balances demanded by the public.
    D. an increase in the value of money.

30. An increase in nominal gross domestic product entails an increase in
    A. the price level.
    B. the production of commodities and services.
    C. one or the other of A and B above, but not both.
    D. one or both of A and B above.

31. Which of the following would show a stable demand for money?
    A. A fairly constant stock of money supplied to the public
    B. A fairly constant stock of money in the hands of the public
    C. A fairly constant ratio between the stock of money and nominal gross domestic product
    D. A fairly constant rate of spending by the public

32. People will ordinarily choose to hold smaller amounts of money when
    A. interest rates are high.
    B. they expect the price level to rise substantially in the near future.
    C. either of the above is the case.
    D. they have no pressing demand for goods that can be purchased with money.

33. If people come to expect very rapid increases in the price level in the near future, they will want to hold
    A. more money than before, thus causing the demand for other goods to increase.
    B. more money than before, thus causing the demand for other goods to decrease.
    C. less money than before, thus causing the demand for other goods to decrease.
    D. less money than before, thus causing the demand for other goods to increase.

34. If nominal gross domestic product rises in response to the creation of a larger money stock by the monetary authorities,
    A. real output will necessarily increase.
    B. inflation will inevitably occur.
    C. a recession cannot occur.
    D. none of the above is correct.

35. Economists who believe that the demand for money is stable usually argue that it is stable
    A. under all circumstances.
    B. in the short run but not in the long run.
    C. enough to permit the monetary authorities to control nominal gross domestic product with considerable precision.
    D. in the long run if monetary policy is properly managed.

D. Answers to the Review Questions in Chapter 21

1. C	6. E	11. D	16. D	21. B	26. C	31. C
2. C	7. D	12. B	17. A	22. D	27. B	32. C
3. B	8. C	13. B	18. B	23. D	28. B	33. D
4. C	9. B	14. C	19. B	24. C	29. B	34. D
5. B	10. C	15. C	20. A	25. D	30. D	35. D

E. Changes in Money Supply and Demand: Processes and Effects

1. (a) If the public wants to hold money balances (M1) equal to 15 percent of nominal GDP, and the Bank of Canada sets and holds the money supply at $90 billion, toward what level will GDP move? Why? By what process?

   (b) If the Bank of Canada allows the money supply to grow by 10 percent and if the demand for money remains unchanged, toward what level will GDP move?

(c) How will this increase be distributed between real GDP and prices?

2. (a) Assume that the stock of money in the hands of the public is $90 billion, nominal GDP is $600 billion, and the public wants to hold money balances equal to 15 percent of GDP. Then, as a result of a widespread shift in expectations (perhaps people begin to anticipate a severe recession), the demand for money increases: The public now wants to hold money balances equal to 16 percent of GDP. If the Bank of Canada holds the money stock steady at $90 billion, toward what level will nominal GDP move? Why? By what process?

(b) How will this change be distributed between real GDP and prices?

(c) Suppose the Bank of Canada now regrets its decision to maintain the money supply at $90 billion and so takes steps to raise it to $96 billion. If the public continues to want to hold money balances equal to 16 percent of GDP, toward what level will nominal GDP rise?

(d) How will this rise in GDP be distributed between real GDP and prices?

F. Answers to Questions in Section E

1. (a) If GDP is larger than $600 billion, the public will be holding less money than it wants. As it tries to increase its money balances by reducing expenditure, GDP will fall. If GDP is less than $600 billion, the public will be holding more money than it prefers to hold. The attempt to reduce its money holdings will increase GDP.

(b) $99 billion is 15 percent of $660 billion. Until the GDP is $660 billion, the public will not be willing to hold $99 billion in money balances.

(c) Who knows? If an economy were the simple mechanism that some models indicate, the increase would be entirely reflected in real GDP until "full employment" output had been attained. After that it would cause inflation. But this is much too simple and optimistic, as we shall see in subsequent chapters.

2. (a) With only $90 billion available, nominal GDP would have to fall to $562.5 billion for the public to hold money balances equal to 16 percent of GDP. The attempt by the public to increase its money balances would fail; the attempt would instead reduce expenditures, and hence GDP, until the public was willing to hold the quantity of money available to it.

    (b) There are good reasons, such as prices and wages that resist downward pressure, to predict that most of the decline in nominal GDP would come about through a fall in real GDP.

    (c) Nominal GDP would return to $600 billion, which is $96 billion divided by 16 percent.

    (d) It would be a most fortunate but quite unlikely occurrence if real GDP bounced back to its previous level. Why should it? The frustrated expectations that produced the original decline in output will not be immediately and smoothly fulfilled when the Bank of Canada expands the money supply.

All of this is extremely simplified. The following chapters will introduce some of the more important complications.

G. Questions to Think about

1. Is it possible for the total output of new goods to be greater than the total income available for purchasing those goods? Is it possible that people could have enough income to purchase the total output of new goods but not desire to purchase everything that has been produced? What would be happening in such a case to the demand for money?

2. Suppose that people suddenly become more anxious and uncertain about the future and try to protect themselves by increasing their liquidity. How could this provoke a "liquidity crisis"? What occurs in a society in which almost everyone is trying to achieve a more liquid position?

3. Can an economic system be in equilibrium if 15 percent or more of its labour force is unemployed and the rate of current output is less than 75 percent of the rates of output achieved in earlier years?

4. What is the precise difference between the two seemingly contradictory assertions below?
    "The economy does not recover automatically from recessions."
    "Recessions are short-run phenomena from which recovery occurs automatically.

H. Answers to Questions in Section G

1. The total income generated in the production of new goods is necessarily equal to the total value of that output. But the ability to purchase is not the same as the desire to purchase. People who decide to purchase goods at a lower rate than the rate at which they are receiving income will be adding to their holdings of money. An increased demand for money is therefore the same thing as a decreased demand for goods other than money. Turning the analysis around, if a recession is regarded as an unexpected decline in the aggregate demand for goods other than money, it can be regarded as an unexpected increase in the aggregate demand for money.

2. Individuals increase their liquidity by selling other goods for money or by adding to their money holdings by reducing the rate at which they acquire other goods with money income. But every sale entails a purchase, and every reduction in purchases entails a reduction in sales. Each person's determination to hold more money and less of other goods makes it more difficult for others to sell goods in order to acquire money. If no additions are made to the stock of money at a time when the

public wants to enlarge its money holdings, the public will not be able to achieve that objective. Instead, the prices of assets other than money will tend to fall, as more are offered for sale while fewer are wanted.

Would price declines of this sort eventually induce people to increase their purchases of other goods; that is, to reduce their desire for liquidity? The key to understanding this situation is *expectations*. If people expect prices to fall even further, they will not want to reduce their liquidity. But if they think prices have fallen about as far as they are going to fall, they will begin to think about taking advantage of the lower prices.

3. The concept of an equilibrium for an entire economic system may be much too vague and ambiguous to be useful. (Chapter 27 will warn against the use of the equilibrium concept in talking about the international balance of payments.) In referring to a state of affairs as a "disequilibrium," we usually intend to call attention to some process operative in the situation that will change the present state of affairs in some predictable direction. "That's not an equilibrium price" is a statement that usually implies the quantities buyers want to purchase and sellers want to provide are not matched at the current price, so that competition among buyers or among sellers will begin pulling the price up or bringing it down. But what exactly might someone mean by saying that the entire Canadian economy is or is not "in equilibrium"? It might be much better to abandon the equilibrium concept in this context in order to ask specifically what we can or cannot expect to occur with unemployment at 15 percent or GDP far below previous levels. But purely verbal disputes rarely settle anything about the way the world actually works.

4. Here is another example of what may be a purely verbal disagreement. A person making the first statement may actually be saying, "The economy does not recover automatically from recessions in a sufficiently short period of time." That doesn't necessarily contradict the second statement. The issue to be examined in that case becomes the length of time that elapses before a recession ends and a recovery begins, or before the recovery carries income and output back up to pre-recession levels. This way of posing the issue leads to the important question, "Can government intervention shorten that time period?" Keynes assumed in *The General Theory* that it could and was sharply critical of those who recommended that nothing be done to interfere with the "natural" working of the economy. Experience in recent years suggests that the consequences of deliberate government policies to check recession and accelerate recovery are somewhat different from what Keynes, and especially his followers, believed or hoped. (These issues are further explored in subsequent chapters.)

Chapter 22

Fiscal and Monetary Policy

A. Multiple-Choice Questions on the Principal Ideas of Chapter 22

1. Why is a large federal budget deficit likely to be accompanied by a rapid rate of growth in the money stock?

   A. Extensive borrowing by the federal government will tend to crowd out private borrowers unless the Bank of Canada increases chartered bank reserves.
   B. People who fear the inflationary effects of the deficit will be less willing to hold money.
   C. The federal government finances deficits by printing new money.
   D. The federal government always sells new bond issues to the Bank of Canada in order to hold down borrowing costs.
   E. Both A and B are correct.

2. The timing lags that must be predicted and controlled if aggregate demand management is to be an effective stabilization technique are the lags between

   A. the onset of a problem and recognition of the problem.
   B. recognition of a problem and action to deal with the problem.
   C. action to deal with a problem and its effects on spending and output decisions.
   D. all of the above.

3. Changes in tax rates or in government expenditures are unlikely to be effective stabilization techniques because

   A. fiscal policy has been conclusively shown to have no effect on aggregate spending.
   B. monetary policy usually cancels out the effects of fiscal policy.
   C. the political process through which proposed tax or expenditure changes must pass is too slow and too subject to conflicting pressures.
   D. aggregate expenditures on new goods are always, and by definition, equal to total output and income.

4. Automatic or nondiscretionary fiscal policy will operate to stabilize aggregate spending if

   A. Parliament is required by law to balance the budget each year.
   B. Cabinet grants the Bank of Canada authority to raise or reduce tax rates unilaterally.
   C. government appropriations are assigned by formula to areas with high unemployment rates.
   D. tax receipts are dependent on income levels.

5. From the standpoint of those who want discretionary aggregate-demand management by government, monetary policy has one clear advantage over fiscal policy in that it

   A. can be implemented quickly without delays imposed by the democratic political process.
   B. depends entirely on the use of techniques that are now well understood and thoroughly under the control of the aggregate-demand managers.
   C. leads to rapid and predictable changes in total spending.
   D. requires less accurate forecasting of economic events to be stabilizing rather than destabilizing in its effects.

6. What will be the effect on interest rates if the Bank of Canada increases the rate at which it's supplying reserves to the commercial banking system?

    A. Interest rates will fall because interest is the price of money and this policy increases the supply of money.
    B. Interest rates will fall if the Bank of Canada's action induces an economic expansion.
    C. Nominal interest rates may fall, but real interest rates will almost certainly rise.
    D. Economic theory cannot predict the effect with any confidence without more information.

7. If the federal government is to be able to use aggregate demand management to secure high levels of output and employment without inflation, it must be able to influence

    A. nominal gross domestic product.
    B. real gross domestic product.
    C. the price level.
    D. real gross domestic product and the price level independently of each other.

8. Recessions and the increased unemployment that accompany them are the consequences of

    A. high income levels that encourage excessive saving.
    B. high interest rates imposed by the central bank to stop inflation.
    C. inadequate rates of government spending on new goods and on transfer payments.
    D. mistaken predictions on the part of business firms and workers.

9. Which of these factors is likely to have contributed to the increased (comparative) stability of the Canadian economy in the 25 years immediately following World War II?
    A. Improved techniques of monetary management that eliminated liquidity crises caused by financial panics
    B. The stabilization of personal expenditures brought about by higher income levels and a progressive income tax
    C. The stabilization of personal consumption expenditures brought about by higher wealth levels and by a tax and transfer system that dampens the impact of aggregate income changes on the income available to consumers
    D. All of the above

B. Answers to, and Explanations of, Multiple-Choice Questions on the Principal Ideas of Chapter 22

1. **A**. During the Great Depression of the 1930s, the federal government probably could have borrowed extensively and run large deficits without depriving private borrowers of many opportunities to obtain credit or raising the cost to them (the interest rate) significantly. Throughout the 1930s, most chartered banks were holding large excess reserves that the government could have tapped to finance much larger deficits than it did in fact run. Moreover, the 1930s was a decade of extensive unemployed and underemployed resources. But no year since World War II has even come close to duplicating this setting. In fact, extensive government borrowing for roughly the two decades from 1975 until 1995 competed directly against private borrowers. When the Bank of Canada expands bank reserves, it prevents a credit shortage from rationing scarce resources. But the real resources for which governments and private borrowers are competing remain scarce. If they are not rationed by rising interest rates, they will be rationed by rising prices that have been fueled by the increased stock of money that Bank of Canada policies make available. In the end, interest rates will rise anyway in response to expectations of inflation. (Chapter 27 will suggest that investment in Canada by foreigners may have prevented some of these dire consequences of the *crowding out* phenomenon.)

2. **D**. Each of these lags taken separately poses a significant challenge to those who want to time fiscal or monetary actions appropriately. Taken together, they may present a nearly insurmountable obstacle to stabilization policies relying on discretionary aggregate demand management.

3.   **C**. Perhaps if economists were rulers (and didn't have lots of meetings and discussions!), tax rates or expenditure projects could be altered quickly enough to make discretionary fiscal policy an effective instrument for stabilizing the level of total expenditures. But in view of the problems presented by all the other time lags plus the uncertainty of most economists about just how fiscal policy works out in practice, we may be fortunate that tax and expenditure policies have to fight their way through all the obstacles of the democratic parliamentary process.

4.   **D**. The requirement of an annually balanced budget would compel a discretionary fiscal policy when fluctuations occurred in aggregate income. That's because tax revenues automatically decline during recessions, generating a deficit, while rising and generating a surplus during periods of prosperity. Nondiscretionary fiscal policy allows the automatic deficits and surpluses that appear — because tax revenues depend on income — to occur and to exert a stabilizing counter pressure on recessions and recoveries.

5.   **A**. The monetary managers are somewhat insulated from partisan or popular political pressures, so that monetary policies can be activated much more promptly than can fiscal policies. This would be a more heartening truth if it were not for the facts that the techniques of money management have not been thoroughly mastered, no one yet knows how to predict the timing of the changes that monetary policy induces in total spending, and a stabilizing, rather than destabilizing, monetary policy may require better forecasting than anyone currently knows how to do.

6.   **D**. Whether interest rates will rise or fall as a consequence of an expansionary monetary policy is going to depend on how the increased supply of credit affects the demand for credit. Interest is the price of credit; the price of money is its purchasing power. If the expansionary policy creates inflationary expectations, nominal interest rates will rise to take account of these expectations even if real interest rates remain constant or even decline. Typically, the short-run effects of *unexpected* increases in the rate of growth of the money supply lead to lower interest rates; and the longer-term effects of *expected* increases in the money supply lead to higher interest rates.

7.   **D**. Few, if any, economists doubt that some combination of fiscal and monetary policies, pursued with sufficient persistence, vengeance, or surprise can alter the level of nominal gross domestic product. But an increase in nominal GDP could mean an increase in real output or it could mean a mere increase in the price level. The trick — the very difficult trick that just possibly cannot be performed, especially not with demand-management policies — is to push real output up without causing inflation and to halt a rise in the price level without causing a recession.

8.   **D**. A recession is an unpredicted and therefore disruptive slowdown in the rate of increase in output and employment. Such a slowdown could be, but is not necessarily, caused by any one factor such as higher interest rates, increased saving, or reduced government expenditures.

9.   **D**. Canada's social programs and progressive income tax have provided strong built-in, or non-discretionary, stabilizers. When overall income levels increase, inflationary pressures are relieved somewhat as people must pay higher taxes and some people receive less in government transfer payments. And when incomes drop, tax collections fall a bit and transfer payments increase, so people don't have to cut back on their consumption spending as much as they would have in an economy without these built-in stabilizers. At the same time, the Bank of Canada is doing a better job of controlling the rate of growth of the money supply.

C.   A Step-by-Step Review of Chapter 22

1.   Fiscal policy means

    A.   real or physical policy as contrasted with monetary policy.

    B.   budget policy.

    C.   deficit financing.

    D.   direct control over relative prices and wages.

2. Aggregate-demand management by means of fiscal policy aims at controlling undesired fluctuations in output and income by changing

    A. the rate of growth of the money stock.
    B. interest rates.
    C. government expenditures and taxes.
    D. profit expectations.

3. Monetary policy aims at controlling undesired fluctuations in aggregate output and income by controlling

    A. relative prices and wages.
    B. currency in circulation.
    C. consumer spending.
    D. chartered bank reserves, which are used as a basis for creating more loans.

4. Monetary policy was used more frequently and consistently than fiscal policy as a stabilization tool in the quarter century following World War II because

    A. most economists thought it was more powerful.
    B. it could be used without changing the beliefs of members of Parliament or the voting public.
    C. monetary policy was known to be more effective against recessions.
    D. it had demonstrated its effectiveness during World War II.

5. When the Bank of Canada buys Canadian treasury bills to help the federal government finance its government expenditures, the Bank of Canada is

    A. adding additional money to the money stock.
    B. adding additional reserves to the stock of commercial bank reserves.
    C. expanding the money stock directly and also adding to the reserves of commercial banks.
    D. causing the price of money to rise.

6. Deficit spending by the federal government will necessarily

    A. reduce the public's holdings of money balances.
    B. raise interest rates.
    C. add to the money stock.
    D. produce some combination of the above effects.

7. In order to move aggregate demand to the level consistent with "full employment" by means of fiscal policy, government officials who set the budget must know

    A. the current level of aggregate demand.
    B. the level of aggregate demand that would be consistent with full employment.
    C. the size of the budget changes required to induce the appropriate-sized changes in aggregate demand.
    D. all of the above.

8. The length and nature of the time lags between fiscal or monetary policy actions and their effects on total spending

    A. can be determined by theory.
    B. can be learned through careful empirical measurement.
    C. can be established by conducting experiments.
    D. may turn out to vary in ways that cannot be predicted.

9. Which of the following is the most serious obstacle to obtaining reliable information on the time it takes for fiscal or monetary policies to have their full effects on private spending and production decisions?

    A. Inadequate data
    B. Insufficiently powerful computers
    C. Lack of interest in the question
    D. The fact that the time lag varies as more or less information becomes available to the public

10. If the prime minister had the legal authority to alter tax rates within certain limits or to initiate spending projects previously approved by cabinet whenever s/he and cabinet concluded that aggregate demand was inadequate, fiscal policy would become a much more effective

    A. companion to monetary policy.
    B. stabilization tool.
    C. tool for influencing the outcome of elections.
    D. weapon against inflation.

11. The common belief that fiscal policy has proved its effectiveness as a stabilization tool in the years since the 1930s is based

    A. on Keynes's *General Theory*.
    B. in large part on a failure to distinguish between stimulus and stabilization.
    C. on the continuous use, by Parliament, of counter-cyclical fiscal policy in the years after World War II.
    D. on the high levels of physical output since the end of the 1930s.

12. The government's budget can contribute toward reducing the effects on total demand of changes in private spending decisions

    A. only if tax rates and appropriations for expenditures are altered in a counter-cyclical direction.
    B. if the government maintains a balanced budget at all times.
    C. if deficits are allowed to occur during recessions and surpluses are allowed to occur during boom periods.
    D. whenever Parliament and the cabinet determine to use the budget for this purpose.

13. If the Bank of Canada makes errors in its use of monetary policy,

    A. it matters very little because the Bank of Canada can quickly shift the direction of its policies.
    B. the Bank of Canada creates destabilizing uncertainties for other decision makers.
    C. the Governor of the Bank of Canada will sustain financial losses.
    D. it may cause inflation but it cannot cause recession.

14. The Bank of Canada is independent of the government of the day in the sense that its managers

    A. ignore the preferences and pressures of elected officials.
    B. can be fired by cabinet, but they have considerable latitude in their decisions since firing them (or insisting on their "resignation") would likely cause quite a political stir.
    C. are chosen by the banking community rather than by Parliament.
    D. are under the control of the private sector of the economy.

15. In addition to the supply-siders' preference for controlling commodity prices, the two principal options that are argued for by those who disagree about the direct targets that monetary policy should aim to control are

    A. monetary aggregates versus interest rates.
    B. chartered bank reserves versus central bank reserves.
    C. the overnight money market rate versus the Bank rate.
    D. the unemployment rate versus the inflation rate.
    E. the *real* versus the *nominal* interest rate.

16. Interest rates are
    A. the price of money and they fall when money becomes more scarce.
    B. the price of money and they rise when money becomes more scarce.
    C. not the price of money; the price of money is its value or purchasing power.
    D. the price of money, but a price controlled by lenders rather than the Bank of Canada.

17. A more rapid rate of increase in the money stock
    A. will not affect interest rates.
    B. will reduce interest rates because it increases the supply of credit.
    C. will raise interest rates because it increases the demand for credit.
    D. may produce higher or lower interest rates depending on its relative effects on the supply of and demand for credit.

18. Inflation will produce higher nominal interest rates if it
    A. reduces the value of money.
    B. produces a recession.
    C. causes borrowers and lenders to expect future declines in the purchasing power of money.
    D. prompts people to believe that prices have risen as far as they're likely to rise and will soon fall.

19. The real interest rate is equal to the nominal interest rate
    A. minus the average return on investment.
    B. minus the expected rate of inflation.
    C. plus the expected rate of inflation.
    D. plus the appropriate risk premium.

20. The very high nominal interest rates that appeared in the late 1970s and 1980s were produced primarily by
    A. tight money policy.
    B. inflationary expectations.
    C. rapid economic growth.
    D. the monopoly power of banks.

21. Those economists who want the Bank of Canada to ignore interest rates in executing monetary policy argue that
    A. interest rates are not important.
    B. the attempt to stabilize interest rates interferes with the more important task of stabilizing the monetary aggregates.
    C. no one knows what interest rates are until it's too late.
    D. setting interest rates is properly the job of cabinet, not the Bank of Canada.

22. Can government attempts to stabilize aggregate demand actually cause it to be less stable?
    A. Hardly
    B. Yes, because the government messes everything up
    C. Not if government officials accept the advice of economists instead of sociologists
    D. Yes, because shifts in government policy can increase uncertainty for private decision makers

23. Which of the major monetary aggregates seems to be the best leading indicator of future changes in real GDP?
    A. M1
    B. M2
    C. M2+
    D. M3
    E. M16

24. Since World War II, personal consumption expenditures have been

    A. a major source of aggregate-demand fluctuations.
    B. a steady and stabilizing component of aggregate demand.
    C. a highly unstable component of aggregate demand.
    D. insufficient to maintain full employment.

25. Highly aggregative economic theories

    A. were widely used by economists prior to the Great Depression in the 1930s.
    B. help us understand the role of uncertainty in causing economic fluctuations.
    C. have been useful in enabling policymakers to "fine-tune" the economy.
    D. All of the above are true.
    E. None of the above is true.

D. Answers to the Review Questions in Chapter 22

1. B	6. D	11. B	16. C	21. B
2. C	7. D	12. C	17. D	22. D
3. D	8. D	13. B	18. C	23. A
4. B	9. D	14. B	19. B	24. B
5. C	10. C	15. A	20. B	25. E

E. Nominal and Real Interest Rates

The rate of return on short-term Canadian government bonds is a fairly good indicator of the nominal interest rate at any time. Because there is no appreciable risk of default on these financial assets, and the costs of arranging the transaction (a loan to the federal government) are trivial, the yield on government bonds approximates the "pure" (nominal) interest rate. Table 22.1 on the next page shows, for the beginning of selected years, the average annual yield on one-to-three year Canadian government bonds and the average annual inflation rate in Canada as measured by year-on-year rates of change in the CPI:

1. What was the real rate of return on these bonds in the years shown? Calculate and write your answers in the right-hand column of the table.

2. Why did investors agree to lend money in 1975 at a real interest rate of minus 5.74 percent?

3. When the inflation rate again jumped up to 12.05 percent in 1981, the yield on these bonds was 6.9 percentage points higher than it had been in 1975, when the inflation rate was "only" 11.9%. Why?

4. When the inflation rate declined sharply from 1983 through 1986, the interest rate on these bonds declined much more slowly. Why did investors demand a nominal return of roughly 10 percent in order to hold government bonds from 1983 to 1986?

5. Why was the real rate of return so high from 1989 through 1993, and why did it decline in the late 1990s?

Table 22.1

Year	Yield (in %)	Inflation Rate (in %)	Real Rate of Return
1960	4.89	1.10	
1965	4.01	2.06	
1970	7.95	4.80	
1971	5.05	1.25	
1972	4.76	4.94	
1973	5.48	5.49	
1974	6.75	9.29	
1975	6.16	11.90	
1976	8.13	9.73	
1977	7.57	6.09	
1978	7.70	9.14	
1979	10.08	8.61	
1980	12.79	9.69	
1981	13.06	12.05	
1982	15.95	11.29	
1983	10.28	8.37	
1984	10.23	5.35	
1985	10.27	3.67	
1986	9.88	4.35	
1987	7.85	3.91	
1988	9.04	4.14	
1989	10.58	4.34	
1990	10.81	5.43	
1991	10.09	6.90	
1992	7.54	1.54	
1993	7.09	2.12	
1994	4.18	1.28	
1995	8.85	0.59	
1996	5.48	1.65	
1997	4.28	2.10	
1998	4.90	1.12	
1999	4.83	0.65	

F. Answers to Questions in Section E

1. Subtract the inflation rate from the nominal yield rate to obtain the real rate of return. Some people prefer to call this the "realized" rate of return because it is the yield that investors realized, after the fact, on their investment. It is not necessarily the "real" yield they *expected* to receive when they bought T-bills. This real, or realized, rate of return ranged from 3.79 percent in 1960 down to minus 5.74 percent in 1975 and up to 6.6 percent in 1989 and 7.26 percent in 1995.

2. They did not expect the inflation rate to be anywhere near that high in 1975. The table shows the real interest that was actually received (the "realized" rate of return); but lenders (and borrowers) made their decisions in 1975 on the basis of their expectations about inflation. The real interest rate, as distinct from the after-the-fact (or "realized") rate of return, is the nominal interest rate minus the *expected* rate of inflation.

3. Investors learn from experience, and they alter their expectations as their experiences change. By 1981, after having experienced serious inflation for several years, they no longer believed it was prudent to hold government bonds that were paying only 6.16% percent a year.

4. Experience in the 1970s and the first three years of the 1980s taught people to expect continuing high rates of inflation. They regarded the sharp decline in 1983 as an aberration. It took many years of much lower inflation rates — well into the 1990s — to persuade investors that they could obtain as much as a 3 or 4 percent real return on government bonds by lending at nominal interest rates as low as 7 percent.

5. One explanation is that people were still expecting higher rates of inflation than were materializing. Another possibility is that the rapid declines in the growth rates of M1 and M2 (see Figures 22.1 - 22.4 in the textbook) caused rapid declines in the supply of lendable funds, which in turn led to higher interest rates. Both explanations probably have some merit.

G. Questions to Think about

What can we learn about the future by looking backward? Those who try to use monetary or fiscal policy to stabilize the economy have available to them data similar to those you will find in Table 22.2 on the next page. The data provide a statistical summary of the Canadian economy's performance from the first quarter of 1988 through the first quarter of 1991. The data show quarterly percentage changes in real gross domestic product, total civilian employment, the price level, and personal consumption expenditures. The last column shows unemployment rates for each quarter.

1. If you were in charge of aggregate-demand management and were looking at these data in the early months of 1991, what kind of policy would you want to implement? Assume your goal is to foster a high but sustainable rate of growth in output and employment without setting off renewed inflation. Would you favour stimulus — more reserves for the banking system, lower interest rates, tax cuts, increased government spending? Or would you lean toward a restrictive policy? (Remember that it's 1991! You don't have any data for 1992 or subsequent years.)

2. The performance of the consumer price index in the last quarter of 1990 and the first quarter of 1991 certainly gives cause for alarm. Does it presage a renewal of the high inflation rates that plagued the Canadian economy just a few years earlier?

Note that the data in the table are mixed: the numbers for real GDP and for the unemployment rate are seasonally adjusted. The numbers for civilian employment and personal consumption spending are not. Notice that the seasonally adjusted data series show much less volatility over time.

Table 22.2

year	quarter	Real GDP	Civilian Employment	Rate of Inflation	Personal Consumption	Unemployment Rate
1988	2	4.54%	4.03%	4.30%	9.00%	7.7
1988	3	0.41%	2.33%	3.78%	0.00%	7.8
1988	4	3.09%	-3.03%	2.81%	8.96%	7.7
1989	1	4.51%	-0.78%	6.97%	-9.20%	7.6
1989	2	1.77%	-4.72%	7.31%	9.77%	7.6
1989	3	0.91%	11.57%	3.59%	-0.11%	7.3
1989	4	0.57%	-2.96%	2.67%	6.85%	7.6
1990	1	2.61%	-1.53%	7.06%	-7.43%	7.6
1990	2	-1.13%	3.10%	3.90%	6.48%	7.5
1990	3	-2.20%	1.50%	3.01%	-0.62%	8.3
1990	4	-3.63%	-3.70%	5.54%	6.75%	9.2
1991	1	-5.33%	-3.85%	12.20%	-9.44%	10.2
Calculations based on Statistics Canada Series:		D14872	D980120	P100000	D980745	D15666

H. Answers to Questions in Section G

1. There are no correct answers, but we can make some useful observations. First, the slowdown in real GDP growth appears to have been serious. We had four straight quarters of negative real growth in the economy, and the unemployment rate was rising dramatically. Yet, look at the behaviour of prices in the last two quarters shown in the table. We certainly don't want to trigger a resurgence of inflation. What will we do if we prescribe stimulus and the economy has already embarked upon a strong expansion? Or if we do nothing and the economy has already slipped into a steep recession? We cannot necessarily make up for our earlier mistakes by applying a stronger dose of the proper remedy later. That may only aggravate uncertainty and instability. Because price levels had begun to rise seriously again just as unemployment rates were rising, many people feared that we were in for another bout of "stagflation" — economic stagnation combined with inflation.

2. We know after the fact that 1992 was a very serious recession year, but it was also the beginning of a long period of economic growth, declining unemployment rates, and very low inflation rates. It was difficult and unpopular for policy makers to avoid making extreme policy choices in the face of these data, but they did so, with results that have been beneficial to most Canadians.

Chapter 23

Supply-Side Perspectives

A. Multiple-Choice Questions on the Principal Ideas of Chapter 23

1. The economists referred to in the text as *supply-side economists* are united in the belief that
   A. aggregate-demand management is not by itself an effective way to bring about high employment with price stability.
   B. markets work much less effectively than demand-side economists assume.
   C. markets work much more effectively than demand-side economists assume.
   D. tax cuts are the best way to produce high employment with price stability.

2. Price and wage controls imposed during a period when aggregate demand is expanding faster than the ability of the economy to supply goods to satisfy that demand
   A. create shortages.
   B. prevent speculation.
   C. promote justice or fairness.
   D. reduce profiteering.

3. Do sellers cause inflation by raising their prices?
   A. No, because all sellers face some competition
   B. No, because no sellers have any interest in higher prices if it also means higher costs
   C. Yes, because most goods are sold by price searchers
   D. Yes, if their actions lead in some way to an increase in the money stock

4. An increase in aggregate demand will increase output and employment if
   A. it persuades some producers that the relative demand for their products has increased.
   B. producers discover that aggregate demand has increased.
   C. there is any excess capacity in the economy.
   D. there is substantial unemployment.

5. A policy that aims at reducing the unemployment rate by deliberately causing inflation
   A. can succeed if policymakers are willing to accept the required rate of inflation.
   B. can succeed only so long as people underestimate the rate at which inflation is occurring.
   C. cannot succeed because inflation undermines investor confidence.
   D. has never actually been tried but would probably work because it is an historical fact that lower unemployment rates are associated with periods of inflation.

6. A policy of slowing down the rate of growth in aggregate demand in order to halt an inflation that has been going on for several years
   A. is likely to cause the unemployment rate to rise until people correctly adjust their expectations to the slower rate of increase in the price level.
   B. is not likely to have a significant effect on the unemployment rate.
   C. is the best way to avoid a recession.
   D. will necessitate the acceptance of a permanently higher unemployment rate.

7. At a time when the federal government is already running a budget deficit, reducing federal tax rates on personal and corporate income without reducing government expenditures
    A. is more likely to result in a reduced deficit after several years, if ever, than in the next year.
    B. may not increase the deficit but cannot reduce it.
    C. will increase the tax base by more than enough to compensate for the decreased tax rates, thus reducing the deficit.
    D. will necessarily increase the size of the deficit.

8. If the Canadian federal government found that it could *not* "roll over" the public debt as it matured, this would be evidence that
    A. investors had lost confidence in the federal government.
    B. the debt had grown too large to refinance.
    C. the government was offering too low a yield on new bonds.
    D. the public preferred consumption to saving.

9. An increase in taxes that reduces the government's budget deficit will
    A. increase private-sector output and employment.
    B. lower interest rates.
    C. reduce the crowding-out effect on private investment.
    D. not necessarily result in any of the above.

B.   Answers to, and Explanations of, Multiple-Choice Questions on the Principal Ideas of Chapter 23

1.   **A**. As commonly used, the term *supply-side* economists refers to economists who generally believe markets work quite well and want government to avoid creating strong disincentives to producers through high tax rates and disabling regulations. In this chapter, however, the concept is expanded to include economists whose lack of confidence in markets prompts them to recommend direct controls on wages and prices. The common conviction among supply-side economists, as the term is used here, is that controlling aggregate demand will not produce the results long promised by demand-side economists.

2.   **A**. Repressed inflation makes inflation worse by preventing the price system from working. It changes the forms that speculation and profiteering take but certainly does not eliminate them. The hope that controls will prevent "unfair" price increases no doubt has a lot to do with their popularity. This is a hope that seems fundamentally impervious to evidence about the injustices that price and wage controls actually cause.

3.   **D**. If sellers with market power use their prices and thereby cause surpluses and increased unemployment, and if the monetary managers respond by increasing the money stock, the market power of the sellers could be called a cause of inflation. Sellers who raise their prices would prefer that their costs not increase; but they also know that their own selling-price decisions will have no discernible effect on the prices they must pay for their inputs.

4.   **A**. Terms like excess capacity and substantial unemployment are not very clear. Almost all producers believe that they have the capacity to expand their output and hence some excess capacity, which they will want to employ if price and cost considerations are appropriate. An increase in aggregate demand has no significance in itself for any producer. Producers will decide to expand their contribution to output and employment when their anticipated marginal revenues shift appropriately relative to their anticipated marginal costs.

5.   **B**. Few knowledgeable people still believe that the unemployment rate can be lowered simply by accepting some higher rate of inflation. The unemployment rate will tend to decline only so long as people underestimate the rate at which inflation is occurring and so overestimate the value of prevailing wages and prices. The fact that lower unemployment rates are historically linked with

higher inflation rates does not imply that we can reduce unemployment by causing inflation, as we learned the hard way in the 1970s and 1980s.

6. **A.** Sellers of both goods and labour who have become accustomed to inflation must revise their expectations if and when inflation stops or slows down. If they hold out for wages or prices higher than prospective purchasers are willing to pay, they won't find buyers. How long will it take for experience to alter their views in appropriate ways? The answer may depend in large part on their confidence in the new policy.

7. **A.** Advocates of supply-side tax cuts want **C** to be the case. This is more likely to be true, if true at all, in the long run than in the short run. Opponents of supply-side tax cuts tend to insist that **D** is correct. It is extremely difficult to test propositions like this because the time period over which the effect is to be observed must be agreed upon. In addition, defenders of the refuted hypothesis must not be able to salvage their claim by asserting that something else changed to bring about the "wrong" outcome.

8. **C.** People will buy and hold government bonds only when they believe that doing so is the best available use of their assets. By offering a slightly higher interest rate, the federal treasury can readily attract additional funds from potential investors. If the federal government ran such enormous deficits that investors became convinced that rapid inflation was ahead, a substantial rise in the interest rate would be required to get them to buy the government bonds; such a rise would be in the nominal rate, not in the real interest rate.

9. **D**. Everything depends on the effect of the higher taxes. Government can crowd out private investment just as effectively through taxation as through borrowing. Moreover, the government's obtaining funds by taxation has a set of effects on the incentives of potential savers different from the effects of increased government borrowing. Most of the time, we tend to think of **C** as the correct answer, but it isn't necessarily correct.

C.   A Step-by-Step Review of Chapter 23

1. Adam Smith was a "supply-side economist" because he believed

   A. a society would always have as much money as it could use.
   B. additional saving would automatically generate additional investment.
   C. economic growth depended primarily upon maintaining profit incentives for producers.
   D. all of the above.
   E. none of the above.

2. The term supply-side economics was coined in the 1970s to describe the advocacy of growth and employment policies emphasizing

   A. fine-tuning.
   B. fiscal policy.
   C. incentives to producers.
   D. monetary policy.

3. Wage and price controls imposed in response to an inflation caused by increases in aggregate demand produce

   A. efficiency but not equity.
   B. equity but not efficiency.
   C. both equity and efficiency.
   D. inequities and inefficiencies.

4. OPEC could not have increased the *relative* price of all goods by raising the price of oil in the 1970s because

    A. OPEC was not a monopoly.
    B. it had no power to increase the price of oil.
    C. the cost of producing some goods does not depend in any way on the price of oil.
    D. an increase in the relative prices of all goods is a logical impossibility.

5. In a barter economy where money was not used, the OPEC-induced price increases of the 1970s would have caused increases in the prices of

    A. nothing but crude petroleum and its refined products.
    B. all goods.
    C. goods that use relatively more oil and decreases in the prices of goods that use relatively less oil.
    D. no goods at all.

6. Relative price changes in a money economy

    A. ought to be prevented because they cause uncertainty.
    B. require that some prices fall and others rise in money terms.
    C. can occur with no money-price decreases if the stock of money increases sufficiently.
    D. cannot really occur despite the money illusion.

7. Rising unemployment caused by the exercise of market power puts the Bank of Canada under pressure to

    A. raise the Bank Rate.
    B. increase the money stock.
    C. raise interest rates.
    D. refuse to lend to the federal government, directly or indirectly.

8. If organized interest groups in Canada today have the power to set their own prices for goods and labour without regard to the public interest,

    A. a contractionary fiscal and monetary policy will be needed to prevent inflation.
    B. an expansionary fiscal and monetary policy will be needed to prevent inflation.
    C. government will be able to prevent inflation through wage and price controls that limit the income of each interest group.
    D. it is likely that they would be able to block any political efforts to control their incomes through government wage or price setting.

9. People who make price and production decisions respond to

    A. aggregate demand.
    B. fiscal policy.
    C. monetary policy.
    D. the observed demand for their own products.

10. A policy of expanding aggregate demand could induce particular suppliers to increase their output if

    A. it caused costs to increase.
    B. it caused prices to fall.
    C. they knew what policy the government was pursuing.
    D. they misread it as a relative increase in the demand for their own product.

11. The relationship established by A. W. Phillips, which became the basis of the "Phillips Curve," was

    A. an inverse relationship between unemployment rates and rates of change in money wages.
    B. a direct relationship between worker productivity and depression.
    C. an inverse relationship between worker productivity and inflation.
    D. a direct relationship between productivity and economic growth.

12. The relationship Phillips found in the United Kingdom between the variables he studied
    A. contradicts the predictions of economic theory, which assert that inflation causes unemployment.
    B. contradicts the predictions of economic theory, which assert that inflation reduces worker productivity.
    C. is compatible with the predictions of economic theory, which assert that scarcity causes prices to rise.
    D. has no relationship to economic theory because it was an empirical relationship.

13. If we consistently observe an association between low unemployment rates and high inflation rates, we may reasonably conclude
    A. that inflation causes high employment rates.
    B. that high employment rates cause inflation.
    C. that both of the above are the case.
    D. none of the above because some third factor may be causing the association.

14. If year after year we observe decorated evergreen trees in almost all Canadian houses on the shortest day of the year, we may reasonably conclude
    A. that putting decorated evergreen trees inside houses shortens the days.
    B. that shorter days cause decorated evergreen trees to grow indoors in Canada.
    C. that both of the above are the case.
    D. none of the above because some third factor may be causing the association.

15. Prices and wages are more likely to drift upward when the economy is operating closer to capacity because
    A. high-capacity operation generates additional economic friction.
    B. high-capacity operations are associated with sellers' markets, in which buyers will more often be willing to pay a premium to avoid the high cost of searching for alternatives.
    C. upward drifting prices and wages encourage higher output.
    D. they will be drawn up by higher interest rates.

16. A policy of deliberately increasing the inflation rate in order to lower the unemployment rate
    A. has been effective wherever it's been seriously tried.
    B. cannot be effective.
    C. might lower the unemployment rate temporarily by causing workers to overestimate the real value of employment offers.
    D. can bring the unemployment rate down permanently to the optimal level if it's tried, but it has never yet been tried.

17. A critical flaw in the policy of deliberately accelerating the inflation rate in order to bring down the unemployment rate is that
    A. inflation does more harm than unemployment does.
    B. successful public policy in a democracy cannot be constructed on the assumption that the citizens can be permanently deceived.
    C. the unemployment rate could fall too low if the inflation rate got out of control.
    D. the public prefers inflation to unemployment and wouldn't know where to stop.

18. A policy of slowing down the rate of growth in aggregate demand in order to halt an inflation that has been going on for several years will tend to reduce output and employment
    A. before it slows down the inflation rate.
    B. after it slows down the inflation rate.
    C. without having any effect on the inflation rate.
    D. in proportion to any reduction in the price level.

19. Why do changes in the rate of growth in aggregate demand tend to affect real GDP before they affect the price level?
    A. Because real GDP is a real variable and the price level is only a nominal variable
    B. Because output-related changes are commonly the signal through which price setters learn that demand has changed
    C. Because prices are no longer determined by the forces of supply and demand in modern industrial economies
    D. Because Parliament has mandated this relationship in Bill C-121

20. Those supply-side economists who predicted that tax rate reductions would produce increases in tax revenue often based their predictions partly on the assumption of
    A. a large underground economy that would begin using the market more if tax rates were reduced.
    B. compensating increases in sales taxes.
    C. compensating increases in property taxes.
    D. expanded government spending to stimulate economic growth.

21. Persons and institutions own Canadian federal government bonds today primarily because
    A. the government continues to delay redemption of the bonds.
    B. the government has refused to redeem the bonds.
    C. they consider the bonds good investments.
    D. they do not want to precipitate an economic collapse from which they would be the first to lose.

22. If the attractiveness of government bonds to investors declines, perhaps because other investments become more attractive,
    A. the price of the bonds will fall and the percentage yield on the purchase of the bonds will rise.
    B. the price of the bonds will fall as will the percentage yield on the purchase of the bonds.
    C. the price of the bonds will rise and the percentage yield on the purchase of the bonds will fall.
    D. the price of the bonds will rise as will the percentage yield on the purchase of the bonds.

23. The federal government may be able to run, for many years in succession, annual operating deficits equal to a large percentage of its revenues because
    A. creditors are convinced it will not default on its debt obligations.
    B. it has agreed to pay its debts upon demand in gold or silver.
    C. it owns so much public land that can function as security for its debts.
    D. it runs on Keynesian principles.

24. The most serious danger created by extensive government borrowing is
    A. the increased risk of deflation.
    B. decline of the infrastructure.
    C. decline of the infrared spectrum.
    D. potential national bankruptcy.
    E. the crowding out of other borrowers.

25. If the Bank of Canada tries to make enough credit available for everyone at a time when the federal government is borrowing almost 30 percent of total personal and business savings, it is likely to cause
    A. a higher inflation rate and higher interest rates.
    B. a higher inflation rate but no increase in interest rates.
    C. a higher nominal interest rate but no inflation.
    D. a large decline in the nominal cost to the government of rolling over the national debt.

26. The most optimistic version of the supply-side argument for lower taxes asserts lower tax rates will
    A. eliminate fluctuations in output and income.
    B. increase tax revenue.
    C. promote prayer in the public schools.
    D. strengthen separatist sentiments in Québec.

27. Government budget deficits can do damage by absorbing too large a proportion of the flow of savings; whether raising taxes will ameliorate this problem depends upon the effect of higher taxes upon

    A. the demand for savings.
    B. the supply of savings.
    C. the supply as well as the demand for savings.
    D. the total size of the deficit.

28. Supply-side economists who advocated tax cuts in the early 1980s to stimulate economic growth also wanted monetary policy to produce

    A. a slow growth in the monetary aggregates.
    B. a stable price level as measured by the price of gold or some index of standard commodity prices.
    C. a steady growth rate in the monetary aggregates.
    D. high interest rates.

29. Disagreements between and among demand-side and supply-side economists are often hard to resolve
    A. because there is substantial disagreement about the facts.
    B. because there is substantial disagreement about the theoretical framework most appropriate for the study of these issues.
    C. because there is substantial disagreement about the goals that public policy ought to pursue.
    D. for all of the reasons above.

30. Why has the Phillips Curve for Canada shifted around so much since the 1970s?
    A. Price changes caused the demand to change for most products.
    B. Increasingly lucrative social programs led to lower unemployment rates.
    C. People's expectations about the rate of inflation changed as we experienced different rates of inflation.
    D. The fear of contracting AIDS led people to spend less money.

D. Answers to the Review Questions in Chapter 23

1. D	6. C	11. A	16. C	21. C	26. B
2. C	7. B	12. C	17. B	22. A	27. C
3. D	8. D	13. D	18. A	23. A	28. B
4. D	9. D	14. D	19. B	24. E	29. D
5. C	10. D	15. B	20. A	25. A	30. C

E. The Federal Government Debt

Despite the widely advertised campaigns urging Canadians to buy and hold Canadian Savings Bonds, these bonds actually make up only a small fraction of the Canadian federal government's debt. Most of the debt, actually, is in the form of government bonds of varying lengths of maturity, mostly short-term. The shortest-term are called *treasury bills* or T-bills and have a maturity of only 91 days. Other government bonds have maturities of 6 months, a year, 3 years, five years, etc. These bonds are typically held by (a) the Bank of Canada and government agencies, (b) Canadian financial institutions, (c) large corporations and money managers, and (d) foreigners.

1. Is there any danger that foreigners might suddenly decide they no longer want to be creditors of the Canadian government and so demand immediate repayment?

2. Does the fact that the Bank of Canada and government agencies hold government debt mean the government owes much of the debt to itself?

F. Answers to Questions in Section E

1. The share of the federal debt held by foreigners has been increasing over the past thirty years. While it is unlikely that any substantial number of foreigners would suddenly reach a common conclusion to cease being creditors of the Canadian government, they might. Fears of Québec separation often trigger such concerns. So do rapid, unanticipated inflations and high budget deficits. Suppose foreigners did decide they didn't want to hold Canadian government debt any longer. What would happen? A lower global demand for Canadian government obligations would mean a lower price for them, which entails a higher percentage return for anyone who is willing to hold these bonds. As the return on the bonds rises, investors will want to hold larger quantities of them and the problem will correct itself, albeit at a higher market rate of interest for the bonds. The fear that foreigners might suddenly decide to cash in all their Canadian bonds, while groundless on the face of it, helps to create some market pressures on Canadian interest rates.

2. We don't want to wave this portion of the debt away with the simplistic claim that the government owes it to itself. First, the Bank of Canada is technically a separate entity from the federal government. Second, remember that when the Bank of Canada adds to its holdings of government bonds, bank reserves and the money supply increase.

G. Questions to Think about

1. How can a democratic government institute an "incomes policy"? Think about it concretely. It is easy to talk about setting something called "wage rates" and something else called "prices"; but, in reality, millions of separate wage rates and prices would have to be set if the government were to successfully control incomes in an effort to prevent inflation without causing unemployment.

2. What government policies might induce Canadians to reduce the proportion of their personal income going toward consumption and consequently increase their rate of personal saving?

H. Answers to Questions in Section G

1. The easiest procedure is to impose a "freeze": All prices and wages are fixed at whatever they happen to be when the incomes policy is initiated. Of course, this rewards those who raised their wages or prices before the freeze and penalizes those who were less astute, less greedy, or perhaps just more reluctant to give in to inflationary pressures. Moreover, new circumstances inevitably evolve calling for new *relative* prices and wages. If changes are not allowed, shortages and surpluses will develop, with consequent inefficiencies and eventually evasions of the law. But if changes are necessary, who will authorize them, using what information? When supply and demand processes are judged unacceptable, what can substitute to generate information about relative scarcities and to provide coordinating signals? Finally, how will all of this be accomplished when those charged with setting prices and wages "in the public interest" are constantly subject to intense private-interest pressures?

2. Lots of people wish they knew. Lowering the rate of time preference would contribute. But how can the government induce people to place a relatively greater value on future satisfactions and less on present gratification? If government policies lead people to believe that they will somehow be taken care of in the event of accident, illness, economic misfortune, or other adversity, they become less willing to save. The intent to provide for children seems to encourage a higher rate of saving, so a declining birth rate could reduce the desire to save. What about higher interest rates? They have to be higher *real* rates, which means that inflationary expectations (and the effects of taxes on nominal incomes) enter the picture. People also save in order to invest directly in projects of their own; but does government know how to encourage the cultivation of such personal projects? How important, relatively, are the prospective monetary return on such projects and the return in terms of direct satisfaction? You probably can think of some additional reasons to be unsure about the answer to this question. You might even ask whether increasing the rate of personal saving is an appropriate task for the government of a free society.

Chapter 24

Aggregate Demand and Supply:
An Overview

A. Multiple-Choice Questions on the Principal Ideas of Chapter 24

1. When job searchers expect the economy to be booming, but it isn't, what happens to their job search decisions and to the unemployment rate?

   A. They search less, and the unemployment rate declines.
   B. They search less, and the unemployment rate increases.
   C. They search more, and the unemployment rate declines.
   D. They search more, and the unemployment rate increases.

2. What is so "natural" about the *natural unemployment rate*?

   A. It is the unemployment rate we observe when people's expectations are in line with reality.
   B. It is the unemployment rate that is observed in all leading industrialized countries.
   C. It is the unemployment rate observed among animals in nature.
   D. It is the historical average unemployment rate for the past fifty years.

3. It is possible to move along the short-run Phillips Curve because

   A. when the federal government implements a demand-management policy, it becomes law.
   B. when aggregate demand is unexpectedly greater than the aggregate rate of production, output goes up and unemployment drops.
   C. high rates of inflation cause the unemployment rate to decline.
   D. low rates of inflation cause the unemployment rate to increase.
   E. all of the above.

4. The long-run Phillips Curve is vertical because

   A. even at high rates of inflation, the economy tends toward the natural unemployment rate.
   B. it is impossible to maintain the unemployment rate below the natural rate for very long, even when aggregate demand policies are used to keep increasing the rate of inflation.
   C. "you can't fool all the people all the time."
   D. all of the above.

5. The *non-accelerating inflation rate of unemployment* (NAIRU) increased from less than four percent in the 1950s to over eight percent in the early 1990s because

   A. the rate of inflation was reduced, causing the economy to move along the short-run Phillips Curve.
   B. the federal government decided to raise the unemployment rate.
   C. on average, people chose to search longer for jobs.
   D. information about job opportunities became more costly to find, causing people to remain unemployed longer.
   E. there was a growth in the number of discouraged workers in the Canadian economy.

6. How is the aggregate supply curve related to the Phillips Curve?
    A. In the long run, both curves are vertical.
    B. Both curves are sloped in the short-run because in the short-run, people's expectations are sometimes not in line with reality.
    C. The aggregate supply curve deals with prices; the Phillips Curve with the rate of inflation.
    D. The aggregate supply curve deals with output; the Phillips Curve with unemployment.
    E. All of the above.

7. Why does the aggregate demand curve slope downward from left to right?
    A. When prices of goods rise and incomes stay constant, the quantity demanded falls.
    B. When prices of goods fall and incomes stay constant, the quantity demanded rises.
    C. When prices remain constant and income rises, the quantity demanded rises.
    D. When prices remain constant and income falls, the quantity demanded falls.
    E. When prices rise, the purchasing power of financial assets declines and people demand less.

8. What happens, *ceteris paribus*, in the aggregate demand - aggregate supply framework when the supply of money is increased?
    A. The aggregate demand curve shifts to the right, output increases in the short run, and prices rise in the long run.
    B. The aggregate demand curve shifts to the left, output decreases in the short run, and prices fall in the long run.
    C. The aggregate supply curve shifts to the right, output increases in the short run, and prices fall in the long run.
    D. The aggregate supply curve shifts to the left, output decreases in the short run, and prices rise in the long run.

B. Answers to, and Explanations of Multiple-Choice Questions on the Principal Ideas of Chapter 24

1. **D**. When people expect the economy to be booming, they typically expect to be able to find good jobs, too. If their expectations are incorrect, they will keep looking for these good jobs, which don't seem to materialize for many job searchers. On average, people search longer for jobs, and when that happens, the total number of people unemployed goes up.

2. **A**. There is nothing "natural" about the natural unemployment rate. It is clearly different in different countries, and it has been quite different at different times in our own recent history, rising from about 4 percent in the 1950s to over 8 percent in the 1980s. The one unifying characteristic of all these numbers is that they represent an educated guess of what the unemployment rate would be if people's expectations about the state of the economy were pretty much in line with the actual state of the economy.

3. **B**. High or low inflation rates don't *cause* different unemployment rates. Instead, it is more informative to think of changes in both the rate of inflation and the unemployment rate as the result of other changes in aggregate supply and aggregate demand. For example, when aggregate demand decreases unexpectedly, people search longer for jobs, output declines, the unemployment rate rises, and there is downward pressure on the rate of inflation.

4. **D**. A vertical long-run Phillips Curve indicates that the economy tends toward one particular unemployment rate, regardless of whether the rate of inflation is very high or very low. We move off this vertical long-run Phillips Curve only in the short run, when people's expectations are not in synch with economic reality. But people's expectations always adapt to economic reality, sometimes quite quickly and sometimes only after a lengthy adjustment period.

5. **C**. People chose to search longer because, on average, the expected marginal benefits of additional job search increased, and the expected marginal costs of additional job search decreased. These

changes occurred, in part, because of the changes that raised the height of Canada's social safety net, because of continued rural-urban migration, and because of the growth of two-income families, meaning that such families still had one income while someone who was unemployed could search longer.

6. **E.** While the aggregate supply curves and the Phillips Curves are related, they show similar phenomena using different economic variables. Aggregate supply curves are more static, in that they deal with overall price *levels*, whereas Phillips Curves deal with the *rate* of change of prices. Also, aggregate supply curves focus on output in the economy, whereas Phillips Curves deal with the unemployment rate.

7. **E.** The price level measured on the vertical axis is the overall price level, including not just the prices of all goods and services, but also salaries, wages, and rents. So when the price level increases, people's incomes increase, too. Standard consumer theory says that when prices and incomes increase at the same rate, then people won't change their consumption behaviour, but this theory overlooks the impact of rising prices on the purchasing power of financial assets. If prices and your income both rise, but the number of dollars you are holding in your bank account don't change, you will be worse off. The money you are holding will have less purchasing power; your *real* money balances will have declined, with the result that you will tend to purchase less when overall price levels increase.

8. **A.** When the money supply increases, people try to convert their increased money holdings into other things they value — stocks, bonds, cars, stereos, cleaning services, whatever. Aggregate demand for goods and services increases. If this increase is unexpected, the initial effect is likely to be an increase in output and a decline in the unemployment rate, but as shortages appear at the old price level, prices will begin to creep upward.

C. A Step-by-Step Review of Chapter 24

1. The unemployment that the economic way of thinking considers "optimal" is that rate for which
   A. no one is unemployed.
   B. the amount of unemployment is minimized.
   C. the amount of job search is minimized.
   D. the amount of job search is what job searchers choose, given realistic expectations.

2. What would be the effect of raising the amount of compensation and the number of weeks during which unemployed persons can receive employment insurance?
   A. The costs of additional search would increase, and people would remain unemployed less.
   B. The costs of additional search would increase, and people would remain unemployed more.
   C. The costs of additional search would decrease, and people would remain unemployed less.
   D. The costs of additional search would decrease, and people would remain unemployed more.

3. Why is the short-run Phillips Curve downward sloping from left to right?
   A. Unanticipated increases in aggregate supply cause the rate of inflation to increase.
   B. Anticipated decreases in aggregate demand cause the rate of inflation to increase.
   C. Unanticipated increases in aggregate demand cause the unemployment rate to decrease.
   D. Anticipated decreases in aggregate supply cause the unemployment rate to increase.

4. What is true about people's inflationary expectations along the short-run Phillips Curve?
   A. At lower unemployment rates, people are expecting lower rates of inflation.
   B. At lower unemployment rates, people are expecting higher rates of inflation.
   C. At higher unemployment rates, people are expecting lower rates of inflation.
   D. At higher unemployment rates, people are expecting higher rates of inflation.
   E. Inflationary expectations are constant along a short-run Phillips Curve.

5. What does it mean when we observe that this year the economy is not on the same short-run Phillips Curve that has been traced out over the previous five years?

    A. The rate of inflation has changed.
    B. Expectations about the rate of inflation have changed.
    C. The unemployment rate has changed.
    D. Expectations about the unemployment rate have changed.
    E. All of the above.

6. When the short-run Phillips Curve slides downward along the long-run Phillips Curve,

    A. the expected rate of inflation is declining.
    B. the expected rate of inflation is increasing.
    C. the expected unemployment rate is declining.
    D. the expected unemployment rate is increasing

7. If the federal government were to implement some sort of expansionary fiscal policy to stimulate the economy, what would be the most likely outcome?

    A. The natural unemployment rate would increase.
    B. The natural unemployment rate would decrease.
    C. Prices would rise.
    D. NAIRU would rise.
    E. NAIRU would decline.

8. Which of the following statements describes a *movement* upward and to the right along the short-run aggregate supply curve?

    A. Rising prices have led to lower rates of output and more unemployment.
    B. Rising prices have led to higher rates of output and less unemployment.
    C. Rising prices have caused inflationary expectations to rise, leading to more unemployment.
    D. Rising prices have caused inflationary expectations to decline, leading to less unemployment.

9. Which of the following statements describes a *leftward shift* of the short-run aggregate supply curve?

    A. Rising prices have led to lower rates of output and more unemployment.
    B. Rising prices have led to higher rates of output and less unemployment.
    C. Rising prices have caused inflationary expectations to rise, leading to more unemployment.
    D. Rising prices have caused inflationary expectations to decline, leading to less unemployment.

10. In the "Keynesian" version of aggregate demand and aggregate supply analysis,

    A. increases in aggregate supply lead to lower prices and higher rates of output.
    B. increases in aggregate demand lead to lower prices and higher rates of output.
    C. increases in aggregate supply lead to higher prices and lower rates of output.
    D. increases in aggregate demand lead to higher prices and higher rates of output.
    E. none of the above.

11. In the "Classical" version of aggregate demand and aggregate supply analysis,

    A. increases in aggregate supply lead to lower prices and higher rates of output.
    B. increases in aggregate demand lead to lower prices and higher rates of output.
    C. increases in aggregate supply lead to higher prices and lower rates of output.
    D. increases in aggregate demand lead to higher prices and higher rates of output.
    E. none of the above.

12. In the typical **AS-AD** model, with a positively sloped **AS** curve, what happens when interest rates decline?
    A. More people choose to save more and spend less, the **AD** curve shifts leftward, and prices decline.
    B. Consumption and investment spending increase; prices and output rise in the short run.
    C. People chose to hold less money, and aggregate demand declines, causing a recession.
    D. Aggregate demand increases, causing unemployment to decline, but having no effect on the price level.

13. Along a positively sloped aggregate supply curve, what price level are people, on average, expecting?
    A. the price level consistent with the current rate of production.
    B. the price level consistent with an unemployment rate of zero.
    C. the price level indicated by the intersection of the short-run and long-run **AS** curves.
    D. the current price level, whatever it happens to be.

14. Which of the following aggregate demand management policies will lead to a lasting reduction in the unemployment rate?
    A. an increase in the rate of growth of the money supply
    B. an increase in government spending on goods and services
    C. a reduction in tax rates
    D. all of the above
    E. none of the above

15. What would it take to shift the long-run aggregate supply curve to the right?
    A. an increase in aggregate demand
    B. a reduction in job search costs
    C. an embargo on oil imposed by OPEC
    D. a severe, worldwide drought.

D. Answers to the Review Questions in Chapter 24

1. D	4. E	7. C	10. E	13. C
2. D	5. B	8. B	11. E	14. E
3. C	6. A	9. C	12. B	15. B

E. Understanding the Phillips Curve

1. Figure 24.1 on the next page shows the present short-run Phillips Curve for an economy.

   (a) What should be the label on the vertical axis? _____.

   (b) What should be the label on the horizontal axis? _____.

   (c) Suppose that the current NAIRU for this economy is seven percent. In the figure, draw in the present long-run Phillips Curve. If this economy is in long-run equilibrium, what rate of inflation are people currently experiencing? _____. Indicate the long-run equilibrium as point **D**.

   (d) What rate(s) of inflation are people expecting in this economy at points **A, B,** and **C**? _____
   (e) How do you know that these are their expectations?

   (f) Suppose that policy-makers would like to reduce the unemployment rate from seven percent to five percent. How might they do this in the short run?

Figure 24.1

Long-run and Short-run Phillips Curves

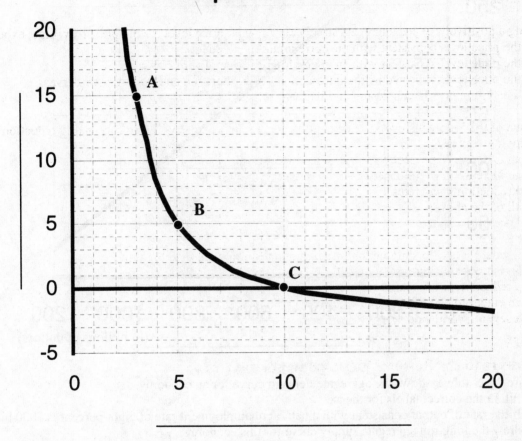

(g) Once the economy is at point **B**, if its NAIRU is still seven percent, the economy will not be able to stay at point **B** for long. Why not?

(h) What will the unemployment rate and the inflation rate be eventually if policy makers maintain the policies you described in (f) above? Label this point **E** on the graph.

(i) If policy makers find a five percent rate of inflation intolerable, what policies might they pursue?

(j) Sketch a new short run Phillips Curve on the graph, and indicate the likely short-run effects of the policies you described in (i).

(k) What are the likely long-run effects of the policies?

Figure 24.2

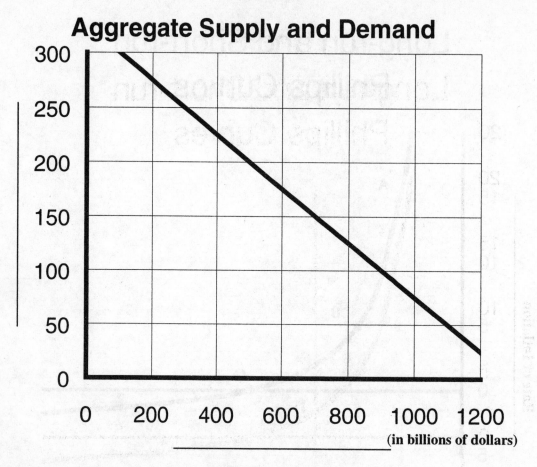

Aggregate Supply and Demand

(in billions of dollars)

2. Figure 24.2, above, shows the aggregate demand curve for an economy.
   (a) Fill in the correct labels for the axes.
   (b) If the rate of output consistent with a natural unemployment rate of eight percent is $800 billion, draw the long-run aggregate supply curve for this economy.
   (c) Based on your answer in (b), assume the economy is in long-run equilibrium, and draw a short-run aggregate supply curve that reflects the "Keynesian" assumptions about output and prices.
   (d) Show the short-run effects on these curves of an expansionary policy designed to increase real output to $1.2 trillion.
   (e) Why is it unlikely that the price level will remain at 125? Sketch a more reasonable short-run supply curve to show price increases as output expands.

   (f) As prices begin to rise, what happens to people's expectations initially? What happens after they experience the higher price levels for awhile?

   (g) As people come to expect higher price levels, what will happen to the short-run aggregate supply curve? Show this change on the graph.

   (h) When this economy reaches its new, long-run equilibrium, what will be the new price level for this economy?

   (i) In the new long-run equilibrium, what will be the economy's rate of output?

   (j) What, if anything, was accomplished by the expansionary policy?

F. Answers to the Questions in Section E

Figure 24.3

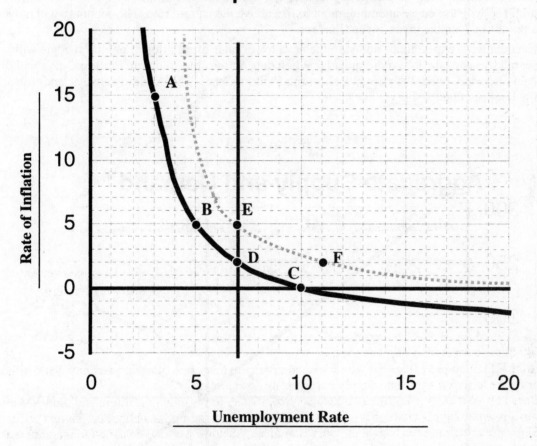

Long-run and Short-run Phillips Curves

1. (a) The vertical axis shows the rate of inflation.
   (b) The horizontal axis shows the unemployment rate.
   (c) When the economy is in long-run equilibrium the long-run Phillips Curve and the short-run Phillips Curve intersect at a point where the expected rate of inflation equals the actual rate of inflation. At this point, the current and the expected rate of inflation are two percent, and people's expectations are in line with reality.
   (d) Two percent at each point.
   (e) (d) is a trick question. The expected rate of inflation is the same, all along a given short run Phillips Curve, and it is equal to the rate of inflation shown by the intersection of the short-run and long-run Phillips Curves.
   (f) Any expansionary policy might work in the short run: increasing the money supply or the federal deficit.
   (g) At point **B**, people are expecting a rate of inflation of only 2% but experiencing a rate of inflation of 5%. They will eventually adjust their expectations to the new reality. As they adjust their expectations, the economy moves to a new short-run Phillips Curve.

(h) As expectations adjust to a five percent rate of inflation, the short-run Phillips Curve drifts rightward until it intersects the long-run Phillips Curve at five percent. At this point, both the expected and the actual rates of inflation are five percent. Unfortunately, however, the unemployment rate has also returned to the natural rate of seven percent. The policy had the effect of reducing unemployment in the short run, but in the long run, its only effect was to increase the rate of inflation.

(i) Contractionary monetary or fiscal policies: reducing the rate of growth of the money supply or reducing the deficit.

(j) Contractionary policies will move the economy downward and to the right along the new, dotted short-run Phillips Curve. The policy makers can reduce the rate of inflation, but in the short run, doing so will also cause unemployment to rise above the natural rate. The economy will move to a point like **F** on the graph in the short run.

(k) Eventually, as expectations adjust to the new, lower rates of inflation at point **F**, people will search less and take jobs more quickly. When they do this, the short-run Phillips Curve will drift back, leftward, toward the original short-run Phillips Curve. The economy always tends toward the long-run Phillips Curve.

2.

Figure 24.3

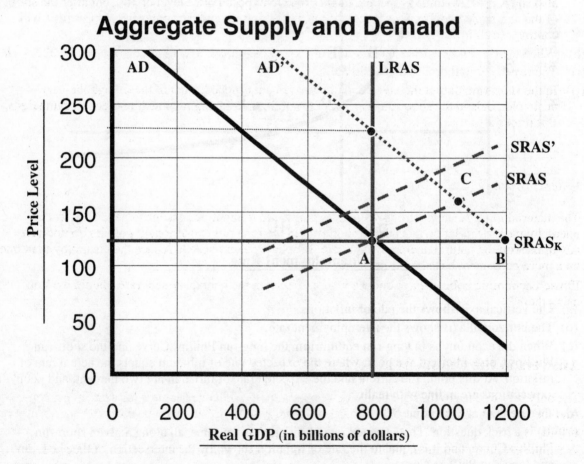

(a) The vertical axis shows the price *level*, not the rate of inflation; the horizontal shows the rate of output in the economy, not the unemployment rate, even though it has a close inverse correlation with the unemployment rate.

(b) The long-run aggregate supply curve, labeled **LRAS**, is vertical above a real GDP of $800b.

(c) The "Keynesian" aggregate supply curve, **SRAS$_K$** is horizontal at the current price level. It is drawn under the assumption that the overall price level does not change. If the economy is experiencing little or no inflation, then this curve may have some short-run predictive power.

(d) It is somewhat unsettling to realize that policy makers might actually attempt this feat — increase real GDP quickly and expect to have no impact on the price level. Judging from campaign speeches, though, it seems as if they think many voters have such an expectation. Expansionary policies shift the aggregate demand curve to the right from **AD** to **AD'**. The shift isn't necessarily parallel, as we have shown it, but a parallel shift is easier to use in this case. The policy, if it worked, would move the economy from point **A** to point **B** on the graph.

(e) The policy would not work for long, though. Shortages would develop, and prices would begin to rise to help allocate the scarce resources to their more valuable uses. A more reasonable short-run aggregate supply curve would be positively sloped through point **A**. The short-run equilibrium would be at point **C**. Here, the price level has crept up to 160, and real output has increased to 1050. This happens because people still expect an overall price level of 125, and their expectations have not yet fully incorporated their observations about current prices.

(f) Initially people don't revise their expectations much, if at all, not knowing whether the higher prices are random blips in the economy or something to be expected for some time. Eventually, however, they revise their price expectations upward.

(g) As people's expectations about prices are revised upward, the short-run aggregate supply curve also shifts upward. Initially, people might come to expect a price level of 160, but after the shift of the aggregate supply curve, prices will rise even further and the aggregate supply curve will continue to shift upward.

(h) When the economy reaches its new long-run equilibrium, the overall price level will be 225.

(i) The real GDP will drop back to $800 billion.

(j) In the short run, output increased and unemployment dropped. Both of these might be very desirable goals in the short run, especially for politicians facing imminent re-election campaigns. But prices also rose.

G. Questions to Think about

1. The material in this chapter strongly suggests that while it might be possible to have an effect on unemployment or inflation rates in the short run, in the long run expansionary policies do not have any impact on the natural unemployment rate. If policy makers wish to reduce the unemployment rate on a more permanent basis, what must they do?

2. If macroeconomic policies have only short-run effects on the unemployment rate, should we stop using them?

H. Answers to the Questions in Section G

1. The only way to change the natural unemployment rate is to change people's job search decisions. And the only way to affect these decisions is to change the expected marginal costs or benefits of job search.

2. When the economy is deep in the throes of a recession, as it was in the early 1930s, 1980s and 1990s, it is difficult, and perhaps cruel and heartless, to do nothing about the suffering of people who are unemployed. At times like these, well-meaning people strongly advocate expansionary policies, urging policy makers to ignore or downplay potential future inflationary effects. Whether you agree with them or not, it is likely that most economists would agree that we can also avoid this suffering if we make sure we don't pursue policies that will create rapid inflations to begin with. If we follow this strategy, then we will not have to dampen aggregate demand to choke off the inflation, causing recessions, as we did in the early 1980s and early 1990s.

Chapter 25

Efficiency, Exchange, and Comparative Advantage

A. Multiple-Choice Questions on the Principal Ideas of Chapter 25

1. The efficiency of any process is measured by the relationship between the
   A. energy turned out and the energy invested.
   B. quantity of goods produced and the quantity of goods used to produce them.
   C. value of the output and the value of the input.
   D. permanent product and the nonrenewable resources consumed.

2. Does trade create wealth?
   A. Yes, because trade makes available to people more of what they value.
   B. Yes, because trade permits the production of more material goods.
   C. No, because trade does not cause anything new to be created.
   D. Yes, but only for the one party in an exchange that takes advantage of the other party.

3. An informed and voluntary exchange is an exchange of equal values
   A. or it leaves one party worse off than before.
   B. if it is a fair exchange.
   C. on all occasions.
   D. on no occasions.

4. If Willie Loman has a comparative advantage in selling over repairing, this means that
   A. Willie can obtain more of what he wants by specializing in selling and then trading for repair services.
   B. the value of what Willie obtains relative to what he gives up in the process is greater when he sells goods than when he repairs them.
   C. some other producer with whom Willie is able to trade has a comparative advantage in repairing over selling.
   D. all of the above are the case.

5. Someone who has a strong comparative advantage in producing hand-painted ceramic tile will benefit from
   A. increases in the efficiency of others who also have a comparative advantage in producing hand-painted ceramic tile.
   B. reduced efficiency on the part of those who produce goods other than hand-painted ceramic tile.
   C. a decline in the number of hand-painted ceramic tiles that exchange for a fixed quantity of other goods.
   D. a fall in the demand for hand-painted ceramic tile.

6. Julius outbids Augustus in an auction of a recently discovered painting by Monet. Does this prove that Julius assigns a higher value than does Augustus to ownership of the painting?

    A. Yes, because Julius was willing to give up more money to obtain it.

    B. No, because either Julius or Augustus may have been mistaken about how much they will enjoy owning this painting.

    C. No, because neither one can be absolutely certain that the painting is a genuine Monet .

    D. No, because Julius' willingness to offer more money for the painting could reflect the fact that Julius places a lower marginal value on money

7. Efficient social cooperation among the participants in an economic system is promoted when

    A. everyone attempts to maximize leisure.

    B. everyone attempts to minimize energy consumption.

    C. people refrain from pursuing their comparative advantages.

    D. people receive correct information about relative costs along with incentives to take these costs fully into account in making their decisions.

B. Answers to, and Explanations of, Multiple-Choice Questions on the Principal Ideas of Chapter 25

1. **C.** Any working definition of efficiency will refer implicitly, if not explicitly, to someone's evaluations of inputs and outputs.

2. **A.** Wealth can be created without the fabrication of material objects.

3. **D.** Two adequately informed people would not voluntarily exchange unless both expected to obtain more in value than they were giving up. Why does the notion persist that a fair exchange is an exchange of equal values? That's an interesting question to think about.

4. **D.** All three statements are attempts to summarize the same situation. The key is available opportunities.

5. **C.** The price of tiles and hence the income of tile producers rises when fewer tiles exchange for the same quantity of other goods. Such an improvement in the terms of trade could come about through lower output by other tile producers as a result of decreased efficiency, through increased efficiency and hence higher output on the part of those who produce other goods, or through a change in people's tastes that increases the demand for tile.

6. **D.** While **D** is the best answer, you could make a good argument for each of the other options. It works well in most circumstances to accept the convention that relative willingness to pay money measures the relative value different people place on goods or activities — which would make **A** correct. Because people do not always correctly assess their own interests or behave in ways that further their long-run well-being, **B** is correct. We often make mistakes because we have received faulty information; so **C** is also correct. The text emphasizes the fact that a monetary value on a good reflects the relative value of that good and of money. People with large incomes typically assign a lower marginal value to money than do people with small incomes.

7. **D.** Much of the current controversy over what is efficient and what is not arises from the fact that relative prices accurately reflect evaluations that some people strongly disapprove of. It is a troublesome truth that any evaluation of an economic system will be in part an evaluation of the values of the people who comprise it.

C. A Step-by-Step Review of Chapter 25

1. Technological efficiency, defined in terms of completely objective relationships, is

    A. easier to measure than is economic efficiency.
    B. more important in the long run than economic efficiency.
    C. a confused concept because efficiency is always a relationship between evaluations.
    D. the key to rapid economic growth.

2. When efficiency is defined by engineers as the ratio between the energy developed by a machine and the energy supplied to that machine, the

    A. definition is a strictly objective one.
    B. energy developed is measured by the useful or valued energy developed.
    C. ratio will always be less than one if energy output and input are defined in strictly objective physical terms.
    D. definition depends entirely on technological considerations.

3. The definition of efficiency as the ratio between the value of output and the value of input implies that

    A. efficiency is unattainable.
    B. efficiency is inescapably an evaluative concept.
    C. objective or physical facts have no effect on efficiency.
    D. people will never be able to agree on what is more or less efficient.

4. A woman who decides to drive to work rather than take the bus

    A. is behaving inefficiently.
    B. decides that driving is more efficient for her.
    C. is probably paying attention to personal comfort and convenience rather than efficiency.
    D. is wasting scarce resources.

5. A man who estimates that he would save money by driving to work rather than taking the bus, but who nonetheless elects to take the bus because driving in rush-hour traffic frightens him, is

    A. behaving inefficiently.
    B. choosing what is for him the most efficient way to commute.
    C. rejecting economic efficiency for personal reasons.
    D. wasting scarce resources.

6. Is cutting down a tree in 2 hours with an axe more efficient than cutting it down in 10 minutes with a gasoline-powered chain saw?

    A. No, because time is valuable.
    B. Yes, because hand tools conserve nonrenewable energy resources.
    C. It could be, if the person cutting down the tree places a high enough value on exercise.
    D. There is no way to answer the question.

7. *"Material" wealth* cannot be distinguished in any useful way from *wealth* (with no modifying adjective) because

    A. all wealth consists ultimately of valued events or experiences.
    B. wealth is ultimately whatever can be purchased with money.
    C. material objects rarely contribute and are certainly not essential to the creation of wealth.
    D. we are a thoroughly materialist society.

8. The word *productive*, as applied to agriculture or manufacturing activities,

    A. merely implies that they are *more* productive than trade.
    B. cannot properly be applied to trade because mere exchange is not productive.
    C. applies equally to trade because exchange is productive in the same ways that agriculture and manufacturing are productive.
    D. is misleading because neither creates genuinely new material.

9. An activity is productive if it

    A. adds to the stock of material objects.
    B. adds to the sum of valued events.
    C. increases people's money income.
    D. reduces the use of nonrenewable resources.

10. Can a successful novelist produce a house with a typewriter?

    A. Only if the typewriter is used to pound in nails
    B. Of course not
    C. Yes, by "manufacturing" a novel and exchanging it for money that is then exchanged for a house
    D. Yes, but only a paper house, which won't be very durable

11. If the people who patronize a particular post office branch collectively place a value of $500 on the time they spend each day standing in line and one additional clerk who could be hired for a total cost of $100 per day could eliminate that line, is the post office branch being managed inefficiently?

    A. Yes, because an output valued at $500 could be obtained with an input valued at $100.
    B. Yes, because standing in line is a deadweight cost.
    C. No, because government activities are not properly evaluated by monetary criteria.
    D. From the perspective of the customers the operation may seem inefficient, but the present arrangement must be deemed efficient from the perspective of the branch manager, who has chosen not to hire an additional clerk.

12. Why don't the customers in the preceding question simply pay the branch manager to hire an additional clerk?

    A. It should not be necessary to bribe someone to get him to do what is efficient.
    B. Such a payment would constitute an unethical bribe.
    C. The customers have a right to expect good service without any additional payment.
    D. The transaction costs under current institutional arrangements would exceed $400 per day.

13. The absolute or ultimate measure of value in the opportunity-cost perspective

    A. is labour embodied in goods.
    B. is natural resources consumed.
    C. is leisure given up.
    D. does not exist.

14. The terms of trade between goods produced and exchanged by people with varying comparative advantages depend

    A. entirely on their bargaining abilities.
    B. entirely on their relative skills.
    C. entirely on the relative quantities supplied.
    D. in part on the demand for the different goods.

15. For one country to be more efficient than another in the production of everything

    A. is logically impossible.
    B. requires that one country have lower labour costs than the other.
    C. requires that the money prices of all goods be lower in one country than in the other.
    D. implies that one country will consume more of everything than the other.

16. Can a person become a less efficient producer of one good merely by becoming a more effective producer of a second good?

    A. No, because greater productivity must increase efficiency.
    B. No, but that might make the person choose to stop producing the first good.
    C. No, because more is always better than less.
    D. Yes, because the cost of producing the first good depends in part on the person's ability to produce the second good.

17. The least expensive option in money terms is the most efficient option

    A. from the standpoint of society as a whole.
    B. because efficiency is basically an economic concept.
    C. if money prices accurately reflect all costs to the decision maker.
    D. unless the person choosing places no value on efficiency.

18. Ignoring costs to other people in making one's own decisions

    A. is efficient.
    B. is inefficient.
    C. cannot be judged efficient or inefficient without first deciding from whose perspective efficiency is being assessed.
    D. has nothing to do with efficiency.

19. Conflict between those who want to extract valuable mineral resources from western lands and those who want to prevent development in order to preserve recreational opportunities reflects conflict between

    A. different values and interests.
    B. ecology and economy.
    C. material wants and nonmaterial wants.
    D. wealth and the environment.

20. Disagreements in society about the relative efficiency of particular projects

    A. make social cooperation impossible until they are resolved.
    B. are often disagreements about the relative value to be assigned to particular goods.
    C. often prevent us from determining their true objective efficiency.
    D. must be resolved by majority vote.

21. Which one of the statements below is false?

    A. Scarcity is reflected in the relationship between demand and supply.
    B. Demand and supply depend on people's evaluations of alternative opportunities.
    C. Any defensible estimate of efficiency presupposes evaluations.
    D. Clear and reliable indicators of relative scarcity make social cooperation possible on a much more extensive scale.
    E. Relative money prices serve as correct indicators of the actual scarcity of all goods at any time.

22. The pursuit of comparative advantage

    A. interferes with the efficient assignment of resources among their alternative uses.
    B. leads decision makers to employ resources in the most efficient way if the relative costs that decision makers must pay reflect opportunity costs.
    C. implies a high value on comparative status.
    D. implies a high value on comparative wealth.

23. In the Taha-Ben-Cal case used in the textbook to illustrate the principle of comparative advantage, Cal has a comparative advantage in the production of spiritual goods because

    A. he can produce them faster than can Taha or Ben.
    B. he can produce more of them than can Taha or Ben.
    C. he enjoys producing them rather than producing material goods.
    D. he is such an ineffective producer of material goods.

24. We can conclude that Cal is more efficient than Taha or Ben at producing spiritual goods if Cal

    A. produces them faster than Taha or Ben.
    B. produces more of them than Taha or Ben.
    C. says he would rather be producing spiritual goods than the material goods he actually produces.
    D. chooses to produce exclusively spiritual goods even though he personally prefers to consume material goods.

D. Answers to the Review Questions in Chapter 25

1. C	5. B	9. B	13. D	17. C	21. E
2. B	6. C	10. C	14. D	18. C	22. B
3. B	7. A	11. D	15. A	19. A	23. D
4. B	8. C	12. D	16. D	20. B	24. D

E. Comparative Advantage, Relative Costs, and Supply

Doe, Ray, Mia, and So are stranded at sea in a lifeboat. They have kits for distilling fresh water from salt water, and they have fishing lines with hooks. In order to survive until they are rescued, they must obtain fresh water and fish each day. Their skills as water distillers and fish catchers vary considerably. The table below shows what each one is capable of in a day. Doe can distil two litres of water per day or catch two kilograms of fish. Ray can distil two litres of water per day or catch four kilograms of fish, etc.:

Daily Capabilities

	Water Distilling (litres)		Fish Catching (kilograms)
Doe	2	or	2
Ray	2	or	4
Mia	4	or	2
So	4	or	1

1. What does it cost the group in kilograms of fish forgone when Doe distils one litre of water? When Ray distils one litre of water? Mia? So? Fill in the cost of production table below with this information.

Cost of Producing One Litre of Water
(In Kilograms of Fish)

Doe _____

Ray _____

Mia _____

So _____

2. Who is the lowest-cost water producer? _____ Who is the highest-cost water producer? _____
3. What does it cost the group in litres of water forgone when each catches one kilogram of fish? Fill in the cost of fish-production table below:

Cost of Producing One Kilogram of Fish
(In Litres of Water)

Doe   _____

Ray   _____

Mia   _____

So   _____

4. Who is the lowest-cost fish producer? Who is the highest-cost fish producer?

5. Graph the marginal opportunity cost curve of each good.

Figure 25.1

Cost per Litre (in Kgms of Fish)

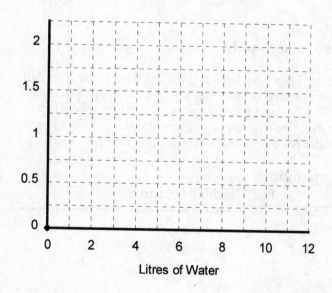

Cost per Kgm (In Litres of Water)

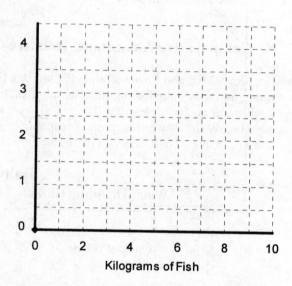

6. If the group decides it wants six litres of water per day (one and a half litres apiece), who should be assigned to water production? How many kilograms of fish can they then have?

7. If they want only one kilogram of fish per day per person, or four kilograms altogether, whom should they assign to fish catching? How many litres of water will they obtain?

8. The group decides it wants more food and decides to obtain an additional two kilograms of fish (for a total of six). When Doe is asked to join Ray in fishing, Mia protests that she is just as productive in fishing as Doe and wants to be transferred to fishing. Use the concept of comparative advantage to explain to Mia why she is a less efficient fish catcher than Doe.

9. Mia responds that she loves to fish and hates to distil water. What effect, if any, does this information have on your assessment of Mia's relative efficiency at the two tasks?

F. Answers to Questions in Section E

1. One kilogram of fish is sacrificed for each litre of water distilled by Doe, two kilograms per litre when Ray distils, one-half kilogram per litre when Mia distils, and one-fourth kilogram per litre when So distils.

2. The answers to the first question should make it obvious that So produces water at the lowest cost and Ray at the highest cost.

3. Doe: one litre
   Ray: one-half litre
   Mia: two litres
   So: four litres

4. Ray is the lowest-cost producer of fish, and So is the highest-cost producer.

5.

Figure 25.2

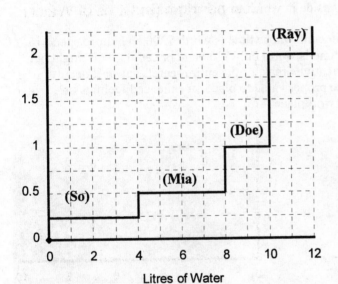

Cost per Litre (in Kgms of Fish)

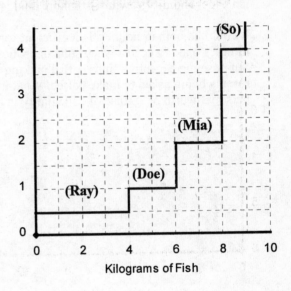

Cost per Kgm (In Litres of Water)

6. So and Mia can produce six litres of water at a cost of only two kilograms of fish given up. Consequently, So will specialize entirely in distilling and Mia will divide her day between the two activities. This will allow them seven kilograms of fish per day.

7. Ray is the most efficient at fishing. He can produce the four kilograms of fish at a cost of only two litres of water, which will allow the group ten litres of water per day.

8. Mia catches a kilogram of fish at a cost of two litres of water, Doe at a cost of only one litre. It is, of course, Mia's skill at distilling that makes her relatively inefficient at fishing.

9. Mia's statement makes it impossible for us to determine each person's costs of production from the data given. She introduces a third good, enjoyment of the work, which enormously complicates the analysis. In the real world, people's enjoyment of, or aversion to, particular tasks does influence supply curves and affect relative prices.

G. Questions to Think about

1. How much of the land in the Northwest and Yukon Territories should be open for commercial uses, and how much should be set aside as wilderness? You aren't expected to answer that question but rather this one: Does the controversy hinge on the importance of economic growth?

2. Should business executives ask their secretaries to make and serve coffee? Is this an efficient practice, or is it a sexist practice, reflecting the fact that most business executives are men, most secretaries are women, and many men expect women to serve them?

H. Answers to Questions in Section G

1. What exactly is it that grows when economic growth occurs? Who wants it to grow and why? Who does not want it to grow and why? The controversy is rooted in conflicting evaluations that different people place on various goods, and the debate would become far more constructive if we could clearly identify the specific preferences that are contending. Talking about "economic growth" usually conceals the issues. If it's economic growth when more backpacks are manufactured, why isn't it economic growth when more land is set aside in which to go backpacking?

2. It could be both or neither. Is it efficient for someone whose time is worth $200 an hour to spend 15 minutes making coffee when someone whose time is worth only $15 an hour can do it? It might be! Suppose the executive finds coffee making a creative break, or the entire secretarial staff deeply resents being asked to make coffee. What is the proper value to place on enhanced feelings of personal worth or a sense of collegiality in the workplace?

Chapter 26
International Trade Policy

A. Multiple-Choice Questions on the Principal Ideas of Chapter 26

1. When Canadians buy automobiles from another country, what do they export?

    A. Claims against something in Canada.
    B. Canadian dollars.
    C. Promises that the sellers of the automobiles may cash in in the future.
    D. All of the above.

2. The idea that we need import restrictions in order to "protect jobs for Canadians"

    A. makes no sense because import controls don't ever protect anyone's jobs.
    B. overlooks the fact that Canada has a wealth of natural resources.
    C. is absurd because in the extreme it would have Canadians producing those things at which our labour is *least* efficient.
    D. has the best interests of Canadian consumers at heart.

3. The major reason there are barriers to trade is

    A. to protect jobs.
    B. to promote the public interest.
    C. to promote some well-organized private interests.
    D. All of the above.

4. When it is argued that we need protection because otherwise some other country could outperform Canada in the production of everything, we know this argument

    A. might be correct if the cost of hiring labour in that other country is sufficiently low.
    B. ignores the concept of comparative advantage
    C. has been developed in order to protect consumer interests.
    D. has probably been used to form the basis of the national-defence argument for increased protection.

5. Who are often the real beneficiaries of policies that restrict competition from foreign producers?

    A. highly mobile workers who can find jobs in other industries.
    B. owners of firms that would lose the value of their capital stock if driven out of business by lower-priced competitors.
    C. consumers, who don't realize that they are better off being required to buy Canadian products.
    D. foreign producers who then turn their attention to producing other products for which they have a comparative advantage.

6. An important problem with the "infant industry" argument favouring protecting Canadian industries is that

    A. it assumes that policy makers are better able than private investors, risking their own capital, to forecast which industries will grow the fastest in the future.
    B. industries that are protected as "infants" never seem to grow up.
    C. policy makers who choose to protect a particular industry are choosing to tax consumers to support a small group of inefficient producers.
    D. All of the above.

B. Answers to, and Explanations of, the Multiple-Choice Questions on the Principal Ideas of Chapter 26

1. **D**. While the buyers might not export Canadian dollars directly, they either export IOUs or they export some other claim. The only reason that the sellers will accept these claims in exchange for automobiles is that they expect to want to use the dollars or other claims to acquire something in Canada in the future. Most often, the sellers will use the claims (or trade them to someone else who will use them) in the future to purchase goods and services produced in Canada. If Canadians weren't producing anything that people in other countries want to buy, the sellers would not be willing to accept Canadian dollars or Canadian dollar-denominated claims in exchange for the goods they are selling to Canadians.

2. **C**. Import restrictions keep prices higher than they would otherwise be — they do not protect consumers. They might protect jobs in some industries where employees do not have alternatives that are very good. But if pushed to an extreme, the argument that we need import restrictions to create and protect jobs would have Canadians using very labour-intensive production techniques just to create jobs. For example, we would hire scribes to hand copy all the copies of this study guide. The result would be that we would not be using our scarce resources efficiently, and we would not be able to produce or consume as much.

3. **C**. Nearly all barriers to trade provide protection to specific interest groups. This protection reduces competition and raises the prices they are able to charge. Members of special-interest groups have an incentive to organize and lobby for protection from competition because the expected gains to them from specific protection outweigh the costs. But consumers have little incentive to lobby against protection because for each consumer, the expected benefits from freer trade are perceived to be small even though they would be quite large if we could add up all the benefits across all consumers.

4. **B**. It is impossible for another country or group of countries to be more efficient than Canada in the production of *everything*. Because of scarcity, the producers in other countries must make choices as to what goods to produce, and their decisions must also take opportunity costs into account. Efficiency has to refer to *comparative* advantage to have any meaning.

5. **B**. Frequently when an industry is competed out of business, the workers can find other jobs. But the plant and equipment may not have many alternative uses except as scrap. Someone who owns the plant and equipment would lose a great deal of money (compared with how much they could earn if they had protection from competition) if they suddenly had no use for it other than as scrap.

6. **D**. The infant industry argument is often invoked by people who wish to be protected from global competition. The problem is that the protection also induces inefficient operations to stay in the industry. The longer they are in the industry, the more they become entrenched, and the more difficult it is to remove the protection later, when they are no longer "infants". At the same time, policy designed to protect specific industries must, either explicitly or implicitly, choose which industries are more deserving than others of this protection. There is no reason to believe that people making this choice and not risking their own money would make any better choices than people who *do* risk their own money.

C. A Step-by-Step Review of Chapter 26

1. If we import more than we export, then
    A. we won't be able to buy as much from foreigners as we would like.
    B. we will make loans to foreigners so they can buy our goods.
    C. we will borrow from foreigners so we can buy their goods.
    D. the Bank of Canada will have to increase the money supply to support the additional international payments flowing out of Canada

2. The theory of comparative advantage predicts that with unencumbered trade, a good will be produced in that region or country where
   A. the opportunity cost of producing it is lowest.
   B. the opportunity cost of producing it is highest.
   C. tariff barriers are the highest.
   D. tariff barriers are the lowest.
   E. wages are the lowest.

3. Why has Canada's trade with other countries grown so rapidly during the twentieth century?
   A. Transportation and communication costs, as a proportion of the cost of manufacturing goods, have fallen.
   B. Canada's major trading partners have experienced high average economic growth rates.
   C. There have been more opportunities for specialization and division of labour.
   D. Trade barriers have been reduced through international treaties.
   E. All of the above.

4. What group of products accounts for approximately two-thirds of Canada's exports?
   A. lumber and sawmill products
   B. automobiles and other manufactured goods
   C. pulp and paper products
   D. water
   E. gas, oil, and other energy resources

5. Which country receives most of Canada's exports?
   A. The United States
   B. The United Kingdom
   C. Japan
   D. Germany
   E. Ghana

6. Why is there such a large wage differential between Mexico and Canada?
   A. Mexicans have a much lower standard of living and can afford to live on lower incomes.
   B. The Canadian cost of living is higher than the cost of living in Mexico.
   C. Canadian taxes are so much higher than Mexican taxes that after taxes are subtracted, the wage rates in the two countries are nearly equal.
   D. Canada is a capital- and resource-intensive economy, making workers here more productive.
   E. All of the above.

7. Which of the following arguments is the only valid argument for instituting trade barriers?
   A. The infant industry argument
   B. The national security argument
   C. Comparative advantage
   D. The job-loss argument
   E. None of the above is a valid argument for protectionism

8. The implementation of the North American Free Trade Agreement (NAFTA) has had the following result:
   A. Canada has been severely damaged by the loss of production and loss of jobs.
   B. Canada's exports have grown dramatically in every industry.
   C. Economists have been forced to face the fact that free trade does not work.
   D. All the losers from our movement toward freer trade have been compensated.
   E. There has been a rise in the volume of trade with our NAFTA partners, benefiting consumers, but at the cost of dislocations in some industries.

9. When Canada imposes a tariff on the import of goods produced in other countries, who captures the difference between the high price paid by Canadians and the cost of production in the other countries?

    A. Canadian consumers
    B. the Canadian government
    C. the company that has the right to import the good
    D. the foreign exporters
    E. the governments of the foreign producers

10. When Canada imposes an import quota, restricting the quantity of goods produced elsewhere that Canadians are allowed to import, the difference between the high price paid by Canadians and the cost of production in the other countries is captured by

    A. Canadian consumers
    B. the Canadian government
    C. the company that has the right to import the good
    D. the foreign exporters
    E. the governments of the foreign producers

11. Which of the following statements about international trade is *true*?

    A. Tariffs protect and create jobs in our export industries.
    B. Quotas are preferable to tariffs because they don't raise prices as much as tariffs do.
    C. Freer trade leads to more output and lower prices for consumers.
    D. We need trade barriers to protect our workers against cheap foreign labour.
    E. When a poor nation and a rich nation trade with each other, the rich get richer and the poor get poorer.

12. The most efficient way to protect Canada's unique social and cultural fabric is via

    A. direct subsidies to the culture producers.
    B. import tariffs.
    C. import quotas.
    D. limitations on the amount of U.S. television that Canadians are allowed to watch.
    E. limitations on magazine and steel competition.

13. What are the benefits of free trade?

    A. Because of comparative advantage, it promotes efficient allocation of global resources.
    B. It leads to more rapid economic growth.
    C. It provides consumers with greater product diversity from which to choose.
    D. It increases competition, leading to lower consumer prices.
    E. All of the above.

14. Suppose the demand curve for a good in Canada is downward-sloping, and the supply curve of that good, produced by manufacturers in a foreign country, is upward-sloping. What will be the effect of Canada's imposing a 20% tariff on imports of that good into Canada?

    A. Canadian demand for the good will increase.
    B. Revenues of the foreign manufacturers will decrease.
    C. Prices in Canada will decline.
    D. Profits of the foreign manufacturers will increase.
    E. None of the above.

15. If the natural unemployment rate is determined by job search decisions within a country, how can barriers to trade protect and create jobs?

    A. They can't.
    B. By raising the cost to Canadians of consuming goods produced elsewhere, they increase Canadian demand for domestically produced goods and services.
    C. They generate additional income for the workers and businesses in the protected industries; these people, in turn, spend the extra income on Canadian-produced goods and services.
    D. They induce the Bank of Canada to increase the money supply, which sets off an economic expansion.
    E. All of the above.

16. If wages are lower in Mexico than they are in Canada,

    A. Canadian consumers will benefit by purchasing lower-cost goods produced in Mexico.
    B. Canadian workers will need to have tariffs imposed on Mexican goods to protect their jobs.
    C. Mexico will have a comparative advantage in the production of all goods and services.
    D. Canada will have a comparative disadvantage in the production of all goods and services.

17. The argument that imports destroy jobs is

    A. completely false.
    B. partially true, in that foreign competition does eliminate some jobs.
    C. irrelevant to policymaking because exports create as many jobs as imports destroy.
    D. never made because it is in no one's interest to make it.

18. Consumers are generally less effective than producers in influencing government policies on international trade because

    A. producers have more money than consumers do.
    B. most people think producers are more important than consumers.
    C. consumers as a group have less to gain from trade policy than do producers as a group.
    D. the cost of organizing consumers for effective political action is usually much higher than the cost of organizing producers.

19. The owners and employees of a firm that is unable to survive in the face of competition

    A. will be better off if they shift to another industry rather than seek government protection.
    B. are entitled to government protection only if the competition is from foreign producers.
    C. are more likely to receive government protection if the competition is from foreign rather than domestic producers.
    D. are protected by the Charter of Rights in their permanent "right to work."

20. The principle of comparative advantage asserts

    A. that no producer can be more efficient than another producer in the production of everything.
    B. that the cost of obtaining a good is the value of what is given up in order to obtain it.
    C. both of the above.
    D. neither of the above.

21. Frederic Bastiat's famous satire on protectionist lobbying called for legislation that would prohibit

    A. banks, to protect goldsmiths.
    B. eating apples, to protect doctors.
    C. publication of books, to protect teachers.
    D. windows, to protect candlemakers.

D. Answers to the Review questions in Chapter 26

1. C	4. D	7. E	10. D	13. E	16. A	19. C
2. A	5. A	8. E	11. C	14. B	17. B	20. C
3. E	6. D	9. B	12. A	15. A	18. D	21. D

E. Using Supply and Demand to Understand the Effects of Trade Barriers

Tariff protection is a very visible type of protection, like many taxes that people must pay. Sometimes, instead of tariffs, the federal government negotiates "voluntary export restrictions" (VERs) with the exporters and their government. To compare and contrast the two types of trade protection, consider the following hypothetical example.

Suppose that in Canada we import leather belts from Mexico. These belts are imported by distributors or wholesalers in Canada who, in turn, sell them to retailers across the country. The supply and demand conditions for this product are shown in Figure 26.1 below. Given these conditions, the wholesalers import 66 667 leather belts per year from Mexico and pay the Mexican producers $6 per belt.

1. (a) What would happen in this market if the Canadian government were to levy a tariff of $2.50 per belt on these importers? Would this tariff affect supply or demand?

    (b) Show this effect by shifting the appropriate curve in Figure 26.1 in the correct direction and by the correct amount.

    (c) What will be the new equilibrium price and quantity transacted? What price will Canadian importers be paying? What price will Mexican exporters be receiving?

    (d) How much of the $2.50 tariff will wholesalers end up bearing? How much will the Mexican producers end up bearing?

    (e) How much will the Canadian government receive in tariff revenues?

    (f) What will happen to the demand for leather belts produced in Canada? to the demand for workers to produce leather belts in Canada?

Figure 26.1
The Market in Canada for Leather Belts from Mexico

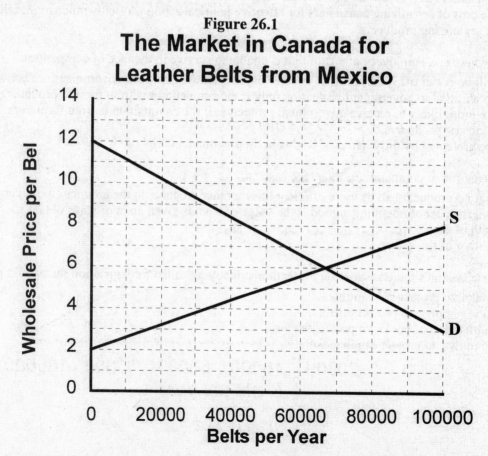

2. Now suppose that instead of a tariff, the federal government negotiates a VER with the Mexican producers of leather belts. They agree to restrict their imports of leather belts to Canada to only 50 000 per year.

    (a) Would this quota restriction affect supply or demand?

    (b) Show this effect by shifting the appropriate curve in Figure 26.1 in the correct direction and by the correct amount.

    (c) What will be the new equilibrium price and quantity transacted? What price will Canadian importers be paying? What price will Mexican exporters be receiving?

    (d) How much of the resulting higher price will wholesalers end up bearing? How much will the Mexican producers end up bearing?

    (e) How much will the Canadian government receive in tariff revenues?

    (f) What will happen to the demand for leather belts produced in Canada? to the demand for workers to produce leather belts in Canada?

    (g) What is the primary difference between a tariff and a VER?

F. Answers to the Questions in Section E

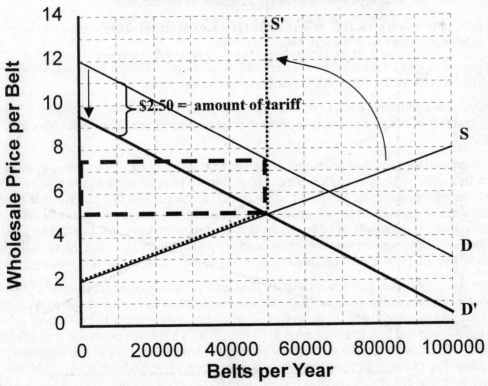

The Market in Canada for Leather Belts from Mexico

Figure 26.2

The graphs in Figure 26.2 look pretty daunting, but work through each part of the question, one step at a time to sort them out. They are put altogether in this one figure to make it easier to see the similarities and differences between the two different types of trade protection.

1. (a) Levying a $2.50 tariff on the importers means that for any quantity they will now be willing to pay the producers in Mexico $2.50 less than they were before. For example, before the tariff, the importers were willing and able to pay $6 per belt for 66 667 belts. Now, they are still willing to pay that same amount in total, but that means they must $2.50 per belt to the Canadian government and are willing and able to pay only $3.50 to the Mexican producers. Similarly, before the tariff, they would have been willing to buy 50 000 belts if the price had been $7.50; after the tariff, however, they are willing to pay only $5 per belt to the producers because they must also pay $2.50 to the Canadian government. The entire demand curve is affected.

   (b) The demand curve shifts downward by $2.50 from **D** to **D'**, as shown in Figure 26.2.

   (c) The new equilibrium price is $5.00 per belt paid by wholesaler-importers in Canada to Mexican belt producers. The importers must also pay $2.50 to the Canadian government. The total amount paid by Canadian importers, including the tariff, is $7.50, but the total amount received by the Mexican producers is $5. The difference is a wedge driven between the producers' price and the importers' price by the tariff.

   (d) After the tariff, producers sell their belts for $1 less than they did before the tariff, and importers buy the belts for $1.50 more (including the tariff) than they did before the tariff.

   (e) The Canadian government will receive 50 000 x $2.50 = $125 000 per year in tariff revenues.

   (f) The demand for substitutes, and for the resources used to produce those substitutes, will increase, which probably helps explain who would be the strongest supporters of such tariffs.

2. (a) The quota will restrict supply. The Mexican producers will not be able to sell more than 50 000 belts to Canadian importers. If, however, the price paid the producers were to drop below $5 per belt, the Mexican producers would cut back on the quantity supplied along the old supply curve.

   (b) The supply curve would rotate and become vertical for all prices above $5 per belt. The entire supply curve would now be the dashed line labeled **S'** in Figure 26.2.

   (c) The new equilibrium price will be $7.50. That is what the Canadian importers will be paying, and that is what the Mexican producers will be receiving.

   (d) The price will go up for both the importers and the producers. The producers in Mexico will actually be made better off by this Canadian protectionist policy.

   (e) Because it is a quota and not a tariff, the Canadian government will receive nothing. The $125 000 that went to the Canadian government under a tariff now goes to the Mexican producers.

   (f) The impact on the Canadian producers of leather belts will be exactly the same, whether this quota or a tariff of $2.50 is implemented. Either form of protection raises the total price that Canadian wholesalers must pay for Mexican belts from $6 per belt to $7.50 per belt. And this higher price of Mexican belts will increase the demand for Canadian belts and for those who produce them. If the supply of labour to the belt-producing industry in Canada is highly elastic, as seems reasonable, then the wages of those workers will not increase much. Most of the increased demand will affect owners of the businesses and potential entrants into the industry.

   (g) The primary difference is that with a tariff, the Canadian government receives $125 000 in extra tax revenues, but, with a quota or VER, those revenues go to foreign produces as additions to their net revenues. With a tariff, there will be taxpayers and members of Parliament debating what to do with and how to allocate the $125 000. With a VER, the producers and government in Mexico will be debating who should have the right to have what share of the increased net revenues. The interesting effect of VERs is that they provide a mechanism *enforced the Canadian government* that effectively requires the Mexican producers to collude to keep prices high and output low.

G. Questions to Think about

1. There are many bogus, self-serving arguments that appear virtually all the time from people seeking special protection from foreign competition. The argument in favour of freer trade almost always relies on comparative advantage. Can you think of any other arguments in favour of freer trade?

2. If the economic arguments favouring free trade are so strong, why don't more voters support free trade?

H. Answers to the Questions in Section G

1. Arguments favouring free trade all tend to be versions of the comparative advantage argument, once you think about them carefully. With freer trade, consumer prices are lower; sellers face more competition, increasing the likelihood of better service; consumers have more to choose from, increasing the variety and scope of quality and service they can choose. On the producer side, free trade allows Canadian producers to specialize, expand, and exploit economies of scale in producing for foreign markets; it also creates jobs in our export industries.

2. Consumers are rarely aware of how and how much trade barriers elevate the prices of things we buy. We go to the store, see a price, and either buy the product or don't buy the product. We don't see a price tag that says, "The price of this product is 20% higher than it would be if Canada didn't have barriers to trade." Furthermore, because each consumer knows that it is unlikely s/he can have any effect on international trade policy, most of us have little or no incentive to find out the facts and to lobby in favour of freer trade, even though as consumers we would be better off with it. Finally, the idea of comparative advantage, while simple to see in the textbook examples, is difficult to see if you are a worker faced with losing your job because of more intense foreign competition.

Chapter 27

National Policies and International Exchange

A. Multiple-Choice Questions on the Principal Ideas of Chapter 27

1. Balance-of-payments accounting will assign an international transaction to a nation's credits column if the transaction
   A. brings useful goods into the nation.
   B. entails a financial payment to some party in the nation.
   C. makes the nation wealthier.
   D. reduces the nation's foreign indebtedness.
   E. reflects comparative advantage.

2. If the calculated credits in a nation's balance of international payments happened to be greater than the calculated debits over the course of a quarter, we would know that the
   A. balance of payments was not in equilibrium during that quarter.
   B. nation had a favourable balance of trade during that quarter.
   C. nation's currency was undervalued in the foreign exchange market.
   D. data compilers had missed more debits than credits in their counting during that quarter.

3. The contention that a nation's balance of payments is in deficit implies that the
   A. debits in the nation's balance of payments exceed the credits.
   B. nation is a net loser from international trade.
   C. nation is importing more than it's exporting.
   D. person making the claim disapproves of something in the current pattern of international transactions.

4. A decline in the foreign exchange value of a nation's currency (e.g. a decline in the U.S. dollar price of a Canadian dollar)
   A. makes foreign goods appear cheaper to that nation's citizens.
   B. makes that nation's goods appear more expensive to foreigners.
   C. reflects a reduced demand for that nation's currency on the part of holders of other currencies.
   D. results from a deficit in that nation's balance of international payments.

5. The rate at which two currencies exchange for each other most closely reflects
   A. the ratio of exports to imports in each nation's international trade.
   B. the ratio of debits to credits in each nation's balance of international payments.
   C. the current domestic purchasing power of each currency.
   D. the expected purchasing power of each currency.

6. Do national governments have the power to control the exchange rate between their currency and other key currencies?
   A. Yes, because currency values are established by law
   B. Yes, because they can always buy or sell their own currency to set its value at any level they choose
   C. Yes, if they are willing and able to pursue a monetary policy consistent with the exchange rate they select
   D. No, because exchange rates are set by supply and demand

7. Floating or flexible exchange rates have been the rule for most nations since the early 1970s
    A. because central banks were opposed to fixed exchange rates.
    B. because economic analysis has demonstrated that resource allocation is more efficient under floating than under fixed rates.
    C. because national governments were unable to agree on policies that were consistent with fixed exchange rates.
    D. despite the fact that they provide no mechanism for the coordination of international exchange.

8. When interest rates are higher in Canada than they are in Switzerland, why don't people invest all their money in Canada and none in Switzerland?
    A. Swiss bankers are more trustworthy than Canadian bankers.
    B. The international branches of Canada's chartered banks are less efficient than Swiss bank branches.
    C. They expect a lower rate of inflation in Canada than they expect in Switzerland.
    D. They expect the Swiss-Franc price of the Canadian dollar to fall in the future.

B. Answers to, and Explanations of, Multiple-Choice Questions on the Principal Ideas of Chapter 27

1. **B.** The accounting focuses on payments. If a nation of starving people were to export food, that would be a credit item because the food would have to be paid for. Balance-of-payments accounting says nothing about usefulness, wealth, or comparative advantage. A reduction in indebtedness would reflect payments out of a nation and would consequently be a debit item.

2. **D.** Many items are inevitably missed in the attempt to measure all the international transactions of a nation. Any divergence between the total of credits and the total of debits must be the result of measurement errors because the totals are equal by definition of the concepts used in constructing a balance of international payments.

3. **D.** A nation cannot import more than it exports when all debits and credits are counted. But someone can certainly decide that a particular set of transactions ought not to be counted in constructing the balance, which is what's occurring whenever someone alleges there is a deficit in the balance of payments. The gain from international trade is the increased wealth that it brings to participants, which has almost nothing to do with any nation's balance of payments.

4. **C.** The first two options would be the consequence of an increase, rather than a decline, in the foreign exchange value of a nation's currency. Only those who define balance-of-payments equilibrium in terms of a stable exchange rate will be able to use the decline as evidence of a deficit. Whatever the causes or consequences, however, the decline reflects a reduced demand for that nation's currency on the part of holders of other currencies.

5. **D.** The rate of exchange between two currencies can and will differ substantially from (the inverse of) their current purchasing powers whenever it comes to be believed that one currency or the other is going to change in relative value in the future. As a consequence, domestic monetary policy can alter foreign exchange rates before it has its effect on domestic price levels.

6. **C.** Exchange rates are set by supply and demand, but government can affect supply and demand. It is through its monetary policy that each government determines the supply of its own currency and hence affects the price at which it will exchange for other currencies. What a government cannot do for very long is pursue an expansionary monetary policy at home and at the same time prevent the foreign-exchange value of its currency from falling by purchasing it on the foreign-exchange markets. The policies must finally be consistent with each other.

7. **C.** Central bankers were, in fact, the principal advocates of fixed exchange rates, perhaps in part because they were the ones responsible for doing the "fixing." Many economic analysts were arguing

in the 1960s that floating rates would be more efficient than fixed rates in conjunction with national policies incompatible with fixed rates, which is far from a demonstration that floating rates produce more efficient resource use than do fixed rates. The arguments of economists were less powerful in any event than the realities of different national policies incompatible with the preservation of fixed and stable exchange rates. Floating rates provide a coordinating mechanism that works in the absence of international agreements, which may be their chief virtue.

8. **D**. Receiving a high rate of return on your investment isn't very attractive if you expect it will be paid in a currency that has a reduced purchasing power. For example, if you expect the purchasing power of the Canadian dollar to fall by two percent over the next year but don't expect any inflation at all in Switzerland, you might reasonably then expect the Swiss Franc price of a Canadian dollar to fall by about two percentage points over the next year. To compensate you for this expected change in exchange rates, you will likely insist on receiving a premium of about two percentage points on your Canadian investments.

C. A Step-by-Step Review of Chapter 27

1. The governmental policies that control international exchange today are

    A. established and enforced by the International Monetary Fund.
    B. designed by national governments to achieve domestic objectives.
    C. completely ineffective at diverting the patterns of trade away from what they would have been otherwise.
    D. designed to promote as much international trade as possible.

2. Which of the following sets is composed entirely of transactions that are credit items in a nation's balance of international payments?

    A. Merchandise imports, gold purchases, lending abroad
    B. Merchandise exports, gold purchases, borrowing from abroad
    C. Merchandise exports, gold sales, lending abroad
    D. Merchandise exports, gold sales, borrowing from abroad

3. Which transaction does not belong with the other four in the same column of the Canadian balance of international payments?

    A. Canadians buy Toyotas from Japan.
    B. Canadians vacation in Disneyland in California.
    C. Canadians purchase shares of stock in a West German automobile manufacturer.
    D. Canadians deposit income from illegal business operations in Swiss banks.
    E. Canadians receive income from investments in Australian sheep ranches.

4. If a nation exported no merchandise or services, received no investment income, gift income, or other unilateral transfers from abroad, and owned no financial assets acceptable in international exchange, could that nation import merchandise from abroad?

    A. No, because imports presuppose earlier exports
    B. No, because the balance of payments must always balance
    C. Yes, but only if other nations failed to recognize the actual situation
    D. Yes, if other nations were willing to extend credit

5. The large deficits in the late 1980s and early 1990s in Canada's current account were in large part the result of

    A. an undervalued Canadian dollar.
    B. declining Canadian productivity.
    C. large surpluses in the preceding decade.
    D. the willingness of foreigners to increase their investments in Canada.

6. The fact that Canada had such large surpluses in its capital account in the late 1980s and early 1990s implies
    A. that Canadians were living beyond their means in the 1980s.
    B. that foreigners now own more of the wealth of Canada than do Canadian residents.
    C. that the rest of the world exploited Canada.
    D. that Canada exploited the rest of the world.
    E. none of the above.

7. A nation's balance of international payments
    A. balances only in equilibrium.
    B. is balanced only when the exchange rate is stable.
    C. is always and necessarily in balance.
    D. cannot ever be in balance.

8. The concept of a disequilibrium in economic theory always refers to a gap between
    A. the amount purchased and the amount sold.
    B. the actual occurrence and the most desirable or ideal occurrence.
    C. what actually happened and what people intended to happen.
    D. what actually happened and what economists predicted.

9. If the dollar price of a German mark changes from 65¢ to 70¢, the dollar has
    A. appreciated and German goods are now more expensive to Canadians.
    B. appreciated and German goods are now less expensive to Canadians.
    C. depreciated and German goods are now more expensive to Canadians.
    D. depreciated and German goods are now less expensive to Canadians.

10. If the Belgian franc changes in price from 3¢ to 2¢, the franc has
    A. appreciated and Canadian goods are now more expensive to Belgians.
    B. appreciated and Canadian goods are now less expensive to Belgians.
    C. depreciated and Canadian goods are now more expensive to Belgians.
    D. depreciated and Canadian goods are now less expensive to Belgians.

11. A widespread belief that the purchasing power of the dollar will decline more rapidly than the purchasing power of the Japanese yen during the next year is going to cause the current value of the dollar relative to the yen to be
    A. lower than it would otherwise be.
    B. higher than it would otherwise be.
    C. the same as it would otherwise be because future changes cannot affect current exchange rates.
    D. highly uncertain because banks won't want to exchange dollars for yen.

12. The principal cause of the large decrease in the foreign-exchange value of the Canadian dollar between 1974 and 1985 was
    A. changed expectations regarding future Canadian inflation rates relative to other major currencies.
    B. surpluses in the Canadian balance of merchandise trade.
    C. deficits in the Canadian government budget.
    D. government policies aimed at fixing exchange rates.
    E. changes in policies of the International Monetary Fund.

13. A major *effect* of the large decrease in the foreign-exchange value of the Canadian dollar between 1974 and 1985 was
    A. a lower rate of inflation in Canada.
    B. a virtual end to Canadian international trade as Canadians were priced out of foreign markets.
    C. inability of Canadian firms to attract foreign investment.
    D. higher prices for Canadian consumers.

14. Pressure on a government to devalue its national currency would most likely come from
    A. consumers eager to obtain cheaper imports.
    B. producers eager to obtain a price advantage against foreign competitors.
    C. members of the opposition political party.
    D. those who believe that we place too much value on money.
    E. the chartered banks.

15. A central bank can devalue the national currency by
    A. prohibiting foreign-exchange transactions.
    B. buying foreign currencies with domestic currency.
    C. selling foreign currencies for domestic currency.
    D. simply announcing a new exchange rate.

16. A central bank policy of buying foreign currencies in order to keep their price up relative to the domestic currency will tend to
    A. create a permanently favourable balance of trade.
    B. lower the domestic price level, thereby encouraging exports and discouraging imports.
    C. raise the domestic price level, thereby discouraging exports and encouraging imports.
    D. produce a surplus in the balance of international payments.

17. The Bretton Woods system for managing international monetary relationships was designed to
    A. maintain stable foreign exchange rates.
    B. enable foreign exchange rates to fluctuate in response to constantly changing conditions of supply and demand.
    C. encourage national governments to devalue their currency when domestic policies called for an increase in net exports.
    D. prevent countries from using the dollar as an international reserve currency.

18. When the governments of nation-states are pursuing mutually incompatible policies,
    A. they must maintain fixed exchange rates for international coordination.
    B. fixed exchange rates reduce the impact of these policies on the flow of international exchange.
    C. floating exchange rates reduce the impact of these policies on the flow of international exchange.
    D. international trade requires managed exchange rates and cannot occur under either fixed or floating exchange rates.

19. The text argues that the ideal foreign-exchange system is one of
    A. floating rates because they respect supply and demand.
    B. floating rates because they give maximum freedom to domestic policymakers.
    C. fixed rates if domestic policies are consistent with fixed rates.
    D. fixed rates because they result in less uncertainty for those who engage in international trade.

20. If interest rates in Canada are lower than interest rates in Italy, interest-rate parity implies that
    A. the inflation rate is higher in Canada.
    B. Italian financial assets are poor investments.
    C. Canadian financial assets are poor investments.
    D. the Italian lira is expected to appreciate against the dollar.
    E. the Canadian dollar is expected to appreciate against the lira.

Look this one up!

21. Suppose people begin to expect prices in Australia to increase by 15 percent while prices in Canada remain relatively stable. What would you expect to happen in the foreign exchange markets for these two currencies?
    A. The demand for Canadian dollars will increase and the supply of Canadian dollars will also increase.
    B. The demand for Canadian dollars will increase and the supply of Canadian dollars will decrease.
    C. The demand for Canadian dollars will decrease and the supply of Canadian dollars will increase.
    D. The demand for Canadian dollars will decrease and the supply of Canadian dollars will decrease.

D. Answers to the Review Questions in Chapter 27

1. B	4. D	7. C	10. C	13. D	16. C	19. C
2. D	5. D	8. C	11. A	14. B	17. A	20. E
3. E	6. E	9. C	12. A	15. B	18. C	21. B

E. Foreign Exchange Rates and International Transactions

The table below shows the average prices of various major national currencies *in cents* of Canadian currency in 1970, 1975, 1980, 1985, 1990, 1995, and June of 1999.

Year	British Pound	French Franc	German Mark	Italian Lira	Japanese Yen	Swiss Franc	US Dollar
1970	250.0	18.8	28.1	0.1667	0.292	24.0	104.2
1975	226.5	23.5	41.8	0.1531	0.347	39.8	102.0
1980	270.9	27.9	64.0	0.1395	0.512	69.8	116.3
1985	174.3	13.5	40.5	0.0676	0.514	48.6	135.1
1990	224.4	23.3	77.9	0.1047	0.860	90.7	116.3
1995	216.4	27.4	95.9	0.0822	1.452	116.4	137.0
1999	232.2	23.3	78.1	0.0789	1.206	95.4	147.1

1. Which currencies depreciated and which appreciated against the Canadian dollar from 1970 to 1980? From 1970 to 1999? From 1995 to 1999?

2. How can you determine whether these changes in rates of exchange resulted from something happening in Canada or in the other country?

3. Assuming that nothing else had changed from 1970 to 1999 except the exchange rate, what would a Canadian film distributor have had to pay at each of these times to obtain the rights to show an Italian movie that was available for one million lire? What would a Roman film distributor have had to pay for a Canadian film that cost $1,000?

4. Is it likely that nothing relevant to Canadian-Italian transactions happened during this period except for these movements in the exchange rate?

5. What would have been the Canadian dollar price in 1985 and again in 1995 of a Japanese car priced at two million yen? Who in Canada was made better off by this large movement in the exchange rate? Who was made worse off?

6. When the price of the British pound goes from $1.75 to $2.25, do Canadians buy more or fewer British goods? Does the total number of dollars spent on these purchases rise or decline?

F. Answers to Questions in Section E

1. When a unit of foreign currency exchanges for more Canadian money than previously, that currency has appreciated relative to the dollar. Thus, only the Italian lira depreciated against the Canadian dollar from 1970 to 1980 — all the others in the table appreciated against the Canadian dollar. Over the entire time period shown, only the British pound and the Italian lira depreciated against the Canadian dollar. But in recent years, from 1995 to June 1999, only the British pound and the U.S. dollar appreciated against the Canadian dollar and the rest *de*preciated.

2. There is no simple way to answer this question, because all change is relative to something else. A useful standard against which to measure change might be the price index for some combination of widely used and internationally traded commodities. If we employed such a standard, we would find that all of the currencies depreciated over the period. But they did so at rates that varied enormously. The basic cause of exchange rate fluctuations is the actual and anticipated changes in the relative purchasing power of the currencies. Another way of saying this is that country-to-country differences in the actual and expected rates of inflation have an enormous impact on exchange rates.

3. One million lire would have cost $1667 in 1970 but only $789 in 1999. One thousand dollars would have cost about 600,000 lire in 1970 and about 1.27 million lire in 1999.

4. It is very unlikely that exchange rate changes of this magnitude could have occurred over such a prolonged period without very sizable differences in the relative inflation rates of the two countries. In fact, the domestic price level in Italy rose far faster over this period than in Canada.

5. A Japanese car costing two million yen would jump in price from $10 280 to $24 120 if the sellers allowed that to occur. Since Japanese exporters and Canadian dealers did not want to wreak havoc in their market, they absorbed a portion of the cost increases brought about by the appreciation of the yen against the Canadian dollar. (Or, which is the same thing, depreciation of the dollar against the yen.) All firms and workers supplying cars to the North American market in competition with the Japanese found the exchange rate movement to be an enormous blessing. North American consumers, however, had to pay more for Japanese cars, and for all other cars, too, as the rising cost of Japanese cars permitted competitors to increase their markups.

6. We cannot predict the effects without additional information. The law of demand presumably holds, so that Canadians will buy a smaller quantity of British goods. But how elastic are Canadian demands for British goods? With an inelastic demand, Canadians would end up paying more dollars in total for fewer goods. One implication of an inelastic demand, however, is that the seller has not done an astute job of price searching. Sellers can always increase their net revenues by raising their prices to buyers whose demand is relatively inelastic at the prevailing price. Also, for most goods traded internationally, there are many substitutes available. These two facts probably lead to generally elastic demands, so that the quantity of domestic currency supplied in the process of purchasing foreign goods will move in the opposite direction from the prices of the goods in the case of most internationally traded goods. This is a longer-run effect, however. In the short run, international purchases may be quite inelastic with respect to price changes.

G. Questions to Think about

1. If you look up the word *dump* in any large and recent dictionary of the English language, you will find one definition that goes something like this: "To sell goods in foreign countries at low prices." Why is this "dumping" rather than "conducting a sale"? Why does the term apply only to selling in foreign countries? Why aren't book publishers "dumping" when they "remainder" books, that is, offer their remaining stock to bookstores at very low prices when sales fall off?

2. What is favourable about a "favourable balance of trade"?

H. Answers to Questions in Section G

1. It is easier to obtain legal protection against competition after a disparaging name has been attached to the competitor's practices. We don't think poorly of merchants who conduct sales; we are much more inclined to be suspicious of those who dump. Domestic producers looking for legislative protection from foreign sellers have been sufficiently successful at downgrading foreigners to add a term to the dictionary. Domestic sellers probably escape the label because they are present to defend themselves. The practice of remaindering would become blatant dumping if publishers did it in foreign countries.

    Notice that we have another term that sellers use to disparage domestic competitors who reduce their prices: *predatory pricing* (discussed in Chapter 13). But it is hard to make this label stick to a competitor unless the competitor is a very large firm.

2. The term *favourable* has for so long been applied to an imbalance in which merchandise and service exports exceed imports that few who use it stop to notice that it might be more appropriately called an *un*favourable balance of trade. When an individual, household, or business firm gives up goods of greater value than it receives in return, it is either being generous, being foolish, or investing for the sake of future returns. If we abstract from the first two possibilities, an excess of exports over imports must be in anticipation of some future excess of imports over exports. Promises to pay more later are secured now in return for the additional value surrendered currently. Fans of "favourable" trade balances want to postpone indefinitely the payoff from such investment, a good sign that there is either a loose link in their logic or a hidden motive at work.

Chapter 28

Inflation, Recession, and Political Economy

A. Multiple-Choice Questions on the Principal Ideas of Chapter 28

1. The stabilization policies of the federal government aim primarily at

   A. holding down the rate of inflation.
   B. keeping the budget balanced over the course of the business cycle.
   C. preventing recessions and high unemployment.
   D. no particular target but are rather the outcome of decisions made by elected and appointed officials in pursuit of many diverse interests.

2. Why are sudden and unanticipated changes in aggregate demand likely to affect real output and employment before they affect prices?

   A. Because corporations will use changes in aggregate demand as an occasion to increase their profits
   B. Because it takes a stiff recession and much unemployment to persuade unions to moderate their wage demands
   C. Because prices are usually fixed by law when aggregate demand is changed
   D. Because sellers who misread a change in aggregate demand as a change in the relative demand for their products will tend to adjust their inventories rather than their prices

3. The democratic political process tends to produce government policies that

   A. are jerky with an inflationary bias.
   B. maximize employment and real growth.
   C. minimize unemployment and inflation.
   D. promote the long-run interests of the majority.

4. Why did the federal government run consistent budget deficits from 1975 through 1997?

   A. Political pressures make expenditures difficult to control.
   B. The federal government's control of the money supply through its indirect influence over the Bank of Canada enables it to borrow almost indefinitely without becoming unable to find willing lenders.
   C. The public has accepted the notion that budget deficits can be good for the economy.
   D. A combination of the three factors mentioned above

5. Economists who argue that the government should not engage in discretionary aggregate demand management believe that government

   A. actions do not affect the economy.
   B. actions that are not anticipated destabilize the economy more than they stabilize it.
   C. initiatives to affect the economy are generally canceled out by private actions.
   D. ought not to take any actions that affect the economy.

B. Answers to, and Explanations of, Multiple-Choice Questions on the Principal Ideas of Chapter 28

1. **D**. Federal government policies often aren't "designed" at all, any more than the pattern of rush-hour traffic (discussed in Chapter 1) is designed. They emerge from the interaction among the decisions of individuals who are pursuing the projects in which they are interested. Those projects might very well include, for many government officials, achievement of what *they perceive* to be the public interest. But it will be the public interest as they understand it in the light of their own experiences and interests.

2. **D**. If corporations simply changed their prices in response to a change in aggregate demand, they would generally earn larger profits. But if they often don't realize what is occurring, and they are much more likely to adjust their inventories (which explains why businesses have become increasingly interested in hiring economists to help them understand the macro economy). Knowledge about what's happening is crucial. Unions and union members will also not alter their wage demands if they don't believe anything has occurred to make doing so in their interest. And for everyone in the economy, the rigidities built into long-term contracts often slow the pace of price adjustments, encouraging decision makers to make quantity adjustments rather than price adjustments.

3. **A**. Inflationary policies are popular both because they directly entail actions pleasing to voters and because the stimulating effects on output and employment tend to occur prior to the costs in terms of a higher inflation rate. But democratic governments eventually must deal with the inflation fostered by their own policies; when inflationary policies are reversed or merely suspended, output and employment tend to fall sharply. Popular discontent with the consequences of disinflationary policies can easily induce a government to resume expansionary policies before halting the inflation caused by earlier policies.

4. **D**. The first consideration sets the stage; but the next two are necessary to explain why provincial and municipal governments don't run persistent deficits and why the federal government did not make deficits a way of life much before 1974.

5. **B**. Government actions, including fiscal and monetary policy, certainly influence the economy. The question is whether we can devise institutions that will provide government officials with the knowledge, incentives, and power that will cause them to run a discretionary aggregate-demand management policy in a manner that is actually stabilizing rather than destabilizing. Canadian experience since the late 1960s until the mid-1990s did not provide solid grounds for optimism. The recent sustained growth of the 1990s holds out more hope that policy makers are capable of doing a better job than they did during the previous two decades.

C. A Step-by-Step Review of Chapter 28

1. The economic policies of government most closely reflect
    A. the public interest.
    B. the interests of the majority.
    C. the interests of those in power.
    D. the interest in price stability and full employment.

2. Frequent elections cause politicians to prefer policies that will produce
    A. long-run benefits and long-run costs.
    B. long-run benefits and short-run costs.
    C. short-run benefits and long-run costs.
    D. short-run benefits and short-run costs.

3. Economic theory predicts that if the majority of the voters in a democracy want total government spending reduced,

   A. it will be reduced by the amount they prefer.
   B. it will be reduced, but by less than they prefer.
   C. it may not be reduced at all because there may be no politically acceptable place to cut.
   D. it will actually expand.

4. If the government acts to expand aggregate demand and the public is not fully informed about what it is doing, the result is likely to be an increase in

   A. output and employment but no change in prices.
   B. output and employment followed by an increase in prices.
   C. prices but no change in output and employment.
   D. prices followed by an increase in output and employment.

5. If the government acts to slow the rate of growth in aggregate demand and the public is not fully informed about what it is doing (or doesn't believe the pronouncements that they "really mean it" this time), the result is likely to be a decrease in

   A. output and employment but no change in prices.
   B. output and employment followed by a decrease in prices.
   C. prices but no change in output and employment.
   D. prices followed by a decrease in output and employment.

6. Legislative bodies that are not compelled to maintain expenditures within the long-run bounds established by tax revenues are likely to

   A. request constitutional limitations on their spending power.
   B. adhere to these limits anyway out of a sense of responsibility.
   C. increase expenditures more rapidly than tax revenues because of the political costs to legislators of either cutting back particular expenditures or increasing tax rates.
   D. win the approval of most voters.

7. The federal government can run large deficits for many years without incurring any risk of bankruptcy, whereas Newfoundland cannot do this, because the federal government

   A. spends its money more wisely.
   B. has authority over the money-supply mechanism and therefore can create the means with which to pay its debts.
   C. uses its deficits only to support high output and full employment.
   D. can demonstrate to potential lenders the likelihood of future surpluses.

8. Provincial and municipal governments are unlike the federal government in that they do not run chronic budget deficits. This is because they

   A. all operate under constitutional constraints.
   B. are closer to the people.
   C. are under less political pressure to spend.
   D. have to convince lenders that they will be able to service their debt for the foreseeable future.

9. The text argues that Keynesian analysis promoted budget deficits by

   A. proving that they prevented recessions.
   B. proving that they could not cause inflation.
   C. providing more jobs for professional economists.
   D. undermining the popular belief that budgets ought to be balanced each year.

10. If the voting public strongly dislikes inflation, elected officials will nonetheless often pursue policies that produce inflation

    A. because they know that inflation does little real harm.
    B. because it is unlikely that the voters will be able to trace inflation to the officials whose decisions caused it.
    C. when they know that inflation is in the long-run public interest.
    D. because they believe that recession is more costly to more people.

11. A government pledged to balance the budget over the course of the business cycle would probably be able to avoid fulfilling its pledge and also avoid admitting that it had failed because

    A. no one takes political promises seriously.
    B. the government controls the press and other media.
    C. there is no clear beginning or end to any business cycle.
    D. there is no competition within government to bring out the truth.

12. Although the Bank of Canada has the tools to pursue a restrictive monetary policy while the federal government is running large budget deficits, the Bank is unlikely to do so because

    A. the Governor of the Bank of Canada must resign if s/he disagrees with policy that cabinet would like the Bank to pursue.
    B. Bank of Canada officials are predominantly bankers, and bankers favour higher interest rates.
    C. Bank of Canada officials must run for reelection every time there is a federal election.
    D. even though it has some alleged degree of independence, the Bank of Canada is unlikely to risk open conflict with the policies of elected officials.

13. The belief that recessions can be effectively countered through government action to stimulate aggregate demand

    A. is false under any and all circumstances.
    B. is irrefutable, even though there may be political objections to such a policy.
    C. assumes that government contributions to demand move quickly and smoothly to sectors of the economy where demand is insufficient.
    D. is purely a matter of opinion, and one opinion is as good as any other.

14. The alternative to discretionary fiscal and monetary policies of the fine-tuning variety is

    A. policies based on indiscretions by fiscal and monetary authorities.
    B. no fiscal or monetary policy at all.
    C. policies based on firm commitments to clearly stated rules.
    D. not available because fine-tuning is unavoidable.

15. A constitutional commitment to an annually balanced federal budget

    A. would prevent Parliament and cabinet from manipulating the economy for political purposes.
    B. would require Parliament to make destabilizing budget decisions at times.
    C. rests on the erroneous belief that constitutions are superior to the will of the people.
    D. probably could not be enforced because Parliament is free to ignore the Constitution whenever it wants to.

16. According to the text, the basic question dividing those who disagree on the proper role of government in the economy is:

    A. Should budget deficits be prohibited by a constitutional amendment?
    B. Should the Bank of Canada be required to maintain a stable rate of growth in the monetary base?
    C. Should direct wage and price controls be used against possessors of market power?
    D. How well do markets work?

D. Answers to the Review Questions in Chapter 28

1. C	5. B	9. D	13. C
2. C	6. C	10. B	14. C
3. C	7. B	11. C	15. B
4. B	8. D	12. D	16. D

E. Political Economy during an Election Year

Suppose it is the beginning of a year during which the government of the day will be likely to have to call an election, and the current prime minister, along with most of the members of the ruling party, are eager to be re-elected. The economy is in the second year of a strong expansion. Real gross domestic product rose at a 3.6 percent annual rate a year ago and at a 4.8 percent annual rate in the year just ended. The unemployment rate is at its lowest level in over a quarter of a century and firms are continuing to expand their hiring. Although the various price indexes are starting to creep up — the GDP deflator rose 2.7 percent a year ago and 4.8 percent in the year just past — there is as yet little evidence of public alarm about a resurgence of inflation. The federal government budget was $30 billion in deficit last year and the most optimistic estimates of the government's own advisers predict at least a $20 billion deficit for the current year.

Here are some of the political issues that will come up in the next few months in Parliament: tax reform; crop subsidies for farmers; subsidies to exporters; grants to provincial and municipal governments for a wide range of purposes, from highway and rapid-transit construction through expansion of police services to job-training programs; loans for post-secondary students; old-age assistance and health-care benefit levels.

1. Should cabinet's position on any of the issues mentioned in the preceding paragraph be influenced by the state of the economy as described in the first paragraph above?
2. How likely is it that cabinet, in an election year, will take a stand on these issues that is based primarily on a desire to stabilize the economy?

F. Answers to the Questions in Section E

1. The facts described in the first paragraph strongly suggest that an unsustainable rate of expansion may have begun and that a much higher inflation rate is a serious threat. Further stimulus to the economy in the form of increased government expenditures would seem not to be appropriate at this time if the goal is stabilization.

2. Who can tell? Who really knows what stabilization requires? Maybe the economy is actually beginning to slow down, although it doesn't show up yet in the data, and a little stimulus in the form of increased government expenditures would be just the tonic required to keep the expansion rolling merrily along. Members of a government anticipating a reelection campaign will find this possibility highly probable. They, their advisers, and leading members of the party caucus will be able to think of plausible reasons for reducing taxes, sweetening subsidies to farmers and exporters, extending grants to provincial and municipal governments, liberalizing the student loan program, and raising old age assistance and health-care benefits. A major effect of the election campaign could easily be the destabilization of the economy.

G. Questions for Discussion

1. In the light of the previous discussion, would it be desirable to amend the constitution so that Canada's senate, which doesn't face constant re-election pressures, had more power in the legislative decision making in Ottawa?

2. How well do markets work?

H. Answers to Questions in Section G

1. It would be presumptuous of us to argue one way or the other on this difficult and hotly debated question. We can, however, point out some of the costs and benefits of such a change. First, the benefits of having a legislative body take a longer-term view, as described in the question, are likely to be non-negligible. At the same time, having such a body be appointed for life and not subject to regular checks from the electorate would likely be a cost to this idea. Whether the costs outweigh the benefits is a question that will persist for quite some time to come.

2. They certainly don't work perfectly. But do we know how to construct better arrangements? That's the large and important question that this course should have equipped you to think about more systematically and intelligently.